P9-DMW-829

A BAKER'S TOUR

ALSO BY NICK MALGIERI

Perfect Cakes

Cookies Unlimited

Chocolate

How to Bake

Great Italian Desserts

Nick Malgieri's Perfect Pastry

HarperCollins*Publishers*

A BAKER'S TOUR

NICK MALGIERI

Photographs by Tom Eckerle

For information, address HarperCollins Publishers, 10 East 53rd Street, New York, NY 10022.

Designed by Joel Avirom and Jason Snyder
Design Assistant: Meghan Day Healey
Illustrations: Laura Hartman Maestro
Food Styling: Barbara Bria Pugliese, with Faith Drobbin, Rebecca Millican, Cara Tennenbaum, Andrea Tutunjian
Prop Styling: Ceci Gallini

ISBN 0-06-058263-4 (hc)

The illustration on the title-page spread is of a Pizza Rustica alla Milanese. The illustrations on the table of contents are of (left to right) Tsourekakia and Simit; Blackberry and Apple Pie; and Rigo Jansci.

For my dear friend
Ann Amendolara Nurse

CONTENTS

INTRODUCTION

Though I am no stranger to adapting foreign recipes for American use, creating a book composed entirely of recipes from outside the United States has been an invigorating challenge. I have chosen to include recipes here that meet several criteria.

First and foremost, any recipe you'll find here reflects excellence of flavor and texture. Second, all the recipes are from outside of the United States, my native country. Yes, some of these recipes come from as close as Toronto, and some even come from friends who live in the United States; but I'm not convinced, for example, that ground beef empanadas, made with all the seasonings and techniques with which they are made in Argentina, are now American just because they are also made in New York or Toledo. Spaghetti and meatballs may be an American interpretation of what once was an Italian dish, but a Sicilian cassata, whether made in Palermo, Hong Kong, or Gnome, is still essentially Sicilian, especially if the recipe comes from a real Sicilian source.

Where do these recipes come from? They hail from all over the world and derive from all kinds of sources. I have traveled a fair amount during the thirty-odd years that I have been a professional baker. I have always collected recipes and cookbooks no matter where I went, and some of the recipes here are the result of those travels. Others come from native cooks who have on-site experience at preparing foreign recipes. Still others come from friends and colleagues whose families have long traditions in the baking of a particular culture.

Readers familiar with my work know that I'm fond of adapting recipes from classic cookbooks. In fact, I have an extensive cookbook collection and frequently use it to do research. I don't take a recipe from just any book, nor do I tend to adapt recipes for foods with which I'm not at all familiar—that would make the outcome of the recipe a mystery, and I wouldn't know whether it had turned out properly. Sometimes, when I am searching for a recipe for a beloved cake or pastry, which I've tasted many times on-site, and for which no recipe is available, I have resorted to looking in that country's classic cookbook literature for help. Sometimes books provide results that reproduce the remembered taste and texture accurately, and in those cases I've included the recipe.

All in all, you'll find recipes that come from friends, colleagues, chefs, and home cooks, with some outstanding examples of the cooking literature of other countries. I hope you enjoy reading and following the recipes as much as I did collecting, writing, and preparing them.

Nick Malgieri
New York City
August 2004

INGREDIENTS

What follows here is a list of the ingredients and types used in preparing the recipes in the book. In other books, I have written extensively on the nature of various ingredients. This list will point you in the right direction for purchasing but is not meant to be a treatise on the nature of the ingredients themselves.

In general, quality is often associated with price, and low-priced, good-quality ingredients are an exception, definitely not the rule. Nowadays bulk-purchasing outlets make it easier to buy high-quality ingredients at a low price, and many even carry imported chocolates and other specialty ingredients. Just make sure you can use all you purchase within a reasonable amount of time—buying in bulk and saving ingredients until they become stale is a false economy.

FLOURS AND STARCHES

All-Purpose Flour: My default flour is unbleached all-purpose flour. If a recipe just specifies all-purpose flour, you may use bleached or unbleached all-purpose flour.

Cake Flour: Any cake flour used here is the plain type, not self-rising.

Cornstarch: Plain cornstarch available in the supermarket.

Potato Starch: During Passover, sometimes substituted for cornstarch, which is made from grain and therefore forbidden.

Breadcrumbs: Fine dry breadcrumbs may be bought in the supermarket. Just make sure to buy unflavored ones. Fresh white breadcrumbs are made by removing the crusts from fresh bread, dicing the bread into manageable pieces, and reducing it to crumbs in the food processor.

SUGARS AND SWEETENERS

Granulated Sugar: I use plain granulated sugar in all my recipes, never superfine sugar.

Brown Sugar: In this book, you may use light or dark, whichever you prefer; but remember that dark brown sugar has a more pronounced molasses flavor and light brown sugar a milder one.

Confectioners' Sugar: I use this mainly for sprinkling on finished cakes and pastries, and sometimes as an ingredient in marzipan, meringues, and some specialty pastry doughs. I never use confectioners' sugar for sweetening whipped cream, because it contains cornstarch and imparts a chalky taste to the cream.

Corn Syrup: Light corn syrup may be used as an ingredient in marzipan and some fillings. Dark corn syrup is used when its stronger flavor is required.

Golden Syrup (Lyle's Golden Syrup): A British import, this is sometimes available in British or other specialty stores. It was originally developed as a substitute for honey and was used in British army rations during World War I. If I don't have Golden Syrup, I substitute honey.

Maple Syrup: If you purchase maple syrup where it is made, you'll probably have a choice of grades. Grade A is the best and most expensive, more delicate in flavor, and meant to be used as a table syrup. Grade B, however, is stronger-flavored and much better for baking—and usually a little lower in price.

Honey: I usually buy a dark, full-flavored honey, not necessarily one with a fancy pedigree.

Molasses: I use unsulfured molasses, which tends to be milder in flavor than the other type available, which is usually marked "robust flavor." Most of the recipes in this book that call for molasses use so little that I doubt it would make any difference if you substituted one for the other.

LEAVENERS

Yeast: All the recipes in this book that use yeast call for active dry yeast, and it is measured in volume (teaspoons and tablespoons), not envelopes. I have counted 2½ teaspoons of yeast as an envelope. If you bake often, it is more practical and less expensive to purchase dry yeast in bulk. Just remember to use all the yeast before its expiration date.

Baking Powder: I use double-acting baking powder, for which several reliable brands are available nationwide. Always check the bottom of the can for the expiration date and discard the baking powder and purchase fresh when necessary.

Baking Soda: Plain bicarbonate of soda. Be careful to crush any lumps before measuring and adding to other ingredients.

FLAVORINGS

Salt: I usually use fine sea salt for both baking and salting food I am cooking. When a coarse salt is needed, I use kosher salt available in the supermarket. Occasionally, especially when I receive it as a gift, I use French fleur de sel, a high-quality, coarse-textured, natural, unadulterated sea salt. It's best for sprinkling on things where you want the crunch of a fine-tasting salt crystal.

Extracts: Whether an extract is vanilla or another flavor, make sure the label states that it is pure. Some brands have "pure vanilla extract" in large letters and "with artificial extract added" in smaller ones below. The same is true of almond extract.

Liquors: This is an area where false economy can really influence the flavor of what you are preparing. If a large bottle of good imported rum or another liquor or liqueur is expensive, buy a smaller bottle rather than a lesser brand. Kirsch (sometimes referred to on a label as Kirschwasser) is a clear brandy distilled from cherries. The best types are imported from Switzerland, Alsace in France, Austria, and Germany and are never cheap.

Chocolate: Most of the recipes here specify either bittersweet or semisweet chocolate. In a few recipes the choice is yours. Remember that bittersweet chocolate is not the same thing as unsweetened chocolate. Bittersweet chocolate contains sugar, while unsweetened chocolate does not. See Sources on page 363 for links to interesting chocolates, which are some of the brands I like best.

Cocoa Powder: I still use alkalized (Dutch-process) cocoa exclusively. It's easy to identify: the package will have a Dutch-sounding name (Droste, Van Houten, Bensdorp) or will state that it is alkalized. Hershey's European-style cocoa is alkalized.

Coffee: Either brew triple-strength espresso (3 tablespoons coffee and ¾ cup boiling water) or use instant espresso. The flavor of the latter is improved by dissolving it in brewed coffee.

Herbs and Spices: Whenever possible I like to use fresh, as opposed to dried, herbs. Fresh herbs have certainly become much more available, even in winter in the supermarket, in the past few years. If you use dried herbs, make sure they are not stale and that they have a lively fragrance when you bruise some between your thumb and first finger. Store all herbs and spices in a cool, dark place, away from heat. The flavor in herbs and spices comes from volatile oils that dissipate over time, taking the flavor with them. If you know you have had spices or dried herbs around for more than a year, it's probably time to discard them. Sources (page 363) lists interesting mail-order suppliers of herbs and spices.

ASIAN SEASONINGS

Konn Chun is the brand you want to purchase for any of the following.

Soy Sauce: Made from fermented soybeans, wheat, and yeast, this is sometimes referred to as light soy sauce because of its thin consistency.

Black Soy Sauce: Also called thick soy sauce, this is made like thin soy sauce, but with the addition of molasses. It is less salty than plain soy sauce.

Hoisin Sauce: Made from fermented soybeans, vinegar, sugar, and garlic, this is used as a seasoning or as a table sauce to accompany certain dishes.

NUTS AND NUT PRODUCTS

In general, nutmeats with the skin still on are referred to as natural or unblanched and those with the skin removed are referred to as blanched or skinless.

Almonds, pistachios, and hazelnuts (also called filberts) are available natural and, sometimes, blanched. For convenience it's easier to purchase them already blanched if possible. Otherwise, to remove the skins from almonds or pistachios, put them in a saucepan and cover with water. Bring to a boil and drain. Rub the nutmeats in a towel to loosen the skins, then go over them one by one, to separate them from the skins. Place the blanched nuts on a jelly-roll pan and dry them out for about 10 minutes at 325 degrees, then cool them, especially if you have to grind them afterward. To blanch hazelnuts, put them in a small roasting pan and bake them at 350 degrees for about 15 minutes, or until the skins begin to char slightly and loosen. Rub in a towel and separate from the skins as for almonds. It's not necessary to dry hazelnuts out after blanching.

Pecans and walnuts are not blanched and are not available skinless.

Pine nuts, pignoli in Italian, are used in several recipes. Buy them from a source where you can taste them to make sure they are fresh, as they easily become rancid.

Store all nuts in a plastic bag in the freezer. If you need to grind nuts in a food processor, make sure they are at room temperature. Cold nutmeats clump up and never grind finely enough; warm ones will turn almost immediately to nut butter.

Almond Paste: I like to use the kind of almond paste that comes in a can, because I find that it has the best flavor and performs best in recipes. Sources (page 363) has a supplier for some fine almond paste available in 1-pound cans.

Sesame Seeds: White or black, these are used in a recipe for Japanese rice crackers. The white are toasted first to increase their flavor.

EGGS

All the eggs called for in this book are large eggs, 24 ounces per dozen.

Some recipes, notably those for some meringues that are not subsequently baked, call for egg whites that are just heated, but not completely cooked. If you are concerned about this, substitute pasteurized egg whites, now easily available in the supermarket. I have recently seen pasteurized whole eggs still in the shell. I have no idea how that's done, but it's not a bad idea.

DAIRY PRODUCTS

Butter: All the butter called for here, with one exception, is unsalted butter. Probably the most important ingredient in fine baking, butter needs to be fresh to be good. Unwrap a stick of butter and scratch the surface with the point of a table knife. If the butter is lighter-colored on the inside than on the outside, it has oxidized and become stale. Such butter won't impart anything but a stale flavor to whatever you bake with it. I never use so-called European or extra-anything butters. All the recipes here were tested with plain butter available at the supermarket. If you substitute butter with a higher fat content, you might get different results, especially in cookie batters and pastry doughs. They will have a tendency to spread more during baking and be very fragile afterward.

If you stock up on butter during a sale, by all means store it in the freezer. If you intend to keep it for more than a month or so, wrap the packages in plastic wrap and foil to keep them as airtight as possible.

Milk: All the milk called for here is whole milk.

Cream: All the cream is heavy whipping cream with a fat content of 36 percent. If you have 40 percent cream available, by all means use it; it won't change anything in the recipe.

Evaporated Milk: Canned product meant to be reconstituted before use. I use it as is in some recipes.

Sweetened Condensed Milk: Like evaporated milk, but heavily sweetened and very thick. It is also used to make dulce de leche, the South American milk jam.

Nonfat Dry Milk: Meant to be reconstituted with water to make skim milk. Used in some recipes to boost the solid content of the batter or mixture.

Sour Cream: Full-fat sour cream is called for here.

Yogurt: Either full-fat or low-fat yogurt will work in the recipes that call for it.

Ricotta: Whole-milk and part-skim ricotta are both called for in recipes here. If possible, buy whole-milk ricotta in an Italian store that sells it loose, as it will have a better texture than the supermarket variety. Ricotta impastata is a special, very dry, creamy-textured ricotta especially used in the filling for cannoli. It comes in 10-pound bags; as far as I know, no one sells it in smaller quantities.

Farmer Cheese: A curd cheese that has approximately 10 percent butterfat. I like to use it for cheese strudel filling. You can substitute part–skim milk ricotta if you can't find farmer cheese.

Parmigiano-Reggiano: Fine-flavored, dry Italian cow's milk cheese. Get the real thing and accept no substitutes. Buy a chunk and keep it in the refrigerator wrapped in wax paper and foil so the cheese has a chance to breathe a little. Always grate it immediately before use.

Pecorino Romano: This is a ewe's milk cheese, and a little like parmigiano, but stronger in flavor. It's not a substitute for parmigiano-reggiano, but in some recipes they may be used interchangeably.

Gruyère: This is the real Gruyère from Switzerland, a raw-milk cheese aged until it develops a tangy flavor. There is no substitute for it.

Emmentaler: The Swiss cheese with the holes. If you purchase it at a deli counter in your local supermarket, ask for "Switzerland Swiss" to avoid imitations from other countries.

MEAT PRODUCTS

Every recipe in the chapter on savory pastries (Chapter 6) is very specific about exactly which type of meat or fish to use.

LARD: The best lard for baking is called leaf lard and is rendered from the hard pork fat that encases the kidneys—exactly the same thing as suet in beef. Lard available in the supermarket is a slightly deodorized version rendered from pork fat in general. Outside the United States both lard and suet are extensively used for deep-frying because of their ability to withstand high temperatures for a long time without breaking down.

OILS

VEGETABLE OILS: Canola, corn, and peanut oil can do a good job for deep-frying, and as an ingredient for cooking onions for a filling or as a small-quantity addition to a dough.

OLIVE OIL: I usually use pure olive oil when it is going to be heated, and extra-virgin olive oil when it is going to be drizzled raw on something, such as a salad.

EQUIPMENT

Having the correct equipment makes all the difference in baking. I'm fanatical about having the correct sizes of baking pans for various recipes, but I limit the sizes I use for recipes I write so that it will be easy for you to have the correct pans without going to great expense.

BAKING PANS

Layer Pans: These are round pans 2 inches deep. In this book I call for pans 8, 9, 10, and 12 inches in diameter. If you don't have a 12-inch round pan and don't want to purchase one, you can substitute a 9 × 13 × 2-inch pan.

Sheet Pans: I use both 10 × 15-inch jelly-roll pans and 12 × 18-inch commercial half-sheet pans. If you don't have the latter, an 11 × 17-inch pan will work just as well.

Tube Pans: A tube pan can be a 1- or 2-piece 12-cup (10-inch) tube pan; or a scalloped Bundt pan, also 12-cup capacity.

Rectangular Pans: A 9 × 13 × 2-inch pan is useful for many different recipes. A metal one doubles as a roasting pan for any purpose in this book. I like the glass ones, too, for chilling pastry cream or other fillings I don't want to come into contact with metal. A rectangular glass dish is also a good pan for deep-dish pies.

Cookie Sheets: Cookie sheets that don't have sides are useful, aside from baking, for moving dough and cake layers and for chilling pieces of dough.

Insulated cookie sheets are worthwhile if your oven gives strong bottom heat and has a tendency to burn things on the bottom. Use them only in the bottom of the oven, though. You can produce the same effect by stacking two uninsulated cookie sheets together for baking in the bottom of the oven.

Loaf Pans: I use both 9 × 5 × 3-inch loaf pans and 8½ × 4½ × 2¾-inch pans for recipes here.

Springforms: I use both 9- and 10-inch springform pans. There are relatively new ones manufactured by Kaiser (see Sources, page 363) that have a completely flat bottom, so you can slide your cake or pastry off the pan onto a platter. Old-fashioned springform pans have a lip on the pan bottom, and you have to dig in under it slightly to remove something.

Pie Pans: I prefer Pyrex for a pie pan, and usually use the standard 9-inch size.

Tart Pans: I like to use a removable-bottom tart pan with fluted sides. Recipes here call for 10-, 11-, and 12-inch pans. The latter two are interchangeable, so you need to have only one of those sizes. There are also individual tart pans with removable bottoms that are about 4½ inches in diameter—perfect for individual savory or dessert tarts.

Tartlet Pans: The ones I use most often are about 2½ inches in diameter, have sloping sides, and are made from tinned base metal. To season these pans before using them for the first time, bake them for half an hour at 350 degrees. You may butter them the first few times you use them, but after that it won't be necessary. Just wipe the pans well with a dry cloth or paper towel after each use. Don't wash them, or you'll have to season them again.

Muffin and Mini-Muffin Pans: These can be useful as substitutes for individual tart and tartlet pans. One recipe for an individual cake is baked in a muffin pan.

SPECIALTY PANS

Gugelhupf Pan: A fluted tube pan of 8- to 10-cup capacity. If you have no special mold, you can also use a tube or Bundt pan, although the cake will not be as tall in the larger mold.

Madeleine Pan: This has 12 shell-shaped cavities, which hold about 2 tablespoons each. Madeleine pans come in a variety of sizes from very small (¾-inch madeleines) to quite large (4-inch madeleines). Three-inch ones are average.

PANS FOR COOKING

Though the cooking needed for the recipes here is limited to cooking up a filling or a sauce, here are some suggestions for that.

Enameled Iron Cookware: I like this for a large Dutch oven for deep-frying and also for smaller saucepans and covered casseroles for making syrups and pastry cream. The pans are heavy-bottomed, so delicate mixtures such as pastry cream cook through well without scorching.

Bimetal Cookware: Stainless steel pans with an aluminum core for even heating. Calphalon Tri-Ply is an example of this type of pan and works well for the same purposes as enameled iron.

Sauté Pans: A 10- and a 12-inch sauté pan are useful for a variety of jobs. The smaller one, with its cover, is used for baking the Indian flatbread naan. Both pans can be used for sautéing onions for topping a focaccia or adding to a savory filling.

HAND TOOLS

Knives: Nowadays there is a profusion of different knives to choose from, as close as your local department store or hardware store. You'll need to have a good paring knife, a chopping (or chef's) knife, and a serrated knife for slicing bread and slicing through cake layers. I like to use an offset serrated knife for a variety of slicing and chopping functions. In some knife assortments this is labeled as a sandwich knife. A thin-bladed slicing knife is also useful for slicing cakes and other desserts at serving time.

Spatulas: Small and large offset spatulas are essential for finishing cakes and spreading filling on dough. I also like to have a wide griddle spatula, which can be useful for moving around a finished cake or dessert.

Skimmer: Skimmers, tongs, and slotted spoons are all useful for deep-frying and a variety of other kitchen jobs.

Graters: A box grater with diagonally set holes, large and small, is better than one that has only holes that look as though they were formed by a nail piercing the sheet metal. Microplane and Cuisipro are two brands of graters that come in all sizes and degrees of fineness for grating citrus zests, nutmeg, and cheese, and for shaving chocolate.

Wooden Spoons: I like to keep a wooden spoon or two for stirring sauces or other mixture. Flat-ended wooden spatulas are more useful, since they can sweep evenly across the bottom of a pan, scraping it efficiently.

Pizza Wheel: A plain sharp one and a serrated one (sometimes both come mounted on the same handle) are useful for cutting different doughs.

Thermometers: Use the kind of candy and deep-fry thermometer that looks like a ruler, not the one that looks like a stem with a round dial at the top.

Instant-Read Thermometer: These can be useful for monitoring the internal temperature of baked bread or heated meringue.

Rolling Pin: I prefer the type without handles that is a straight cylinder of wood, about 16 inches long and about 2 inches in diameter. There are also nylon ones in the same shape that resist dough sticking to them.

DECORATING EQUIPMENT

Pastry Bags: These come in nylon or disposable plastic and are easy to find in cookware stores or by mail order. I like a 14- to 16-inch bag as an all-purpose one. Smaller ones are more for tiny piped cake decorating designs, and larger ones are meant to be used for large-quantity production.

Pastry Tubes: I have given the Ateco tube number in every recipe that uses piping. Ateco is the more or less universal supplier of tubes and the brand you'll encounter when you shop for them.

PAPER GOODS

Parchment Paper: After years of production work in professional kitchens, I always use large sheets of parchment paper (18 × 24 inches) that come in a box of 1,000 sheets. These are easy to obtain from paper wholesalers, and a friendly bakery may even sell you a box. You can share the box with several friends who also like to bake, and it's so much more convenient than using dinky paper on a roll.

Extra-Wide Foil: This can also be useful for lining large pans.

Wax Paper: Failing everything else, I have also used buttered wax paper.

Cardboards: These are available in various sizes and shapes. Round ones the same diameter as your cake will make cake finishing a breeze. Rectangular ones can make unmolding large cakes or tarts easy, and can also be used to slide loaves of free-form bread onto a baking stone in the oven.

MEASURING TOOLS

Liquid measures are usually made from glass or clear plastic and are graduated for fractions of cups. New-style measuring cups make it possible to read the quantity from the top, rather than the side of the cup—a definite improvement. I have several each in 1-, 2-, 4-, and 8-cup sizes. Not having to rinse out the cup before measuring another ingredient makes things easier.

Dry-Measure Cups: These are for measuring dry ingredients such as flour, confectioners' sugar, or cornstarch. Spoon the ingredient into the cup and level it off for accurate measurement. Sugar is the only dry ingredient I scoop when measuring.

Measuring Spoons: Graduated metal measuring spoons are essential. I like to have several sets so that if one set gets wet measuring liquid ingredients, there is another set of dry ones waiting.

Scales: There are any number of fairly inexpensive battery-operated scales available. These make quick work of weighing out chocolate or other ingredients measured by weight.

ELECTRICALS

A heavy-duty mixer such as a KitchenAid is essential for the recipes here. I suppose you could get away with a heavy-duty hand mixer, but it would be less convenient to use. If you are investing in a stand mixer, go all the way and buy an extra bowl and whisk. They will save you so much time in the first year you use the mixer that they will more than pay for themselves.

A food processor is essential for grinding nuts and mixing many doughs. My first choice of machine for mixing most pastry doughs is the food processor. Use the metal blade for pureeing, grinding, and pastry doughs, and the plastic one for most yeast doughs.

A blender is useful for pureeing fruit for sauces or fillings. I think it does a faster and more efficient job than a food processor.

MISCELLANEOUS

Baking Stone: This is useful for free-form breads and is not expensive. I like the large rectangular stones. The one I have is about 14 × 16 inches.

A BAKER'S TOUR

1. BREADS

ITALY — LIGURIAN FOCACCIA FROM NOVE LIGURE
Focaccia alla Novese

ARMENIA — CRACKER BREAD
Lavash

INDIA — GRILL- OR GRIDDLE-BAKED FLATBREAD
Naan

ITALY — CRUSTY "SLIPPER" BREAD
Ciabatta

FRANCE — BORDEAUX RUSTIC BREAD
Pain Rustique Bordelais

SWITZERLAND — OLIVE OIL BREAD FROM TICINO
Pane Ticinese

ISRAEL — BRAIDED BREAD
Challah

SWITZERLAND — THICK-CRUSTED PEASANT ROLLS
Buerli

BELGIUM — RAISIN BREAKFAST BREAD
Cramique

DENMARK — SALT PRETZELS
Kringler

THE NETHERLANDS — CURRANT ROLLS
Krentenbollen

ENGLAND — POTATO LOAF BREAD

FRANCE — SPICE BREAD
Pain d'Épices

IRELAND — DARINA ALLEN'S SODA BREAD

SCOTLAND — MRS. MACNAB'S SCONES

Overleaf: Darina Allen's Soda Bread

BREAD IS UNIVERSAL. No matter where you go in the world, you'll find it in some form. It's the most common, as well as the most diverse, baked product available today. Cultures vary greatly with regard to taste and the amount of time available for baking; furthermore, different climates produce different strains of wheat and other grains. Because of these differences and others, radically diverse forms of bread have emerged from various cultures. How fortunate we are today to have the perspective of history, not to mention convenient methods for sharing information, so that we have access to so many types of bread.

The following list gives brief descriptions of the type of breads considered here. It is by no means a complete list of all the breads available in the world, but it does cover many of them.

FLATBREADS: Thin, usually flexible breads that are sometimes wrapped around fillings. Some flatbreads are cooked on a griddle rather than in the oven.

FREE-FORM LOAVES: Breads that are shaped into rounds, long or short ovals, or cylinders. They may be baked in a sheet pan or slid from a peel (dough shovel) or a piece of stiff cardboard directly onto a baking stone heated in the oven.

ROLLS: Small versions of free-form loaves. Rolls make neat individual servings.

PAN BREADS: These are shaped and then placed in pans for a final rising and then for baking. Their shape makes them practical for slicing and toasting, or for sandwiches.

QUICK BREADS: These are leavened with baking powder or baking soda or both, rather than yeast.

Breads can also be divided into one-step breads and two-step breads. For one-step breads, all ingredients are mixed together at the same time. The two-step method—most common with yeast-risen breads—calls for combining part of the flour, part of the liquid, and all or some of the yeast and allowing that initial mixture to rise before adding the remainder of the ingredients. (This initial mixture is called a starter.) The latter method permits the use of less yeast, depending on multiplication of a small amount of yeast to leaven the dough. In some cases, it is also used to create a more complex flavor.

SOME HINTS FOR ACHIEVING GOOD BREAD

1. Measure accurately. Don't expect the dough or the final baked bread to have the right texture if the ingredients haven't been accurately measured. It can be easier to mix a complicated recipe if you measure out all the ingredients first, before you begin. Then you can concentrate on the mixing and you won't be distracted by attempting to do two things at the same time.

2. Mix well. Whether you decide to mix your dough by hand or by machine, make sure you make a smooth, elastic dough. This ensures the best texture for the finished bread.

3. Take your time. Bread doughs need to rise slowly to develop the best flavor and texture. A dough that has not risen enough after mixing will not rise well before or during baking.

4. Neatness counts. Try to keep separate pieces uniform in size. Use pans of the correct size for large loaves so that the loaves rise to their utmost.

5. Watch the oven. Baking times are as accurate as possible, but you should still keep an eye on your bread while it is baking. Bread baking frequently starts out at a high temperature—but if you see that a loaf is getting too dark, by all means lower the temperature by 50 to 75 degrees. Your oven may be heating to a higher temperature than the one it is set to. An instant-read thermometer gives best results in determining doneness for breads: when plunged into the thickest part of the loaf, it should read between 200 and 210 degrees.

6. Cool loaves thoroughly. Make sure to follow the instructions for cooling the loaf. If you wrap or cover the loaf before it has cooled completely, it may become soggy.

7. Enjoy your bread fresh. If you must bake bread days in advance, wrap and freeze it after it has cooled; then defrost, reheat, and cool it before serving. This will give you the best approximation of freshly baked bread, although nothing beats the flavor and texture of fresh bread. More specific instructions for storage appear at the end of some recipes.

MIXING BREAD DOUGH

The recipes in this chapter all give instructions for mixing the dough in a heavy-duty stand mixer. Follow the instructions below for mixing by hand or in the food processor.

Hand Mixing: Use a large rubber spatula to mix the liquid into the dry ingredients. Mix until all the flour has been moistened and a dough is beginning to form, though it will look very rough and uneven.

Scrape the dough out onto a lightly floured work surface and use a bench scraper to repeatedly fold the dough over on itself. It should start to look smoother and become slightly elastic.

To knead the dough, fold the dough in half toward you, folding the far end over to the middle. Use the heels of your hands to press the dough away from you. Turn the dough so that it is perpendicular to its original position and repeat the folding and pushing. If the dough is sticky, lightly flour the work surface and your hands, but avoid adding flour to the dough. Continue for 5 to 10 minutes, or until the dough is smooth and elastic.

To save some time and work, knead the dough for a minute or so, then cover it with a cloth or plastic wrap and let it rest for 10 minutes. When you come back to the dough, it will become smooth and elastic with minimal additional kneading.

Food-Processor Mixing: Use the plastic blade in your food processor for mixing bread doughs. Add the liquid to the dry ingredients in the food processor and pulse the machine on and off at 1-second intervals to form a shaggy ball of dough. Let the dough rest for 10 minutes, then pulse again, using 2- or 3-second pulses, until the dough is smooth and elastic and easily forms a ball.

ITALY

Ligurian Focaccia from Nove Ligure

Focaccia alla Novese

DOUGH

2 teaspoons salt

4 cups all-purpose flour (spoon flour into dry-measure cup and level off)

5 tablespoons lard or olive oil

2 teaspoons active dry yeast

1⅔ cups warm water, about 110 degrees

FINISHING

3 tablespoons olive oil

2 teaspoons coarse or kosher salt

One 10 × 15-inch jelly-roll pan, generously greased with olive oil

In November 1998, I attended the Slow Food conference in Turin with my friends Miriam Brickman and Arthur Boehm. We signed up for the conference at the last minute, so we were unable to attend any of the seminars, but we did manage to spend quite a while on the tasting floor. Of course, I headed straight for the bakery stands, where a baker from Liguria was making and selling this salt-drenched focaccia.

Back home, I re-created that well-enjoyed and well-remembered focaccia—this was not too difficult, given that the list of ingredients had been posted at the stand. Lard turned out to be the secret to tasty, tender results. One of the things I love most about this recipe is that it is easy to prepare by hand—all you need is a rubber spatula. I like to serve focaccia with drinks before a meal; you can dress it up with prosciutto or other cured meats or serve it alone.

One 10 × 15-inch flatbread

1. To make the dough, stir the salt into the flour and rub in the lard or oil with your hands, making sure it is evenly absorbed by the flour.

2. Whisk the yeast into the water and use a large rubber spatula to stir the yeast mixture into the flour mixture. Stir vigorously to make an evenly moistened dough that is not necessarily very smooth.

3. Cover the bowl with plastic wrap and let the dough rise at room temperature until it is doubled in bulk, about 1 hour.

4. Once the dough has risen, scrape it onto the prepared pan and spread it evenly with the palms of your hands. If the dough resists, set the pan aside for 5 minutes to let the dough relax a little, then continue. Cover the dough with oiled plastic wrap and let the dough rise in the pan until it is puffy, about another 30 minutes.

5. About 15 minutes before you are ready to bake the focaccia, set a rack in the lowest level of the oven and preheat the oven to 425 degrees.

6. Use your index finger to dimple the dough at 1½-inch intervals. Drizzle with the olive oil and sprinkle with the salt.

7. Bake the focaccia until it is deep golden in color, about 30 minutes. Before removing the focaccia from the oven, use a spatula to lift the focaccia to make sure the bottom is well-colored and done.

8. Slide the focaccia from the pan onto a rack to cool, or onto a cutting board if you wish to serve it immediately.

Serving: Cut the focaccia into 2- to 3-inch squares.

Storage: Focaccia like this is always best on the day it is made, but if you have leftovers, wrap them tightly in foil. Unwrap them and reheat them in the oven or toaster oven before serving.

ARMENIA

Cracker Bread
Lavash

3¼ cups unbleached all-purpose flour (spoon flour into dry-measure cup and level off)

1½ teaspoons salt

2½ teaspoons active dry yeast

1 cup warm water, about 110 degrees

1 teaspoon sugar

¼ cup olive oil or melted butter

Three 12 × 18-inch jelly-roll pans lined with parchment or foil. (If you don't have 3 pans, you can wait and reuse the same pan—the dough will keep well until you have time to stretch and bake it.)

This is a perfect example of a thin, crisp, Middle Eastern flatbread. It is light, delicate, and easy to prepare. Although the word *lavash* has been picked up to describe soft breads as well, it indicates a crackerlike flatbread. Traditionally, lavash are baked on bricks or on inverted woks.

This lavash may be quite different from others you have seen. Often lavash is moistened with water to make it limp so it can function as a wrap for savory ingredients, just like the rolled sandwiches so popular today. I prefer it crisp. As is typical of ethnic recipes, it's hard to pin down the "true" version of lavash. There's always another side to the story. ***Three 12 × 18-inch sheets of bread***

1. Stir the flour and salt together in the bowl of an electric mixer.
2. Whisk the yeast into the water, then whisk in the sugar and oil. Stir this mixture into the flour with a large rubber spatula, continuing to stir until the flour is evenly moistened and the dough is rough and shaggy-looking.
3. Place the bowl on the mixer with the dough hook and mix on medium speed until dough is even in appearance, about 2 minutes. Stop the mixer and let the dough rest 10 minutes.
4. Continue mixing the dough for another 2 minutes, on low speed, just until the dough is smooth and elastic.

5. Scrape the dough into an oiled bowl and turn it over so that the top of the dough is oiled. Cover with plastic and let the dough rise at room temperature until it is doubled in bulk, about 1 hour.
6. Scrape the dough—avoid folding it over on itself—from the bowl to a floured work surface. Press the dough into an even disk and cut the dough into 3 even wedges. Form each wedge into a ball and allow to rest on the work surface, covered with a towel or plastic wrap, for about 10 minutes.
7. Meanwhile set racks in the upper and lower thirds of the oven and preheat to 350 degrees.
8. Take one of the balls of dough and roll it as thin as possible on a floured work surface. Pick up the dough and gently stretch it over the pan in both length and width until it is a little larger than the pan. Use scissors to cut away the thick edges and discard them.
9. Repeat with the remaining dough. If you don't have 3 pans, just let the remaining dough rest until a pan is available, then stretch and bake the dough.
10. Pierce the dough at 1-inch intervals with the tines of a fork.
11. Bake the bread until evenly golden and crisp, about 20 minutes.
12. Place the pan on a rack to cool.

Serving: Break up the bread into irregular pieces. This is a good accompaniment to Middle Eastern–style hors d'oeuvres; I like to serve it with olives, some feta cheese, and a dish of hummus or charred eggplant salad.

Storage: For short-term storage, keep the bread at room temperature on a pan and loosely covered with plastic wrap. After it has cooled, transfer it to a tin or plastic container with a tight-fitting lid. If it softens and loses its crispness, place it on a cookie sheet and crisp in a 350-degree oven for a few minutes before serving.

INDIA

Grill- or Griddle-Baked Flatbread
Naan

4 cups all-purpose flour (spoon flour into dry-measure cup and level off)

2 teaspoons salt

1 tablespoon sugar

2½ teaspoons active dry yeast

1¼ cups warm water, about 110 degrees

1½ tablespoons vegetable or olive oil

Melted butter for serving

A griddle or nonstick sauté pan for baking the naan, or a charcoal or gas grill

Normally naan is baked in a tandoor, an Indian oven shaped like a beehive. Since these ovens are seldom part of an American home kitchen, I have adapted the recipe to bake the bread on a griddle or sauté pan, or on an outdoor gas or charcoal grill.

I learned to make naan from Mohammed Hussein, the bread expert at Danny Meyer's Indian fusion restaurant, Tabla, in Manhattan. Hussein, as everyone calls him, is from Bangladesh and also has his own Indian restaurant in Woodside, Queens. Chef Floyd Cardoz was kind enough to arrange for me to spend a morning at Tabla with Hussein learning to mix and bake the bread, and I am very grateful to him for having allowed my intrusion into his immaculate kitchens. Making the dough for naan was easy at Tabla, as they have giant mixers to accommodate large quantities. Sticking my arm into a tandoor oven heated to more than 800 degrees was another story. I was so afraid of getting burned that the first time I tried to press the disk of dough against the side of the oven was a dismal failure: the bread wound up on the oven floor and burned. My second naan stuck to the side of the oven almost entirely, and things improved markedly on subsequent tries. Still, using a pan on the stove or an outdoor grill will pretty much duplicate the method for baking naan, and you won't have to stick your arm into a furnace to do it! ***Six 8-inch flatbreads***

1. Stir together the flour, salt, and sugar by hand in the bowl of an electric mixer.

2. Whisk the yeast into the water and add to the bowl. Use a large rubber spatula to stir the ingredients together. Place the bowl on the mixer with the dough hook and mix the dough at the lowest speed for 2 minutes. Add the oil and mix 1 minute longer.

3. Scrape the dough into an oiled bowl and turn it over so that the top is oiled. Press plastic wrap against the surface of the dough and let the dough rise at room temperature until it is doubled in bulk, about 1 hour. You may also let it rise in the refrigerator overnight.

4. Scrape the risen dough out onto a lightly floured work surface and use a knife or bench scraper to divide the dough into 6 equal pieces. Round the pieces of dough under your hand to make smooth spheres, as in the illustration, right. Place on a floured plate or pan and cover with oiled plastic wrap. Let the dough rise for about 1 hour at room temperature or about 3 hours in the refrigerator.

5. To bake the naan on a sauté pan or griddle, place the pan over medium heat and cover the pan with a dome-shaped cover at least 10 inches in diameter. Let the pan heat while you are shaping the naan.

6. On a lightly floured work surface, use your fingertips to press out one of the pieces of dough into a flat disk. Then use the palm of your hand or a rolling pin to flatten the piece of dough to an even disk about 8 inches in diameter.

7. Uncover the pan or griddle and place the dough on it. Cover for 2 minutes and allow to bake. Uncover the pan and turn the dough over to bake on the other side for 2 additional minutes, covering the pan again. Remove the baked naan from the pan and cover the pan and allow it to heat for a couple of minutes before pressing out and baking the next piece of dough. Baking the naan one at a time is time-consuming, but best for flavor and texture.

8. To bake the naan on a grill, make a charcoal fire and allow it to burn to a covering of white ash. Or preheat a gas grill and set the temperature between medium and high.

9. Press out all the pieces of dough and place on the grill all at once. If you can cover the grill, do so for about 30 seconds, and turn the naan over to bake for 30 seconds on the other side.

10. No matter which method you choose, it is important to use good judgment about the baking time. Naan should be blistery and lightly colored, with a few dark spots, so regulate the baking time to make sure they do not burn.

SERVING: Quickly brush the naan with melted butter before serving in wedges (or tearing apart with hands) with Indian food or any highly seasoned food.

STORAGE: Naan is always best when freshly baked and doesn't lend itself to advance preparation, but if you have any left over, by all means wrap it in plastic and refrigerate it. Reheat any leftover naan in the toaster oven and butter it.

VARIATIONS

ONION SEED *NAAN:* Add 1 tablespoon onion seeds (available in Indian markets, or see Sources, page 363) to the dough before the oil.

ROSEMARY *NAAN:* Not a traditional Indian variation, but a popular one at Tabla. Add 1½ tablespoons chopped fresh rosemary to the dough before the oil.

GARLIC *NAAN:* Add 2 teaspoons finely chopped garlic to the dough before the oil.

ITALY

Crusty "Slipper" Bread
Ciabatta

4½ cups unbleached all-purpose flour (spoon flour into dry-measure cup and level off)

2 teaspoons salt

2 teaspoons active dry yeast

2 cups warm water, about 110 degrees

Olive oil for the bowl

Cornmeal for the sliding pan

Baking stone or 2 jelly-roll pans that fit side by side in the oven, plus a cookie sheet with no sides or a piece of stiff cardboard to slide the loaves into the oven

The name *ciabatta*, Italian for slipper, probably derives from the fact that this casually shaped loaf looks like a slipper or shoe. Ciabatta's main characteristic is that it emphasizes crust over crumb: the loaf is almost all crust with a few webs of crumb inside.

The dough is very soft and rather difficult to handle. Not to worry, though. Ciabatta is never perfectly formed, so if your loaf is slightly uneven in shape, it makes no difference. ***Two 8- to 10-inch loaves***

1. Stir together the flour and salt in the bowl of an electric mixer. In a separate bowl, whisk the yeast into the water. Then stir the yeast mixture into the flour.
2. Fit the mixer with the paddle and mix the dough for about 1 minute on lowest speed.
3. Stop the mixer and let the dough rest for 10 minutes.
4. Beat the dough again on medium speed, until smooth and elastic, about 2 to 3 minutes.
5. Oil a 3-quart bowl and scrape the dough into it. Turn the dough over so that the top is also oiled. Press plastic wrap against the surface of the dough and let the dough rise at room temperature until it is doubled in bulk, about 1 hour.

6. About 30 minutes before you are ready to bake the dough, place the baking stone on the middle rack of the oven and preheat to 500 degrees. If you are using pans instead of the stone, invert the two pans side by side on the middle rack of the oven and preheat at the same temperature.

7. To form the loaves, scrape the dough onto a floured work surface, deflating it as little as possible. Gently pat the dough into an 8-inch square. Cut in half to make 2 rectangles.

8. Sprinkle the cookie sheet or cardboard with cornmeal and arrange one of the pieces of dough at the far end, stretching the dough very slightly as you place it on the pan. Open the oven and slide the loaf onto the stone or one of the inverted jelly-roll pans, quickly jerking away the cookie sheet or cardboard. Repeat with the remaining piece of dough.

9. Bake the ciabattas until they are very dark golden and reach an internal temperature of about 200 degrees, about 25 minutes.

10. Cool the breads directly on a rack.

Serving: Cut the loaf into thick vertical slices to serve it with a meal. To use the loaves for sandwiches, split them horizontally.

Storage: See page 26.

Ciabatta (left) and Buerli (page 24).

FRANCE

Bordeaux Rustic Bread
Pain Rustique Bordelais

STARTER

½ teaspoon active dry yeast

¼ cup warm water, about 110 degrees

½ cup unbleached all-purpose flour (spoon flour into dry-measure cup and level off)

DOUGH

1½ cups warm water, about 110 degrees

1 teaspoon active dry yeast

3 cups unbleached all-purpose flour

1 cup medium or whole grain rye flour

2 teaspoons salt

2 jelly-roll pans dusted with cornmeal

This mixed-grain bread is easy to make and also easy to form—it is just cut into several rectangles to be shaped before baking. The mixture of white and rye flour duplicates the nuttier flavor of some European flours. It is an invention of the famous bread expert Raymond Calvel, and this version is adapted from *Pains Spéciaux et Décorés* by Couet and Kayser (Éditions St. Honoré, 1989). ***Three rectangular 5 × 12-inch loaves***

1. For the starter, in a medium bowl, whisk the yeast into the water and then stir in the flour. Cover with plastic wrap and allow to ferment for 8 hours in a cool place. If the room is warm, let the sponge rise at room temperature for 1 hour, then for the remaining 7 hours let it rise in the refrigerator.

2. When the starter is done, make the dough. Place the water in the bowl of an electric mixer and whisk in the yeast by hand. Use a rubber spatula to scrape the starter into the water and mix it in. Add both flours and the salt, and use the rubber spatula to mix the ingredients to a rough dough.

3. Place the bowl on the mixer with the dough hook and mix on lowest speed for 2 minutes. Allow the dough to rest for 10 minutes.

4. Mix on medium speed until it is smooth, elastic, and slightly sticky, about 2 minutes. Scrape the dough into an oiled bowl and turn it over so that the top is oiled. Allow the dough to rise until doubled, about 1 hour.

5. To form the loaves, scrape the dough onto a floured work surface. Shape the dough into a 12-inch square. Cut into three 4 × 12-inch rectangles, using a knife or bench scraper.

6. Transfer the loaves to the prepared pans, placing 2 on one pan and 1 on the other. Cover the loaves with cloth or plastic wrap and allow them to rise at room temperature until doubled, about 1 hour.

7. About 15 minutes before the loaves are completely risen, set racks in the upper and lower thirds of the oven and preheat to 450 degrees.

8. Place the pans in the oven and bake until the loaves are beginning to color well, about 20 minutes. Turn the pans from back to front, then place the top pan on the lower rack and the bottom pan on the upper rack. Close the oven and lower the temperature to 350 degrees.

9. Bake until the loaves are deep golden and the internal temperature reaches about 200 degrees, about 20 additional minutes. Cool the loaves on racks.

Serving: Cut the bread into 1-inch slices. It is a perfect accompaniment to a meal and also makes great toast when sliced thin.

Storage: See page 6.

Olive Oil Bread from Ticino
Pane Ticinese

3 cups bleached all-purpose flour (spoon flour into dry-measure cup and level off)

1½ teaspoons salt

2 teaspoons active dry yeast

1 cup warm water, about 110 degrees

1 teaspoon sugar

2 tablespoons olive oil

Cornmeal for the pan

1 jelly-roll pan dusted with cornmeal

This snowy-white crumbed loaf is reminiscent of the excellent bread at Lino Gabbani's elegant prepared food store on Via Pessina in Lugano. Sometimes this bread is called *pane reale*, or royal bread, in Ticino. ***One 18-inch rectangular loaf***

1. Stir the flour and salt together in the bowl of an electric mixer.
2. Whisk the yeast into the water, then whisk in the sugar and the oil.
3. Use a large rubber spatula to stir the liquid into the flour.
4. Place the bowl on the mixer fitted with the dough hook and mix the dough on low speed for 2 minutes. Stop the mixer and allow the dough to rest for 10 minutes.
5. Mix the dough on medium speed until it is smooth and elastic, about 2 minutes.
6. Scrape the dough into an oiled bowl and turn the dough over so that the top is oiled. Press plastic wrap against the dough and allow it to rise at room temperature until it is doubled in bulk, about 1 hour. After the dough has risen it will be quite soft.
7. After the dough has risen, scrape it onto a lightly floured work surface and press it gently to deflate it. Form the dough into a rough rectangle, then divide it into 7 equal pieces. Form each piece of dough into a blunt oval about 4 inches long.

8. Position the ovals of dough parallel to each other and about ½ inch apart on the prepared pan. Cover with a towel or a piece of oiled plastic wrap and allow the loaf to rise until it is doubled in bulk and the ovals are touching, about 45 minutes to 1 hour.
9. About 15 minutes before the loaf is done rising, set a rack in the middle level of the oven and preheat to 425 degrees.
10. Use a razor blade or a sharp knife to slash the loaf lengthwise down its center, stopping short of the ends.
11. Bake the loaf until it is well risen and deep golden and reaches an internal temperature of about 200 degrees, about 30 minutes.
12. Cool the loaf on a rack.

SERVING: Cut the loaf into 1-inch vertical slices to serve. Its delicate flavor makes it perfect to serve with cheese.

STORAGE: See page 6.

ISRAEL

Braided Bread
Challah

This recipe comes from my dear friend Yocheved Hirsch, who lives in Tel Aviv. It's simple and easy to make. Whether you want it for its primary purpose, to eat with the Jewish sabbath meal, or whether you just want to enjoy an excellent bread, rich with eggs and oil, this fits the bill.

One large loaf, about 16 inches long

SPONGE

2½ teaspoons active dry yeast

⅓ cup warm water, about 110 degrees

½ cup unbleached all-purpose flour (spoon flour into dry-measure cup and level off)

DOUGH

1 cup warm water, about 110 degrees

½ cup vegetable oil, such as corn or canola

2 large eggs

2 large egg yolks

¼ cup sugar

2½ teaspoons salt

5½ cups unbleached all-purpose flour

Egg wash: 1 egg well beaten with a pinch of salt

One 12 × 18-inch jelly-roll pan, lined with parchment or foil

1. For the sponge, in a medium bowl whisk the yeast into the water. Stir in the flour and cover with plastic wrap. Let the sponge rise at room temperature until bubbly, about 15 minutes.
2. After the sponge has risen, scrape it into the bowl of an electric mixer. Use a large rubber spatula to stir in the water, oil, eggs, yolks, sugar, and salt. Finally, stir in the flour.
3. Place the bowl on the mixer with the paddle attachment and mix on low speed for 1 minute. Stop the mixer and let the dough rest for 10 minutes.
4. Mix the dough again on medium speed until it is smooth and elastic, about 4 minutes.

5. Scrape the dough into an oiled bowl and turn it over so that the top is oiled. Press plastic wrap against the surface of the dough and let the dough rise at room temperature until it is doubled, 45 minutes to 1 hour.

6. Scrape the risen dough out onto a lightly floured work surface. Press the dough into a rough square and use a knife or bench scraper to cut the dough into 3 equal pieces.

7. Roll one piece of dough back and forth under the palms of your hands to make it into a cylinder about 12 inches long. Repeat with the other pieces of dough.

8. Arrange the 3 pieces of dough next to each other lengthwise on the prepared pan.

9. Starting in the center, braid the pieces of dough one over the other, avoiding stretching the dough as you are braiding. When you get to the end, pinch the 3 pieces of dough together and turn them about 1 inch under the loaf.

10. Turn the pan so that the unbraided end is facing you and repeat on that side of the loaf.

11. Cover with a cloth or plastic wrap and let rise at room temperature until doubled, about 1 hour.

12. About 15 minutes before the challah is completely risen, set a rack in the middle level of the oven and preheat to 375 degrees.

13. Immediately before placing the challah in the oven, brush it neatly with the egg wash.

14. Bake the challah until it is well risen and deep golden, about 45 minutes. Slide it on the paper from the pan to a rack to cool.

Serving: This is a great breakfast or brunch bread and also makes good toast or French toast.

Storage: See page 6.

Thick-Crusted Peasant Rolls
Buerli

STARTER

2 cups unbleached all-purpose flour (spoon flour into dry-measure cup and level off)

1/4 cup whole wheat flour

1 teaspoon active dry yeast

1 cup warm water, about 110 degrees

DOUGH

1 3/4 cups water

1 1/2 teaspoons active dry yeast

4 cups unbleached all-purpose flour

1/2 cup whole wheat flour

1 tablespoon sugar

2 1/2 teaspoons salt

2 jelly-roll pans dusted heavily with flour

When I first went to Switzerland to work in the early 1970s, buurli were a common sight in all the little restaurants and train station buffets throughout Zurich and eastern Switzerland. Now the quaint little restaurants and the excellent chewy buurli have begun to disappear, but I know I can always get a good buerli, along with an excellent bratwurst, at the Horber stand in the Wednesday market in the train station in Zurich. When I can't go there, I make this version of one of my favorite breads.

Buerli are always baked in couples or quartets. This recipe gives instructions for baking them in couples, because that way they fit more easily on 2 baking pans. They are large rolls that are a perfect accompaniment to hearty food—and they freeze well. ***12 large rolls***

1. For the starter, in a nonreactive bowl large enough to contain the starter after it has tripled in volume, stir both flours together. In a separate small bowl, whisk the yeast into the water. Then stir the yeast mixture thoroughly into the flour mixture. Cover the bowl with plastic wrap and leave to ferment for 3 hours.

2. After the starter has risen, prepare the dough. Put the water into the bowl of an electric mixer and whisk in the yeast by hand. Use a large rubber spatula to scrape in the starter and mix it with the water and yeast. Stir in the flours, sugar, and salt to form a rough dough.

3. Place the bowl on the mixer with the dough hook and mix on lowest speed for two minutes. Stop the mixer and allow the dough to rest for 10 minutes.

4. Mix the dough again on medium speed until it is smooth and elastic, about another 2 minutes. Scrape the dough into an oiled bowl and turn the dough over so that the top is oiled. Press plastic wrap against the surface of the dough and allow it to rise for 30 minutes.

5. Scrape the dough out onto a lightly floured work surface. Fold both ends of the dough in toward the center from opposite sides, then repeat with the other sides of the dough, as in the illustration below.

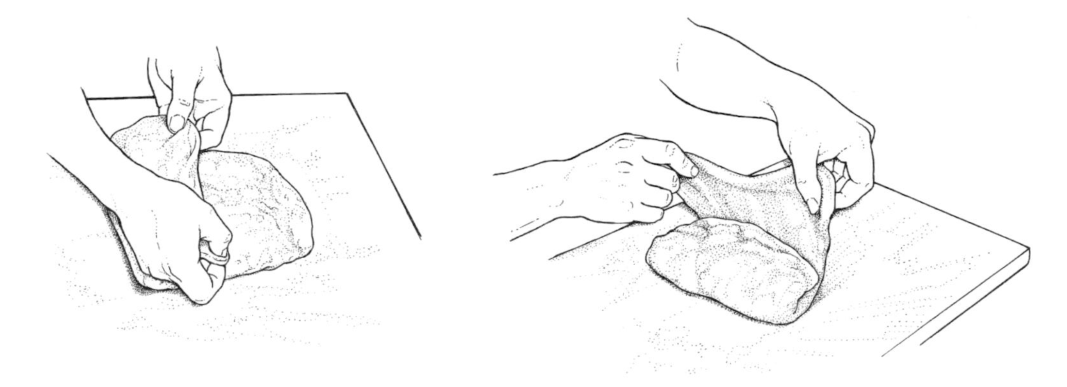

6. Return the dough to the bowl and allow it to rest for 30 minutes, covered loosely with plastic wrap or a towel. Then repeat the folding of the dough.

7. Again, replace the dough in the bowl and cover it loosely with plastic wrap or a towel and let it rise for 30 minutes.

8. To form the buerli, scrape the risen dough onto a lightly floured work surface and cut it into 3 equal pieces. Divide each of the resulting pieces in half to make 6 pieces, then divide each of the 6 pieces in half to make 12.

9. Generously flour the pieces of dough and form them into rough rounds.

10. Place 6 rounds of dough on each of the prepared pans. The rounds for each pair should be 1 inch away from each other to allow for rising. The first pair should be close to one of the short edges of the pan. The second pair should be in the middle of the pan, and the third pair should be close to the bottom edge of the pan. (The paired buerli should touch each other after they're risen, but shouldn't touch the other buerli.)

11. Cover each pan with a cloth and allow the buerli to rise until doubled, about 1 hour.

12. About 15 minutes before the buerli are completely risen, set racks in the upper and lower thirds of the oven and preheat to 500 degrees. Set a roasting pan in the bottom of the oven (to be used for making steam).

13. Place the pans of buerli in the oven and quickly add 2 cups of water to the heated pan in the bottom of the oven, averting your face from the steam. Quickly close the oven to prevent steam from escaping. Bake the buerli about 20 minutes, then turn the pans back to front, and place the pan from the upper shelf on the bottom and the pan from the bottom shelf on the top. Lower the temperature to 400 degrees and bake the buerli until they are very dark—almost black—and their internal temperature reaches 200 degrees, about 15 to 20 minutes longer.

14. Cool the buerli on racks.

SERVING: Buerli are never cut with a knife, but instead are broken apart by hand.

STORAGE: These are best on the day they are baked, but can be wrapped tightly and frozen. Defrost covered. Then bake uncovered for 10 minutes at 350 degrees and cool before serving.

BELGIUM

Raisin Breakfast Bread
Cramique

2 cups unbleached all-purpose flour (spoon flour into dry-measure cup and level off)

2 teaspoons active dry yeast

½ cup warm milk, about 110 degrees

2 large egg yolks

4 tablespoons (½ stick) unsalted butter, very soft

1 teaspoon sugar

¾ teaspoon salt

¾ cup dark raisins

One 8½ × 4½ × 2¾-inch loaf pan, buttered and the bottom lined with a rectangle of parchment paper

This is a popular bread to serve with butter for breakfast in Belgium, but it is also perfect to serve with tea or coffee in the afternoon. It is a lean form of brioche, enriched with just a little butter, sugar, and egg. This version comes from Wittamer, the best pastry shop in Brussels.

One 8½ × 4½ × 2¾-inch loaf

1. Place 1½ cups of the flour in the bowl of an electric mixer.
2. In a medium bowl, whisk the yeast into the milk, then whisk in the yolks. Stir the liquids into the flour.
3. Place the bowl on the mixer fitted with the paddle attachment and mix on lowest speed for 2 minutes. Stop the mixer and let the dough rest for 10 minutes.
4. Add the butter, sugar, and salt to the bowl along with the remaining ½ cup of flour and mix on lowest speed until combined. Mix on medium speed until the dough is smooth and elastic, about another 3 to 4 minutes. Beat in the raisins on lowest speed.
5. Scrape the dough into a buttered bowl and turn the dough over so that the top is buttered. Press plastic wrap against it and allow the dough to rise until doubled, about 1 hour.

6. After the dough is risen, scrape it onto a floured work surface. Press the dough into a rectangle. To form a loaf, make sure the surface of the dough is free of any excess flour, then stretch the dough into a rough rectangle. Fold in the short ends of the dough until it is approximately the length of the pan, then fold the far long edge over to the middle. Fold over the other long side and compress to form a tight cylinder, as in the illustration on page 35. Place the dough in the pan, seam side down. Cover with buttered plastic wrap. Allow the loaf to rise until doubled, about 1 hour.

7. When the loaf is almost doubled, set a rack in the middle level of the oven and preheat to 400 degrees.

8. When the loaf has completely risen, place in the oven and bake until it is deep golden and the internal temperature is about 200 degrees, about 30 minutes.

9. Unmold the loaf to a rack to cool on its side.

SERVING: Cut into thin slices, this bread makes excellent sandwiches and toast.

STORAGE: On the day it is baked, keep the bread loosely covered at room temperature. Tightly wrap in plastic and freeze for longer storage.

VARIATION: *CRAQUELIN*

Replace the raisins in the dough with ⅓ cup pearl sugar (see Sources, page 363). After the dough has risen, form it into a disk about 8 inches in diameter and place it on a cookie sheet lined with parchment or foil. Cover with buttered plastic wrap and allow to rise until doubled. Brush the top of the loaf with beaten egg and cut two concentric circular slashes in the top of the loaf, about 1½ and 3 inches from the edge. Sprinkle more pearl sugar in the cuts. Bake as above.

DENMARK

Salt Pretzels
Kringler

These are an amusing addition to an assortment of dinner rolls. ***12 small pretzels***

DOUGH

2 cups all-purpose flour (spoon flour into dry-measure cup and level off)

½ teaspoon salt

1½ teaspoons sugar

4 tablespoons (½ stick) unsalted butter, softened

2 teaspoons active dry yeast

½ cup warm milk, about 110 degrees

1 large egg

Egg wash: 1 egg well beaten with a pinch of salt

Kosher salt for sprinkling

2 cookie sheets or jelly-roll pans lined with parchment or foil

1. In the bowl of an electric mixer stir together the flour, salt, and sugar. Rub in the butter with your hands or a pastry blender. Whisk the yeast into the milk, then add liquid to the flour mixture. Add the egg and use a large rubber spatula to mix to a rough dough.
2. Place the bowl on the mixer with the dough hook and mix on lowest speed for 2 minutes. Stop the mixer and allow the dough to rest for 10 minutes.
3. Mix the dough again on medium speed until it is smooth and elastic, about 2 or 3 minutes.
4. Scrape the dough into an oiled or buttered bowl and turn it over so that the top is greased. Press plastic wrap against the surface of the dough and allow to rise at room temperature until doubled, about 1 hour.
5. Scrape the risen dough out onto a lightly floured work surface and press it into a rough square. Use a knife or bench scraper to cut the dough into 3 equal pieces. Cut each of the pieces into 4 pieces to make 12 pieces in all.

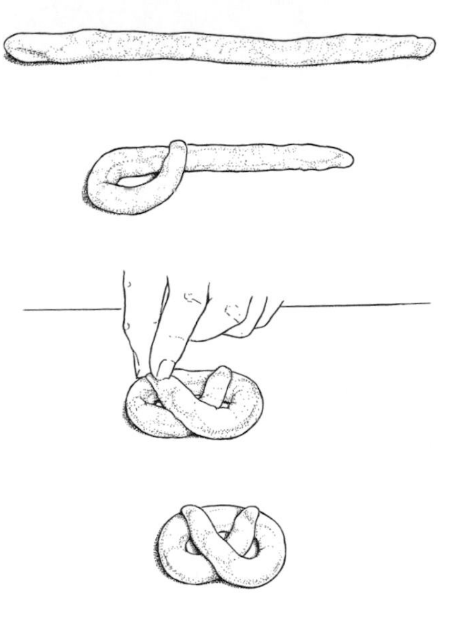

6. Cover the pieces of dough with a towel or plastic wrap. Roll a piece of dough into a strand about 12 inches long.

7. Shape into a pretzel according to the illustration, right, and place on the baking pan. Repeat with the remaining pieces of dough.

8. Brush the pretzels with the beaten egg and sprinkle them lightly with salt. Allow them to rise until they just begin to puff a little, about 30 minutes.

9. About 15 minutes before the pretzels are completely risen, set racks in the upper and lower thirds of the oven and preheat to 400 degrees.

10. Place the pans in the oven and bake for about 10 minutes. Switch the top pan to the lower rack and the bottom pan to the upper rack, also turning the pans back to front when you switch them. Bake the pretzels until they are a light golden color, about 10 to 15 minutes longer.

11. Slide the papers from the pans to racks to cool the pretzels on the papers.

SERVING: These are good with drinks before a meal, especially with a strong cheese or some prosciutto. Or serve them along with other breads as dinner rolls.

STORAGE: Keep the pretzels loosely covered at room temperature the day they are made. Place in plastic bags and freeze for longer storage. Reheat the pretzels and cool them slightly before serving.

THE NETHERLANDS

Currant Rolls
Krentenbollen

1 cup currants

½ cup dark raisins

2 cups unbleached all-purpose flour (spoon flour into dry-measure cup and level off)

1 cup whole wheat flour

2 teaspoons active dry yeast

1 cup warm milk, about 110 degrees

1 teaspoon sugar

1 teaspoon salt

2 tablespoons (¼ stick) unsalted butter, softened

1 large egg

1 large cookie sheet or jelly-roll pan covered with parchment or foil

Though these rolls are full of currants and raisins, they are not particularly sweet. In the Netherlands they are often used to make cheese sandwiches with aged Gouda.

12 medium rolls

1. Cover the currants and raisins with water, bring them to a boil over medium heat, and drain. Cool the dried fruit in a single layer on a pan covered with paper towels.
2. In a large bowl, mix the flour and whole wheat flour, then transfer approximately half of the combined flours to the bowl of an electric mixer.
3. Whisk the yeast into the milk, then stir the liquid into the flour in the mixer bowl, using a large rubber spatula. Cover the bowl with plastic wrap and set it aside until it begins to rise visibly, about 20 minutes.
4. Stir the sponge to deflate it and add the remaining flour, the sugar, salt, butter, and egg and stir them into the sponge with a large rubber spatula.
5. Place the bowl on the mixer with the dough hook and mix on lowest speed for 2 minutes. Stop the mixer and let the dough rest for 10 minutes.

6. Mix the dough on medium speed until it is smooth and elastic, about 2 minutes. Lower the speed to lowest and mix in the cooled currants and raisins.
7. Scrape the dough into a buttered bowl and turn it so that the top is buttered. Press plastic wrap against the dough and let it rise at room temperature until doubled, about 1 hour.
8. Scrape the dough onto a lightly floured work surface and press the dough into a rough square. Use a knife or bench scraper to cut the dough into 12 equal pieces.
9. Round each piece of dough under the cupped palm of your hand to make it into a sphere and to stretch a smooth, even skin around it, as in the illustration on page 13. Arrange the rolls equidistant from each other on the prepared pan.
10. Cover the rolls with a towel or plastic wrap and allow to rise until doubled, about 1 hour.
11. About 15 minutes before the rolls are completely risen, set a rack in the middle level of the oven and preheat to 375 degrees.
12. Bake the rolls until they are well risen and deep golden, about 30 to 35 minutes. The internal temperature should be about 200 degrees.
13. Cool the rolls on a rack.

Serving: Use the rolls for breakfast or brunch, or split and butter them and use them for cheese or other sandwiches as they do in the Netherlands.

Storage: See page 6.

ENGLAND

Potato Loaf Bread

4 cups unbleached all-purpose flour (spoon flour into dry-measure cup and level off)

½ cup warm mashed potato (1 small Idaho potato)

1½ teaspoons active dry yeast

⅔ cup warm milk, about 110 degrees

⅔ cup warm water, about 110 degrees

1 tablespoon salt

Two 8½ × 4½ × 2¾-inch loaf pans, buttered and lined with a rectangle of parchment paper

This is an adaptation of a recipe in Elizabeth David's brilliant *English Bread and Yeast Cookery* (Viking, 1977). The addition of the potato makes the bread more moist and flavorful, and the potato flavor really comes through when the bread is toasted. The potato needs to be warm when added to the other ingredients, so start cooking the potato and then get the other ingredients ready. By the time you are ready to use the potato, it will probably be just right and you may proceed with the recipe. To cook the potato, microwave or boil it; then peel, mash, and measure it. ***Two 8½ × 4½ × 2¾-inch loaves***

1. Combine the flour and potato in the bowl of an electric mixer and place on the mixer fitted with the paddle attachment. Mix on low speed until the flour and potato are smooth.

2. Whisk the yeast into the milk and water and add to the mixer bowl. Mix briefly on lowest speed, then switch to the dough hook. Add the salt and mix for 2 minutes on lowest speed. Stop the mixer and allow the dough to rest for 10 minutes.

3. Mix the dough again on medium speed until it is smooth and elastic, about 2 minutes.

4. Scrape the dough into an oiled bowl and turn the dough over so that the top is oiled. Press plastic wrap against the surface of the dough and let the dough rise at room temperature until doubled in bulk, about 1½ to 2 hours.

5. After the dough has risen, scrape the dough to a floured work surface. Press the dough into a rectangle, then cut it in half. To form a loaf, make sure the surface is free of any excess flour, then stretch the dough into a rough rectangle. Fold in the short ends of the dough until it is approximately the length of the pan, then fold the far long edge over to the middle. Fold over the other long side and compress to form a tight cylinder, as in the illustration, right. Place the dough in the pan, seam side down. Cover with oiled plastic wrap. Repeat with the second piece of dough. Allow to rise until doubled, about 1 to 1½ hours.

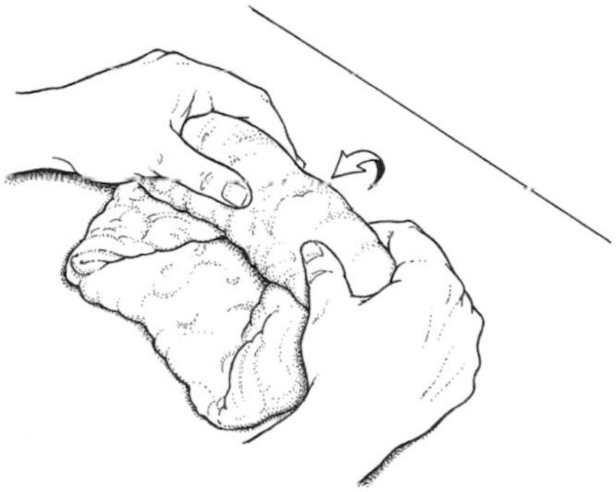

6. When the loaves are almost doubled, set a rack in the middle level of the oven and preheat to 400 degrees.

7. When the loaves have completely risen, place in the oven and bake until they are deep golden and the internal temperature is about 200 degrees, about 30 minutes,.

8. Unmold the loaves onto a rack to cool on their sides.

Serving: Cut into thin slices, this bread makes excellent sandwiches and toast.

Storage: See page 6.

FRANCE

Spice Bread
Pain d'Épices

3 cups bleached all-purpose flour (spoon flour into dry-measure cup and level off)

1 teaspoon dry mustard

1 teaspoon ground cinnamon

1 teaspoon finely crushed or ground aniseed

2½ teaspoons baking powder

½ teaspoon salt

1 cup water

⅔ cup sugar

⅔ cup dark, flavorful honey

1 tablespoon grated orange zest

One 9 × 5 × 3-inch loaf pan buttered and the bottom lined with a rectangle of parchment paper

This simple, tasty loaf is closely associated with the city of Dijon in Burgundy, and for that reason I have always added some dry mustard to the mixture of spices. Because this simple bread contains no fat of any kind, it should be allowed to age for a day or two before serving so that it will be more tender. ***One 9 × 5 × 3-inch loaf***

1. Set a rack in the middle level of the oven and preheat to 375 degrees.
2. In a large bowl mix the flour with the mustard, cinnamon, aniseed, baking powder, and salt. Sift them through a strainer onto a sheet of parchment or wax paper.
3. Combine the water and sugar in a 3-quart saucepan and place over medium heat, stirring occasionally to dissolve sugar, until the syrup comes to a simmer and all the sugar is melted.
4. Remove the syrup from the heat and stir in the honey and orange zest.
5. Resift about ¼ cup of the flour mixture over the sugar and honey mixture in the saucepan and incorporate it with a small whisk. Continue adding small amounts of the flour mixture in this way until about half of it is incorporated. For the remaining flour mixture, continue adding small amounts, but use a rubber spatula to mix it in.

6. Scrape the batter into the prepared pan and bake until a toothpick inserted in the center of the cake emerges dry, about 65 to 75 minutes. Start checking after 1 hour has elapsed so as not to overbake the bread. If the loaf starts to color too deeply on top, reduce the oven temperature to 325 degrees and cover the bread loosely with aluminum foil.

7. Cool the loaf in the pan on a rack for 10 minutes, then unmold and cool completely. Wrap well in foil when cool and age for 1 to 2 days before serving.

SERVING: Serve the pain d'épices in thin slices with tea or coffee. Some people like to butter it, but I like it plain.

STORAGE: When well wrapped in foil, this loaf will keep for a week. Freeze for longer storage.

IRELAND

Darina Allen's Soda Bread

4 cups unbleached all-purpose flour (spoon flour into dry-measure cup and level off)

1 teaspoon salt

1 teaspoon baking soda

1½ cups buttermilk (plus 1 to 2 tablespoons more if necessary)

1 cookie sheet or jelly-roll pan lined with parchment or foil

Most versions of soda bread seen in the United States are fancy, with lots of butter, sugar, raisins, and sometimes caraway seeds added for flavor and richness. Really, however, traditional Irish soda bread is similar to a slightly dry version of a scone. It is very simple and needs to be topped with a little butter and marmalade to make it more interesting. The versions of soda bread that follow are adapted from one of my favorite cookbooks, Darina Allen's *Irish Traditional Cooking* (Kyle Cathie, 1995). Darina runs a highly regarded cooking school and country inn at Ballymaloe in Ireland and is rightly considered the top food authority of that country. ***One 10-inch round loaf***

1. Set a rack in the middle of the oven and preheat to 450 degrees.
2. Stir together the flour, salt, and baking soda in a large bowl. Make a well in the center and add the buttermilk.
3. Use a rubber spatula to gently stir the buttermilk into the flour mixture, scraping up from the bottom of the bowl and using a movement similar to that for folding in egg whites. The flour should be evenly moistened and form a soft dough. If there are dry spots of unmoistened flour after you have mixed in the buttermilk for about 15 seconds, add 1 to 2 additional tablespoons of buttermilk and mix gently again.

4. Scrape the dough out onto a floured work surface and fold it over on itself two or three times. Form the dough into a ball and transfer it to the prepared pan. Press the dough into a 7-inch disk and cut a cross in the top of the dough that extends over the sides of the loaf. (Darina says that this is to let the fairies out!)

5. Bake the soda bread until it begins to color, about 15 minutes. Lower the heat to 400 degrees. Continue baking until the loaf is dark golden and baked through, about 20 to 30 additional minutes. You can test the center for doneness with a toothpick.

6. Slide the soda bread onto a rack to cool slightly before serving. If you want a crisp crust, leave the bread uncovered. If you prefer a tender crust, cover the bread with a towel as it is cooling.

Serving: Cut the soda bread into ½-inch slices and serve with butter and orange marmalade. Strong tea is the traditional beverage.

Storage: Keep the soda bread covered at room temperature. Leftovers may be sliced and toasted.

VARIATIONS

Seedy Bread: Add 1 tablespoon of sugar and 2 teaspoons caraway seeds to the flour mixture. Rub in 4 tablespoons (½ stick) butter with your hands or a pastry blender. Moisten with 1¼ to 1⅓ cups buttermilk (the sugar and butter will make the dough stickier). Shape and bake as above.

Spotted Dog: To the seedy bread, above, add 1 cup of raisins or currants or a mixture of the two and omit the caraway seeds. Beat 1 egg with 1 cup buttermilk and use that to moisten the dough, adding 1 to 2 more tablespoons of buttermilk if necessary. Shape and bake as above.

SCOTLAND

Mrs. Macnab's Scones

4 cups unbleached all-purpose flour (spoon flour into dry-measure cup and level off)

2 tablespoons sugar

1 tablespoon baking powder

4 tablespoons (½ stick) unsalted butter, cold

1 large egg

1¼ cups buttermilk

2 small cookie sheets or jelly-roll pans covered with parchment or foil

This is a famous Scottish scone recipe, which I have adapted from *Scots Kitchen* by F. Marian McNeill (Blackie and Son, 1929–1955). Mrs. Macnab was a farm wife at Ballater, not far from Balmoral, the summer residence of the British royal family. During her lifetime in the late nineteenth century, many of the dignitaries visiting Balmoral, including King Frederick of Prussia, came to tea at Mrs. Macnab's farmhouse because of the excellence of her scones. Now we can all enjoy them!

The recipe is deceptively simple—the whole success of these scones lies in not handling the dough too much, so that it doesn't toughen. Mix them with a light hand and they will be excellent. ***4 cakes of 4 scones each, or 16 individual scones***

1. Set racks in the upper and lower thirds of the oven and preheat to 425 degrees.
2. Stir together the flour, sugar, and baking powder in a large bowl. Rub in the butter finely, using your hands or a pastry blender.
3. Use a fork to beat together the egg and buttermilk. Add them to the flour mixture. Use the fork to gently mix in the liquid, scraping up from the bottom of the bowl, with a movement similar to the one used to fold in egg whites. Continue until all the dry ingredients are evenly moistened.
4. Scrape the dough out onto a floured surface and gently fold it over on itself two or three times.

5. Cut the dough into 4 pieces and press each piece into a 5-inch disk. Place the disks on the prepared pans, 2 disks to a pan. Use a knife or bench scraper to cut each disk into quarters, but don't separate the quarters.
6. Bake the scones until they are well risen and deep golden, about 12 to 15 minutes.
7. Leave the scones on the pans to cool for a few minutes.

SERVING: Serve the scones warm from the oven, but not red-hot, with butter or whipped cream and preserves or marmalade.

STORAGE: Keep the leftovers in a plastic bag in the refrigerator or freezer and warm them up in the oven or toaster oven before eating. (Leftover scones are not fit for guests, however.)

2. YEAST-RISEN CAKES AND PASTRIES

AUSTRIA	YEAST-RISEN COFFEE CAKE *Gugelhupf*
ITALY	CHESTNUT PANETTONE *Panettone alle Castagne*
POLAND	YEAST-RISEN COFFEE CAKE *Babka*
GERMANY	YEAST-RISEN CHRISTMAS CAKE FROM DRESDEN *Dresdner Stollen*
CROATIA	WALNUT-FILLED COFFEE CAKE *Povetica*
SWITZERLAND	ALMOND COFFEE RING FROM BERN *Berner Mandelkranz*
ENGLAND	HOT CROSS BUNS
SWITZERLAND	CHOCOLATE-STUDDED SWEET BUNS FROM BASEL *Schoggiweggli*
CZECH REPUBLIC AND SLOVAKIA	PRUNE-FILLED BUNS *Kolache*

Overleaf: Panettone alle Castagne

SWEET YEAST-RISEN CAKES AND PASTRIES such as Viennese gugelhupf and Italian panettone are a long-standing tradition, particularly in the home kitchens of Europe. These homey treats are not too far from savory yeast-risen breads. They are, generally speaking, forms of bread dough enriched with butter, eggs, and flavorings.

Many old-fashioned recipes start with instructions to procure bread dough from a local baker, but nowadays the recipes for these cakes and pastries are self-contained. Many begin with a sponge or starter, a mixture of yeast, liquid, and flour. The sponge allows the yeast to multiply and strengthen before being combined with rich, heavy ingredients such as sugar, butter, and eggs, making the dough rise more easily once all the ingredients are combined.

As with all home-style foods, the terminology is a bit confusing: a panettone or gugelhupf is considered a cake, whereas in France, brioche and things made from brioche dough are considered pastries. No matter—they all taste wonderful and are well worth the extra rising time they require. Best of all, they are not labor-intensive. Indeed, it's easy to see why home bakers have been preparing yeast-risen cakes and pastries for centuries.

HINTS FOR SUCCESS WITH YEAST-RISEN CAKES AND PASTRIES

1. Don't overheat: Make sure the milk or other liquid for dissolving the yeast is just lukewarm, no more than 110 degrees. Liquid that is too hot will kill the yeast and prevent the dough from rising at all.

2. Don't overchill: Have all ingredients at room temperature before you begin, unless a recipe calls for chilled butter. Starting with cold ingredients will add unnecessarily to the rising time of the dough.

3. Provide a warm rising space: In a few recipes, as marked, the dough needs to be chilled in order for the butter to firm up during the mixing process. For the rest, however, try to let the dough rise at a fairly warm room temperature—75 to 80 degrees is ideal. This saves time.

4. Don't overdo it: Make sure the dough doesn't rise too much before baking, however. Overrisen dough will cave in during the initial stage of baking, ruining your cake or pastry.

5. Use common sense: If the outside starts to color too much during the initial stage of baking, cover the cake or pastry with aluminum foil to prevent more top heat, and lower the oven temperature by 50 degrees. Your cake or pastry will take a little longer to bake, but will not be too dark. Follow instructions for descriptions of doneness in the recipes rather than slavishly adhering to a time schedule for baking.

6. Be patient before storing: Allow cakes and pastries to cool sufficiently before wrapping them. If you wrap them while they are still warm, condensation will form inside the package and make them wet and soggy.

7. Enjoy: Serving suggestions are included in the recipes, but these cakes and pastries fall very much into the "anytime" category. They are good to have on hand to offer to unexpected guests and are a perfect make-ahead item for entertaining. They can be served as dessert, but many are excellent for breakfast, and all are ideal when you are looking for a little something sweet to serve with afternoon coffee or tea.

AUSTRIA

Yeast-Risen Coffee Cake
Gugelhupf

SPONGE

½ cup milk

2½ teaspoons active dry yeast

⅔ cup unbleached all-purpose flour (spoon flour into dry-measure cup and level off)

DOUGH

½ cup raisins

1 tablespoon dark rum

6 tablespoons (¾ stick) unsalted butter, softened

3 tablespoons sugar

½ teaspoon salt

2 teaspoons grated lemon zest

1 teaspoon vanilla extract

2 large egg yolks

1⅓ cups unbleached all-purpose flour (spoon flour into dry-measure cup and level off)

⅓ cup whole blanched almonds, coarsely chopped

¼ cup sliced blanched almonds for lining the mold

One 6- to 8-cup gugelhupf or other decorative tube pan, thickly buttered

This delicate tea and coffee cake is seen all over Vienna in pastry shops and coffeehouses. This recipe is a contemporary version adapted from *Wiener Suss-speisen*, or *Viennese Sweets* (Trauner, 1990), originally written by Eduard Meier. The current edition was revised and expanded by Karl Schumacher, the pastry chef of the Oberlaa spa resort south of Vienna.

One 8- or 9-inch cake, about 12 servings

1. For the sponge, warm the milk over low heat in a small saucepan until it is just lukewarm, about 100 degrees. Pour the milk into a small bowl and whisk in the yeast. Stir in the flour and cover the bowl with plastic wrap. Let the sponge rise until very puffy, about 20 minutes.

2. Meanwhile, stir together the raisins and the rum and let the raisins macerate while you prepare the dough.

3. For the dough, beat the butter with the sugar and salt in an electric mixer fitted with the paddle attachment on medium speed until it is soft and light, about 2 to 3 minutes.

4. Beat in the lemon zest and vanilla.

5. Beat in the egg yolks, one at a time, beating smooth after each addition.

6. Stop the mixer and scrape the sponge into the electric mixer bowl. Beat on lowest speed until incorporated, about 1 minute.

7. Drain the raisins well, reserving the rum. Beat the rum into the dough, then beat in the flour.

8. Beat the dough for 2 minutes on lowest speed, then stop the mixer and let the dough rest for 10 minutes.

9. Beat the dough on medium speed until it is smooth and elastic, about 2 additional minutes. Decrease the speed to lowest and beat in the macerated raisins and the chopped almonds.

10. Scrape the dough into a buttered bowl and turn it over so that the top is buttered. Cover the bowl with plastic wrap and let the dough rise until it just begins to puff, about 20 minutes.

11. To prepare the mold, scatter the sliced almonds all over the buttered inside of the mold, rotating the mold to cover the buttered surface evenly with the almonds. Invert the mold to remove any of the almonds that have not stuck to the butter.

12. Use a large rubber spatula to carefully scrape the dough into the prepared mold, to avoid disturbing the sliced almonds. Cover the mold with a towel or a piece of buttered plastic wrap and let the dough rise until it is doubled. If you are using a 6-cup mold, the risen dough should reach the top of the mold; if you are using an 8-cup mold, the risen dough should reach about ½ inch short of the top.

13. About 15 minutes before the gugelhupf is fully risen, set a rack in the middle level of the oven and preheat to 375 degrees.

14. Bake the gugelhupf until it is well risen and deep golden, about 40 to 45 minutes. Test for doneness by inserting a toothpick halfway between the edge of the mold and the central tube. The toothpick should emerge dry.

15. Cool the gugelhupf in the pan on a rack for 10 minutes, then invert it onto the rack, remove the mold, and cool completely.

SERVING: Use a sharp serrated knife to cut the gugelhupf into slices. Leftover gugelhupf is good toasted and buttered.

STORAGE: Keep the gugelhupf wrapped in plastic. Double-wrap and freeze for longer storage. Defrost and bring to room temperature before serving.

ITALY

Chestnut Panettone
Panettone alle Castagne

SPONGE

½ cup milk

2½ teaspoons active dry yeast

⅔ cup unbleached all-purpose flour (spoon flour into dry-measure cup and level off)

DOUGH

8 tablespoons (1 stick) unsalted butter, softened

⅓ cup sugar

½ teaspoon salt

1 teaspoon finely grated lemon zest

2 teaspoons vanilla extract

1 tablespoon dark rum

3 large eggs, at room temperature

3 large egg yolks, at room temperature

3 cups unbleached all-purpose flour (spoon flour into dry-measure cup and level off)

1 cup candied chestnuts, drained, rinsed, and cut into ¼-inch dice

2 tablespoons unsalted butter, melted, for finishing

One 9-inch springform pan, 3 inches deep, buttered

The classic version of panettone, the traditional Italian Christmas cake, is flavored with raisins and candied orange peel, but today panettone is made in a wide variety of flavors. This one derives from a suggestion from my dear friend Nancy Nicholas, who tasted a chestnut panettone and then described it to me. I had never before thought to add candied chestnuts to panettone. Little did I know, however, when I started working on this recipe that my friend Rose Levy Beranbaum was including a chestnut panettone in her book *The Bread Bible* (Norton, 2003). When Rose and I realized that we were developing parallel recipes, we had a good laugh over great minds working alike. This recipe, however, is completely different from Rose's. ***1 tall 9-inch cake***

1. For the sponge, warm the milk in a small saucepan over low heat until it is just lukewarm, about 100 degrees. Pour the milk into a small bowl and whisk in the yeast. Stir in the flour. Cover the bowl with plastic wrap and set aside to ferment until risen and bubbling, about 20 minutes.

2. For the dough, beat the butter with the sugar and salt on medium speed in the bowl of an electric mixer fitted with the paddle attachment until well mixed, about 1 minute. Beat in the lemon zest, vanilla, and rum.

3. Whisk the eggs and yolks together and add about ⅓ of the egg mixture to the mixer bowl, beating it in until smooth. Decrease to the lowest speed and add about ⅓ of the flour, beating it in until smooth. Beat in another ⅓ of the egg mixture, then another ⅓ of the flour. Stop and scrape down the bowl and paddle. Resume mixing and beat in the remaining egg mixture, then the remaining flour. Stop the mixer and scrape in the risen sponge. Beat on lowest speed for 2 minutes, then stop and allow the dough to rest for 10 minutes.

4. Beat the dough on medium speed until it is smooth and relatively elastic (it will be very soft), about 2 minutes.

5. On lowest speed, beat in the candied chestnut pieces just until they are evenly distributed.

6. Scrape the dough into a large buttered bowl and use a rubber spatula to turn the dough over so that the top is buttered. Cover with plastic wrap and let the dough rise at room temperature until it is doubled in bulk, about 1 to 2 hours.

7. After the dough has risen, stir gently with a large rubber spatula to deflate it. Then scrape it into the prepared pan. Cover the pan with plastic wrap and allow the dough to rise in the pan until it reaches the top, about an hour longer.

8. About 15 minutes before the dough has completely risen, set a rack in the middle level of the oven and preheat to 350 degrees.

9. Bake the panettone until it is well risen and deep golden and a toothpick inserted in the center emerges dry, about 1 hour.

10. Cool in the pan on a rack for 5 minutes, then remove the sides of the springform pan. Use a metal spatula to slide the panettone from the springform base to the rack. Paint the panettone all over with the melted butter. Allow the panettone to cool completely.

SERVING: Cut the panettone into thin wedges to serve. Perfect for breakfast or brunch, this is also an excellent tea cake.

STORAGE: Keep the panettone in plastic wrap and try to use it within 24 hours, because it gets dry rather quickly. Leftovers make good French toast or bread pudding. Freeze the panettone, double-wrapped in plastic wrap, for longer storage. Defrost and bring to room temperature, loosely covered with a towel, before serving.

POLAND

Yeast-Risen Coffee Cake
Babka

SPONGE

1¼ cups milk

4 teaspoons active dry yeast

2 cups unbleached all-purpose flour (spoon flour into dry-measure cup and level off)

DOUGH

8 tablespoons (1 stick) unsalted butter, softened

¾ cup sugar

1 teaspoon salt

1 tablespoon grated lemon zest

2 teaspoons vanilla extract

12 large egg yolks

2 cups unbleached all-purpose flour (spoon flour into dry-measure cup and level off)

1 cup dark raisins

1 cup whole blanched almonds, cut into quarters

One 12-cup tube or Bundt pan, buttered

This is a particularly light, flavorful version of an eastern European standard. Some versions of babka are rolled up with a filling before being placed in the pan, but this one simply mixes all the ingredients together. That makes it easier to prepare. ***One 10-inch tube cake, about 20 servings***

1. For the sponge, warm the milk in a saucepan over low heat until it is just lukewarm, about 110 degrees. Pour the milk into a medium bowl and whisk in the yeast. Stir in the flour and cover the bowl with plastic wrap. Let the sponge rise until it is doubled, about 30 minutes.

2. After the sponge has risen, beat the butter, sugar, and salt in an electric mixer with the paddle on medium speed until soft, about 2 to 3 minutes. Beat in the lemon zest and vanilla.

3. Beat in 6 of the egg yolks, one at a time, beating until smooth after each addition.

4. Beat in about ⅓ of the flour, followed by 2 more egg yolks. Stop and scrape bowl and beater. Beat in another ⅓ of the flour and 2 more of the egg yolks. Stop and scrape. Finally beat in the remaining flour and the remaining 2 egg yolks.

5. Stop the mixer and add the sponge into the mixer bowl. Beat on lowest speed continuously for 2 minutes. Stop the mixer and let the dough rest for 10 minutes.

6. Beat the dough on medium speed until it is smooth and elastic (the dough will be very soft), about 2 minutes. Beat in the raisins and almonds until they are evenly distributed.

7. Scrape the dough into the prepared pan and cover the pan with a towel or a piece of buttered plastic wrap. Let the dough rise until it fills the pan, about 1 hour.

8. About 15 minutes before the dough has completely risen, set a rack in the middle level of the oven and preheat to 350 degrees.

9. Bake the babka until it is well risen and deep golden, about 40 to 45 minutes. To test for doneness, insert a toothpick between the edge of the pan and the central tube. It should emerge dry.

10. Cool in the pan on a rack for 10 minutes, then invert onto a rack and cool completely.

SERVING: Use a sharp serrated knife to cut the babka into slices.

STORAGE: Keep the babka in plastic wrap, or wrap and freeze for longer storage.

GERMANY

Yeast-Risen Christmas Cake from Dresden
Dresdner Stollen

SPONGE

1 cup milk

4 teaspoons active dry yeast

1 cup unbleached all-purpose flour (spoon flour into dry-measure cup and level off)

DOUGH

8 tablespoons (1 stick) unsalted butter, softened

½ cup light brown sugar, firmly packed

½ teaspoon salt

2 tablespoons dark rum

2 teaspoons vanilla extract

2 cups unbleached all-purpose flour (spoon flour into dry-measure cup and level off)

½ cup raisins

½ cup candied orange peel, cut into ¼-inch dice

½ cup whole almonds, blanched or unblanched, coarsely chopped

FINISHING

3 tablespoons unsalted butter, melted

¼ cup sugar

Confectioners' sugar for dusting

1 cookie sheet or jelly-roll pan lined with parchment or foil

Stollen is a popular Christmas treat throughout the German-speaking world. Though many fancy and filled versions have appeared recently, this is a recipe for the classic version. Getting the stollen's characteristic folds just right when shaping requires some care and attention, but the illustration will guide you. ***Two 12-inch-long loaves, about 40 slices***

1. For the sponge, warm the milk in a small saucepan over low heat until it is just lukewarm, about 110 degrees. Pour the milk into a medium bowl and whisk in the yeast. Stir in the flour with a rubber spatula. Cover the bowl with plastic wrap and let the sponge rise until it is very puffy, about 30 minutes.

2. For the dough, beat the butter with the sugar and salt in the bowl of an electric mixer with the paddle attachment on medium speed until it is soft and light, about 2 to 3 minutes.

3. Beat in the rum and vanilla.

4. Stop the mixer and scrape the sponge into the mixing bowl. Add the flour. Beat the dough on lowest speed for 2 minutes, then stop the mixer and let the dough rest for 10 minutes.

5. Beat the dough on medium speed until it is smooth and elastic, about 2 additional minutes. Beat in the raisins, candied peel, and almonds, beating only until they are evenly distributed throughout the dough.

6. Scrape the dough into a buttered bowl and turn the dough over so that the top is buttered. Cover the bowl with plastic wrap and let the dough rise until it is doubled in bulk, about 1½ hours.

7. To shape the stollen, scrape the dough out onto a lightly floured work surface and press it into a rectangle about 5 × 12 inches. With the handle of a wooden spoon or a dowel, make an indentation 1 inch in from the right edge of the long side of the dough. Use a rolling pin to make a 2-inch-wide trough 1 inch in from the left side of the dough. Fold the thick edge of the left side into the indentation on the right side of the dough, as in the illustration below.

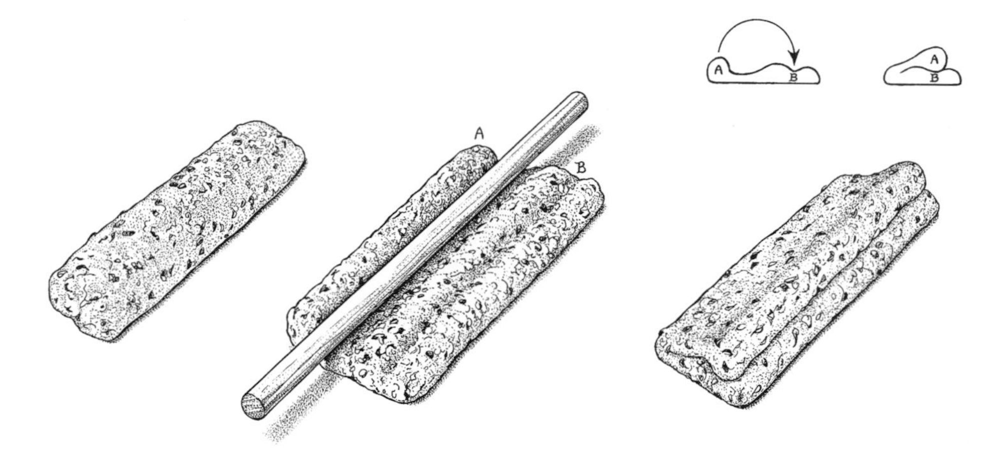

8. Slide your hand under the stollen and transfer it to the prepared pan. Once the stollen is on the pan, neaten the edges so that it is an even rectangle.

9. Cover the stollen with a towel or buttered plastic wrap and let it rise until it just begins to puff, about 30 minutes.

10. About 15 minutes before you are ready to bake the stollen, set a rack in the middle level of the oven and preheat to 375 degrees.

11. Bake the stollen until it is well risen and deep golden and a toothpick inserted in the thickest part emerges dry, about 30 to 40 minutes.

12. Immediately after removing the stollen from the oven, use a pastry brush to paint it with the melted butter. Then sprinkle the sugar on it.

13. Slide the paper from the pan to a rack to cool the stollen.

SERVING: Stollen is a great coffee cake. Dust it with confectioners' sugar and cut it into ½-inch slices just before serving. In Germany, people often butter the slices, though we would probably find stollen rich enough without added butter.

STORAGE: Stollen keeps well. Double-wrap it in plastic wrap and a sheet of aluminum foil and keep it in a cool place—it will keep for weeks.

CROATIA

Walnut-Filled Coffee Cake

Povetica

DOUGH

2½ teaspoons active dry yeast

2 tablespoons sugar

½ cup warm water

2¼ cups unbleached all-purpose flour (spoon flour into dry-measure cup and level off)

½ teaspoon salt

4 tablespoons (½ stick) unsalted butter, chilled and cut into ½-inch cubes

2 large egg yolks

FILLING

2 cups (about 8 ounces) walnut pieces

⅓ cup milk

½ cup sugar

⅓ cup light brown sugar

1½ teaspoons ground cinnamon

1 tablespoon butter

1 teaspoon lemon juice

1 large egg white

3 tablespoons unsalted butter, melted

1½ tablespoons honey

Egg wash: 1 egg well beaten with a pinch of salt

One 9-inch round pan, 2 inches deep, well buttered

This recipe comes from my friend Tim Brennan, who owns Cravings Desserts and Café in St. Louis. His maternal grandmother, Magdalen Suljak, was from Kunic in Croatia and made this as a holiday treat for the family. Tim usually Americanizes the cake by substituting pecans for walnuts, among other small changes, but this recipe is for the classic version.

Throughout the Slavic-influenced area of northeastern Italy and in the former Yugoslavia, there are many versions of these sweet nut-filled strudels. Some, like this one, are made with yeast dough, others with forms of puff pastry. They are all vaguely similar, though there are regional differences in the fillings and the shapes. ***One 9-inch cake, about 12 servings***

1. For the dough, whisk the yeast and sugar into the warm water and set aside for a few minutes until it starts to bubble.

2. In the bowl of an electric mixer, stir together the flour and salt. Add the butter and place the bowl on the mixer. Mix on low speed with the paddle attachment until the butter pieces are slightly reduced in size, about 2 minutes.

3. Add the yolks and the yeast mixture and mix for 2 minutes on lowest speed. Stop the mixer and let the dough rest for 10 minutes.

4. Mix the dough on medium speed until it is smooth and elastic, about 2 minutes.

5. Turn the dough out into a buttered bowl and turn the dough over so that the top is buttered. Cover the bowl with plastic wrap and allow the dough to rise until it is doubled in bulk, about 1 hour.

6. While the dough is rising, prepare the filling. In the food processor, grind the walnuts very fine, almost to a paste. Pour the milk into a 2-quart saucepan and place over low heat. Heat the milk until there are bubbles around the edges. Remove from the heat and stir in the ground walnuts and the remaining ingredients, except the melted butter and honey. Return the filling to the heat and continue cooking, stirring often, until the filling thickens and comes to a boil.

7. Scrape the filling onto a plate or another shallow nonreactive container and chill it until it has cooled completely. The filling may also be prepared earlier in the day or the day before.

8. To form the pastry, scrape the risen dough out onto a floured work surface. Press the dough into a rough rectangle. Roll the dough to a 12 × 18-inch rectangle. Combine the butter and honey and brush them on the dough. Spread the filling evenly on the dough.

9. Roll up the dough, jelly-roll style, from one of the 18-inch ends. Twist the dough into a spiral with the center protruding upward. Drop the dough into the prepared pan and cover it with a towel or buttered plastic wrap.

10. Allow the formed pastry to rise until it fills the pan and is well puffed, about 1 hour.

11. About 15 minutes before the pastry is fully risen, set a rack in the middle level of the oven and preheat to 375 degrees.

12. Brush with the egg wash. Wait 5 minutes, then brush again.

13. Bake the povetica until it is well colored and firm to the touch, about 35 to 40 minutes.

14. Cool in the pan on a rack for about 15 minutes, then turn out, invert again, and cool completely.

Serving: This is a perfect breakfast or brunch pastry. Alternatively, after a light meal serve it for dessert with shots of slivovitz, Yugoslav plum brandy.

Storage: Keep the pastry loosely covered on the day it is baked; it is best when served fresh. For advance preparation, wrap well in plastic wrap and freeze. Defrost and reheat at 350 degrees for about 10 minutes, then cool before serving.

SWITZERLAND

Almond Coffee Ring from Bern
Berner Mandelkranz

DOUGH

3 teaspoons active dry yeast

3 tablespoons warm water, about 110 degrees

½ cup warm milk

4 tablespoons (½ stick) unsalted butter, melted

1 large egg

3 tablespoons sugar

½ teaspoon salt

3 cups unbleached all-purpose flour (spoon flour into dry-measure cup and level off)

FILLING

2 cups whole almonds, blanched or unblanched, finely ground in the food processor

⅔ cup sugar

2 tablespoons lemon juice

2 teaspoons grated lemon zest

¼ teaspoon cinnamon

⅓ cup milk

½ cup raisins

Egg wash: 1 egg well beaten with a pinch of salt

Confectioners' sugar for finishing

1 cookie sheet or jelly-roll pan lined with parchment or foil

This recipe comes from my friend the expert baker, caterer, and cooking teacher Thea Cvijanovich, who lives in Winston-Salem, North Carolina. Thea and I met in the late 1980s when she was the director of a now-defunct cooking school in Winston-Salem. She is a native of Bern, Switzerland, and has been living in the United Sates for more than 40 years. In Thea's family this is known as Noah's Nut Strudel in honor of her grandson, for whom she often bakes it. ***One 8- to 9-inch ring, about 12 generous servings***

1. For the dough, whisk the yeast into the water and set aside while preparing the other ingredients.
2. Pour the milk into the bowl of an electric mixer and whisk in the remaining ingredients, except the flour, by hand, one at a time. Whisk in the yeast mixture.
3. Use a large rubber spatula to stir in the flour.
4. Place the bowl on the mixer with the paddle attachment and beat on lowest speed for 2 minutes. Stop the mixer and let the dough rest for 10 minutes.
5. Beat the dough on medium speed until it is smooth and elastic, about 2 additional minutes.
6. Scrape the dough into a buttered bowl and turn the dough over so that the top is buttered. Cover the bowl with plastic wrap and let the dough rise until it is doubled, about 1 hour.
7. While the dough is rising, prepare the filling. Stir the ground almonds and sugar together in a mixing bowl, using a large rubber spatula. Add the remaining ingredients, except for the raisins, and stir to a smooth paste. Set aside covered until needed.
8. Once the dough has risen, scrape it out onto a lightly floured work surface and flour the dough. Press the dough into a rough rectangle, then roll it out into a rectangle 10 × 15 inches.
9. Using a metal offset spatula, spread the dough with the filling. Distribute the raisins evenly over the surface.
10. Roll up the dough like a jelly roll from one of the 15-inch ends. Transfer it to the pan, seam side down, and form a ring by connecting the ends of the dough, pinching them together where they overlap. Gently adjust the dough into an even circle.

11. Cover the ring with a towel or a piece of buttered plastic wrap and let it rise until it increases in bulk by about half, about 30 minutes. The dough is risen enough when you press gently with a fingertip and the dough does not spring back.

12. About 15 minutes before the ring is fully risen, set a rack in the middle level of the oven and preheat to 375 degrees.

13. Paint the dough evenly with the egg wash, then let the egg wash dry for 5 minutes. Paint the dough again with the remaining egg wash.

14. Bake the ring until it is a deep golden color and feels firm when pressed with a fingertip, about 30 to 40 minutes.

15. Slide the paper from the pan to a rack to cool the ring.

SERVING: Cut the ring into thick slices to serve for breakfast, brunch, or tea.

STORAGE: Keep the ring loosely covered with plastic wrap or a towel on the day it is baked. Double-wrap in plastic wrap and freeze for longer storage. Defrost the ring and bring it to room temperature before serving.

ENGLAND

Hot Cross Buns

SPONGE

½ cup milk

2½ teaspoons active dry yeast

½ cup unbleached all-purpose flour (spoon flour into dry-measure cup and level off)

DOUGH

1⅔ cups unbleached all-purpose flour (spoon flour into dry-measure cup and level off)

⅓ cup sugar

½ teaspoon salt

¼ teaspoon each ground cinnamon, ground cloves, ground nutmeg, and ground ginger

4 tablespoons (½ stick) unsalted butter, softened, cut into 10 pieces

1 large egg

⅔ cup currants or raisins, or a mixture of the two

¼ cup finely diced candied citron or orange peel (see headnote)

GLAZE

2 tablespoons sugar

1 tablespoon water

ICING

⅔ cup confectioners' sugar

2 teaspoons water

1 cookie sheet or jelly-roll pan lined with parchment or foil

Thought to derive from a kind of bun usually served after funerals, hot cross buns have become standard Lenten fare in English-speaking countries. This recipe calls for both currants or raisins and candied fruit. If you prefer, omit the candied fruit and replace it with more raisins or currants. ***12 buns***

1. For the sponge, heat the milk in a small saucepan until it is just lukewarm, no more than 110 degrees. Pour the warm milk into a medium bowl and whisk in the yeast. Use a rubber spatula to stir in the flour, then cover the bowl with plastic wrap. Let the sponge ferment until it is bubbly, about 15 to 20 minutes.

2. Once the sponge is ready, prepare the dough. Combine the flour, sugar, salt, and spices in the bowl of an electric mixer and stir well to mix. Place on the mixer with the paddle attachment and add the butter. Mix until the butter is finely worked in, about 2 minutes.

3. Remove the bowl from the mixer and scrape in the sponge. Add the egg and return to the mixer with the paddle. Mix on lowest speed for 2 minutes. Stop the mixer and allow the dough to rest for 10 minutes.

4. Mix the dough again on medium speed until it is smooth and elastic, about 2 minutes. Reduce the speed to lowest and add the currants or raisins and candied fruit. Mix until they are evenly distributed throughout the dough.

5. Scrape the dough into a buttered bowl and turn the dough over so that the top is buttered. Cover the bowl with plastic wrap and allow the dough to rise until it is doubled in size, about 1 hour.

6. Turn the risen dough out onto a lightly floured work surface and press it into a rough square. Divide the dough into 12 equal pieces with a knife or bench scraper.

7. Round each piece by pressing it under the palm of your hand as you rotate your hand around the dough, as in the illustration on page 13. Arrange the buns on the prepared pan and press a cross into the top of each bun with the back of the blade of a table knife. Cover the pan with a towel or buttered plastic wrap and allow the buns to rise until they are almost doubled, about 45 minutes.

8. About 15 minutes before the buns are completely risen, set a rack in the middle of the oven and preheat to 375 degrees.

9. Bake the buns until they are deep golden and feel light, about 15 to 20 minutes. Just before the buns are finished baking, bring the sugar and water for the glaze to a boil. Brush the glaze on the buns as soon as they come out of the oven.

10. Slide the paper from the pan to a rack to cool the buns.

11. For the icing, combine the confectioners' sugar and water in a small saucepan and stir well to mix. Place over low heat, and stir until the icing is just warm to the touch. Scrape the icing into a paper cone or a small plastic bag and snip the corner. Pipe a cross on the top of each cooled bun, following the indentation made before baking. Let the icing dry for 30 minutes before serving.

Serving: These are perfect for breakfast or brunch.

Storage: Keep the buns under a cake dome at room temperature on the day they are baked. They are really best when perfectly fresh. For advance preparation, bake the buns, but do not apply glaze or icing. Cool the buns, then freeze them in a plastic bag. Before serving, defrost the buns, place them on a cookie sheet, and reheat them at 350 degrees for 5 minutes. Then apply the glaze and icing according to the instructions above.

Hot Cross Bun (front) and Schoggiweggli (page 67).

SWITZERLAND

Chocolate-Studded Sweet Buns from Basel
Schoggiweggli

1 cup milk

2½ teaspoons active dry yeast

3 cups unbleached all-purpose flour (spoon flour into dry-measure cup and level off)

1 tablespoon sugar

2 teaspoons salt

4 tablespoons (½ stick) unsalted butter, softened

6 ounces semisweet chocolate cut into ½-inch chunks, the dusty particles sifted away

Egg wash: 1 egg well beaten with a pinch of salt

2 cookie sheets or jelly-roll pans lined with parchment or foil

These are a specialty of the Confiserie Bachmann in Basel, one of the great pastry shops in a city that has many. The owner, Gregor Bachmann, led me through a tasting of some of his specialties, all of which were terrific. These chocolate-studded buns were my favorites. ***18 buns***

1. Warm the milk in a small saucepan over low heat until it is just lukewarm. Pour it into a small bowl and whisk in the yeast. Set aside while preparing the other ingredients.

2. Combine the flour, sugar, and salt in the bowl of an electric mixer. Place on the mixer fitted with the paddle attachment and mix on lowest speed for 30 seconds. Add the butter and mix until the butter is finely distributed throughout the dry ingredients, about 1 additional minute.

3. Add the yeast mixture and beat the dough on lowest speed for 2 minutes. Stop the mixer and let the dough rest for 10 minutes.

4. Mix the dough on medium speed until smooth and elastic, about 2 minutes. Beat in the chocolate, on lowest speed, until evenly distributed. (Overbeating will melt the chocolate.)

5. Scrape the dough into a buttered bowl and turn the dough over so that the top is buttered. Cover the bowl with plastic wrap and let the dough rise until it is doubled, about 1 hour.

6. Scrape the dough out onto a lightly floured work surface and press it into a rough rectangle. Use a knife or bench scraper to divide the dough into 18 equal pieces.

7. Round each piece by pressing it under the palm of your hand as you rotate your hand around the dough, as in the illustration on page 13. Arrange the rounded buns close together on the work surface, cover them with a towel, and let them rest for 10 minutes.

8. Place one of the buns on the work surface and roll it to create an oval shape. First roll the center with one palm to make it round, then use both palms to point the ends. Arrange the shaped bun on one of the prepared pans. Repeat with the remaining pieces of dough.

9. Cover the buns with buttered plastic wrap and let them rise until doubled, about 1 hour.

10. About 15 minutes before the buns are completely risen, set racks in the upper and lower thirds of the oven and preheat to 375 degrees.

11. Paint the risen buns with egg wash. Use oiled scissors to cut 4 slashes on top of each one, as in the illustration. If a piece of chocolate is in the way, just cut around it.

12. Bake the buns for about 15 minutes, then switch the pan from the top rack to the lower one and the pan from the bottom rack to the upper one, turning the pans back to front at the same time. Bake until well risen and deep golden, about 10 additional minutes. Slide the papers from the pans onto racks to cool the buns.

SERVING: These are good for breakfast, brunch, or a snack.

STORAGE: Keep the buns loosely covered on the day they are baked. Place in plastic bags and freeze for longer storage. Defrost and bring to room temperature before serving.

Prune-Filled Buns
Kolache

These delicate prune buns are a mainstay of eastern European baking. If you're not crazy about prunes, substitute dried apricots for the filling. ***24 buns***

SPONGE

3 teaspoons active dry yeast

½ cup warm water (110 degrees)

1 cup unbleached all-purpose flour (spoon flour into dry-measure cup and level off)

DOUGH

12 tablespoons (1½ sticks) unsalted butter, softened

½ cup sugar

1 teaspoon salt

4 large egg yolks

3½ cups unbleached all-purpose flour (spoon flour into dry-measure cup and level off)

½ cup milk

PRUNE FILLING

2 cups water

2 cups diced pitted prunes

2 tablespoons sugar

Pinch of freshly grated nutmeg

1 tablespoon finely grated orange zest

2 cookie sheets or jelly-roll pans lined with parchment or foil

1. For the sponge, whisk the yeast into the water and stir in the flour. Cover the bowl with plastic wrap and set aside until the sponge is risen and bubbly, about 20 minutes.

2. For the dough, beat the butter with the sugar and salt in the bowl of an electric mixer fitted with the paddle attachment on medium speed until well mixed, about 1 minute. Beat in the yolks, one at a time, beating to incorporate after each addition. Decrease the mixer speed to lowest and beat in about half the flour, beating until it is smoothly incorporated. Beat in the sponge and the milk and continue beating until smooth. Finally, beat in the remaining flour.

3. Beat the dough on low speed for 2 minutes, then stop the mixer. Let the dough rest for 10 minutes.

4. Increase mixer speed to medium and beat until the dough is smooth and elastic, about 2 additional minutes.

5. Scrape the dough out into a buttered bowl and turn the dough over so that the top is buttered. Cover the bowl with plastic wrap and allow the dough to rise until doubled in bulk, about 1 hour.

6. While the dough is rising, make the filling. Combine all ingredients in a 2-quart saucepan and place over medium heat. Bring to a boil and lower heat so that the filling simmers gently. Cook for about 15 minutes, stirring occasionally, until the filling is thick and has the consistency of jam. Cool the filling by spreading it on a plate and refrigerating it.

7. To form the kolache, scrape the risen dough from the bowl to a floured work surface and flour the dough. Pat the dough into a rough rectangle, then roll it into a 12 × 18-inch rectangle.

8. Use a floured 3-inch plain round cutter to cut the dough into disks. As you cut the rounds, place them on the prepared pans 2 inches apart in all directions. Cover the pans with towels or buttered plastic wrap and allow the kolache to rise until almost doubled, about 45 minutes.

9. When the kolache are risen, set racks in the upper and lower thirds of the oven and preheat to 350 degrees.

10. Use the bottom of a small glass or another 1-inch-diameter vessel, floured, to indent the center of each kolache. Fill each indentation with a scant tablespoon of the filling.

11. Bake the kolache for 10 minutes, then switch the pan from the top rack to the lower one and the pan from the bottom rack to the upper one, turning the pans back to front at the same time. Bake until the kolache are a deep golden color and feel firm when pressed with a fingertip, about 10 to 15 additional minutes.

12. Slide the papers from the pans onto racks to cool the kolache on racks.

Serving: Serve the kolache for breakfast, brunch, or a snack. They need no accompaniment.

Storage: Keep the kolache loosely covered on the day they are baked. For longer storage, wrap in plastic wrap and freeze. Defrost them, reheat for 5 minutes at 350 degrees, and cool before serving.

3. COOKIES

THE NETHERLANDS	SPICY ALMOND-STUDDED SQUARES *Jan Hagel*
NEW ZEALAND	TAN FINGERS
ITALY	"UGLY BUT GOOD" HAZELNUT COOKIES *Brutti ma Buoni*
BELGIUM	CRISP SUGAR COOKIES FROM CHARLEROI *Speculoos de Charleroi*
SWITZERLAND AND GERMANY	HONEY CAKES *Lebkuchen*
DENMARK	HONEY CAKES *Honningkager*
PORTUGAL	CINNAMON BUTTER COOKIES *Raivas*
ARMENIA	SESAME SEED RINGS *Simit*
ITALY	TWISTED COOKIES FROM THE VAL D'AOSTA *Torcettini di Saint Vincent*
LEBANON	PISTACHIO-FILLED BUTTER COOKIES *Mamoul*
GREECE	WINE TWISTS *Tsourekakia*
SWITZERLAND	LITTLE SUGARED COOKIES *Zuckerbroetli*
ARGENTINA	CRISP SANDWICH COOKIES FILLED WITH MILK CARAMEL *Alfajores*
AUSTRIA	SANDWICH COOKIES FROM BAD ISCHL *Ischler Toertchen*

Overleaf: Ischler Toertchen

COOKIES ARE TRULY INTERNATIONAL, not to mention popular. In fact, every country has so many varieties that it was difficult to choose among the thousands of recipes available.

Dozens of countries have bar cookies, drop cookies, rolled and cut cookies, hand-molded and filled cookies, piped cookies, and sandwich cookies. Each type of cookie has its merits. As always, my first concern in collecting these recipes was to find those that are both delicious and easy to prepare, but I have also favored cookies that keep well. As a result, many of the recipes included in this chapter are for cookies that are as good when they are a week old as when they are fresh from the oven.

GENERAL INSTRUCTIONS FOR BAKING COOKIES

Some cookie recipes involve baking more than one sheet or pan of cookies at a time. This can lead to uneven baking, since the cookie sheets must be placed in different locations in the oven. Remember to do the following about halfway through the baking time:

1. Change the position of the pans from the upper to lower rack and vice versa.

2. Rotate the pans back to front for more even baking.

Also, if you notice that cookies frequently burn on the bottom when baking in the lower third of the oven, stack two sheets together to insulate the cookies from the excess heat. That should prevent the bottoms from burning. The double-pan arrangement should always be on the bottom rack of the oven, so remember to leave the extra pan there when you switch the two regular pans.

Watch the cookies for signs of doneness and use a fingertip when appropriate to determine when the cookie dough has become firm and baked through. Cookies suffer even more than other baked goods from slavish adherence to a schedule, so use your fingers, eyes, nose, and common sense to determine doneness.

Be careful to cool cookies completely before packing them in tins or other containers. And don't skip placing paper between the layers of cookies; it will prevent them from sticking together should they soften.

If cookies that are meant to be crisp become soft while you are storing them, you can crisp them again by spreading them out in a single layer on a cookie sheet and baking them at 300 degrees for about 7 or 8 minutes. Cool the cookies on the pans on racks. Once cool, they will have regained their snap.

THE NETHERLANDS

Spicy Almond-Studded Squares

Jan Hagel

Any resemblance between these cookies and the American industrially-made version is purely coincidental. This is a real Dutch recipe for delicious, easy-to-prepare cookies. In the Netherlands, one of these arrives on the saucer when you order a cup of coffee in a café. ***About thirty-five 2-inch cookies***

DOUGH

2¼ cups all-purpose flour

1 teaspoon ground cinnamon

½ teaspoon baking powder

½ cup sugar

12 tablespoons (1½ sticks) unsalted butter, chilled and cut into 12 pieces

TOPPING

Water for brushing the dough

1 cup (about 4 ounces) sliced blanched almonds

¼ cup sugar

One 10 × 15-inch jelly-roll pan, buttered and lined, bottom and sides, with parchment or foil

1. Set a rack in the middle level of the oven and preheat to 350 degrees.
2. Place the dry ingredients into the bowl of a food processor fitted with the steel blade and pulse several times to mix. Add the butter and pulse repeatedly until the mixture is reduced to fine crumbs and looks like coarse cornmeal.

3. Evenly scatter the dough mixture in the pan and use the palm of your hand to press it down evenly and to make it adhere together.
4. Paint the dough sparingly with water and evenly scatter the almonds and sugar on the dough, gently pressing them in.
5. Bake the cookies until they are a deep golden color, the almonds have toasted, and the cookies are firm, about 20 to 25 minutes.
6. Immediately pull the paper with the cookie slab on it from the pan and transfer it to a cutting board. Immediately use a sharp serrated knife to cut the baked cookie into 2-inch squares. Use a spatula to transfer them to racks to finish cooling.

STORAGE: Keep the cookies between sheets of parchment or wax paper in a tin or plastic container with a tight-fitting cover.

NEW ZEALAND

Tan Fingers

DOUGH

14 tablespoons (1¾ sticks) unsalted butter, softened

½ cup sugar

¼ teaspoon salt

1 teaspoon vanilla extract

2¼ cups unbleached all-purpose flour (spoon flour into dry-measure cup and level off)

FILLING

5 tablespoons unsalted butter

1 tablespoon light corn syrup

One 14-ounce can sweetened condensed milk

One 9 × 13 × 2-inch pan, buttered and lined, bottom and sides, with buttered parchment or foil

This intriguing bar cookie was shared by my friend Thea Cvijanovich. Her sister Eva Abplanalp, who lives in Kamo-Whangarei, New Zealand, sent the recipe to her. It is a popular New Zealand cookie.

Twenty-four 2-inch squares

1. Set a rack in the lowest level of the oven and preheat to 350 degrees.
2. For the dough, beat the butter with the sugar and salt in an electric mixer fitted with the paddle attachment on medium speed, until soft and light, 2 to 3 minutes.
3. Beat in the vanilla.
4. On lowest speed, beat in the flour, scraping bowl and paddle with a rubber spatula and continuing to mix until the dough is smooth.
5. Remove the bowl from the mixer and scrape three-quarters of the dough into the prepared pan. Use the palm of your hand to press the dough down evenly, without compressing it any more than necessary. Chill the dough-lined pan and reserve the remaining dough at room temperature.

6. For the filling, bring the butter, corn syrup, and sweetened condensed milk to a simmer in a medium saucepan, stirring occasionally. Allow the mixture to boil gently until it starts to thicken and becomes a very light caramel color. Pour the filling into a stainless steel bowl and let it cool for 5 minutes.

7. Remove the dough-lined pan from the refrigerator and scrape the filling onto the dough, using a small offset spatula to spread the filling evenly over the dough. Use the remaining dough to make a crumbly topping: With your fingertips, separate the dough into medium crumbs and evenly scatter them on the caramel filling.

8. Bake until the filling is a deep caramel color and the dough and crumb topping are baked through, about 30 minutes.

9. Cool for about 10 minutes in the pan on a rack. Lift the slab of baked dough out of the pan to a cutting board before it has cooled completely. Then cut the slab into 2-inch squares. (Cut these right on the paper rather than trying to pull the paper off first.)

STORAGE: Keep these at room temperature if you are serving them within a day. If not, wrap and freeze them. Defrost them and bring them to room temperature before serving.

ITALY

"Ugly but Good" Hazelnut Cookies
Brutti ma Buoni

4 large egg whites

Pinch of salt

1⅓ cups sugar

3½ cups (about 14 ounces) whole hazelnuts, finely ground in a food processor

2 cookie sheets or jelly-roll pans lined with parchment or foil

These are popular cookies throughout Italy, though they probably originated in Piemonte. In cooking the batter, the heat must be low to prevent scorching, which would ruin the flavor of the cookies.

About sixty 1½-inch cookies

1. Set racks in the upper and lower thirds of the oven and preheat to 350 degrees.
2. Whip the egg whites and salt in an electric mixer with the whisk on medium speed until they are white and opaque and beginning to hold their shape. Increase the speed to medium high and whip in the sugar 1 tablespoon at a time, continuing to whip the whites until they hold a firm peak. Remove the bowl from the mixer and fold in the ground hazelnuts.
3. Scrape the batter into a medium saucepan and place over low heat. Cook, stirring constantly with a wooden spoon, until the mixture is heated through, about 8 minutes.
4. Use 2 spoons to form ¾-inch cookies. Use one spoon to scoop up some batter and the other to scrape it off the first spoon, rounding it somewhat as you do, and drop the cookies onto the prepared pan, spacing them about 1 inch apart from each other in all directions.
5. Bake the cookies until they are well colored and slightly firm, about 20 to 25 minutes.
6. Cool the cookies on the pan on a rack.

Storage: Store the cookies in a tin or plastic container with a tight-fitting cover.

Crisp Sugar Cookies from Charleroi
Speculoos de Charleroi

2 cups all-purpose flour (spoon flour into dry-measure cup and level off)

½ teaspoon baking powder

½ teaspoon baking soda

6 tablespoons (¾ stick) unsalted butter, softened

¾ cup dark brown sugar, firmly packed

1 large egg

2 cookie sheets or jelly-roll pans lined with parchment or foil

This is a Belgian variation of the classic cookie called speculaas in Dutch. In my book *Cookies Unlimited* I gave a recipe for Dutch speculaas formed in both modern and antique cookie molds, which I traveled to the Netherlands to buy. These Belgian speculoos don't need any special mold, though you'll need round, holiday, or other decorative cutters to form them. They make excellent Christmas cookies. ***About 30 cookies, depending on the size of the cutter***

1. Set racks in the upper and lower thirds of the oven and preheat to 350 degrees.
2. Stir the flour, baking powder, and baking soda together and set aside.
3. Beat the butter and brown sugar with an electric mixer fitted with the paddle attachment on medium speed until well mixed and creamy, about 2 minutes. Beat in the egg and continue beating until the mixture is smooth.
4. Remove the bowl from the mixer and stir in the flour mixture with a large rubber spatula.
5. Scrape the dough out into a lightly floured work surface and use a knife or bench scraper to cut the dough into 3 pieces.

6. Roll one piece at a time until it is about ⅛ inch thick, moving the dough often to prevent it from sticking to the work surface.
7. Use a floured cutter to cut out the cookies. Place them 1 inch apart in all directions on the prepared pans.
8. Bake the cookies until they are light golden and firm (they will continue to crisp as they cool), about 12 minutes. At least once during baking, change the position of the pans in the oven as described at the beginning of this chapter. If your oven gives strong bottom heat, stack 2 pans together for baking on the lower rack, to provide insulation.
9. Cool the cookies on the pans on racks.

Storage: Keep the speculoos between sheets of parchment or wax paper in a tin or plastic container with a tight-fitting cover. They keep well and so may be prepared far in advance. If they lose their crispness, arrange them on a cookie sheet, bake again for 10 minutes at 325 degrees, and cool before serving.

Honey Cakes
Lebkuchen

DOUGH

4 cups unbleached all-purpose flour (spoon flour into dry-measure cup and level off)

1½ teaspoons baking powder

1 teaspoon baking soda

2 teaspoons ground cinnamon

2 teaspoons ground coriander

1 teaspoon ground cloves

½ teaspoon ground nutmeg

½ teaspoon ground ginger

¾ cup honey

½ cup molasses

½ cup sugar

⅓ cup water

GLAZE

½ cup light corn syrup

DECORATION

Sliced blanched almonds

Candied cherries

2 cookie sheets or jelly-roll pans lined with parchment or foil

There are probably as many types of lebkuchen as there are bakers in Switzerland and Germany. Subtle variations in spices and other ingredients can change the flavor and texture, but the result is always recognizable as lebkuchen.

The descendent of medieval honey cakes, lebkuchen were once an important branch of baking all their own. While they are still enjoyed in German-speaking countries today, so many other baked goods are available now that they are nowhere near as prevalent.

The name *Lebkuchen* derives from *leben*, "to live." My teacher Albert Kumin once explained that it reflects the cakes' lasting qualities. In other words, they are long-lived cakes. Lebkuchen are traditionally cut into heart shapes and are rather large. The instructions here are for a smaller cookie, one that we would be more likely to serve. If you don't have a heart-shaped cutter, other shapes are permissible, especially around the holidays. ***About 30 cookies, depending on the size of the cutter***

1. Set racks in the upper and lower thirds of the oven and preheat to 350 degrees.
2. In a large bowl, mix the flour with the baking powder, baking soda, and spices.
3. In a medium saucepan, combine the honey, molasses, and sugar and stir well to mix. Place over medium heat and bring to a full rolling boil. Remove from heat and carefully stir in the water a little at a time.
4. Stir the warm honey mixture into the dry ingredients to form a firm dough. Scrape the dough out onto a lightly floured work surface, cover it with a towel or plastic wrap, and let it cool for a few minutes until it is still warm, but not so hot that you can't handle it comfortably.
5. Use a knife or bench scraper to cut the dough into 3 pieces. Set aside 2 pieces of the dough and cover them with a clean cloth or plastic wrap.
6. Roll one piece of the dough until it is about ¼-inch thick. Use a floured heart-shape or fluted round cutter to cut out the cookies. As they are cut, arrange them on the prepared pans 1 inch apart in all directions.
7. Repeat with the other 2 pieces of dough. Save all the scraps from cutting and sprinkle a few drops of water on them before pressing together and rerolling. Don't reroll the scraps more than once, or the resulting cookies will be tough.
8. Bake the lebkuchen until they are well risen, no longer shiny, and slightly firm when pressed with a fingertip, about 12 to 15 minutes. Change the position of the pans from upper to lower rack and vice versa, also turning them back to front at least once during baking. If your oven gives strong bottom heat, stack 2 pans together for baking on the lower rack, to provide extra insulation.
9. Slide the papers from the pans to racks to cool the lebkuchen.
10. While the lebkuchen are cooling, prepare the glaze. Bring the corn syrup to a boil in a small pan. Brush the hot glaze over each of the cookies, then decorate them with the almonds and cherries. Reheat the glaze if necessary to finish all the lebkuchen.

STORAGE: Keep the lebkuchen between sheets of parchment or wax paper in a tin or plastic container with a tight-fitting cover. They last indefinitely, as the name implies. If you are going to prepare them long in advance, it may be wiser to add the glaze and decorations closer to the time you wish to serve the cookies.

DENMARK

Honey Cakes
Honningkager

The addition of butter and cream to the dough makes these honey cakes very delicate. They are a modern take on cookies that are medieval in origin. These make perfect Christmas cookies. ***About 48 cookies, depending on the size of the cutters***

DOUGH

4 cups unbleached all-purpose flour (spoon flour into dry-measure cup and level off)

1 teaspoon baking soda

1 teaspoon ground cinnamon

½ teaspoon ground cloves

½ cup honey

⅓ cup dark brown sugar, firmly packed

4 tablespoons (½ stick) unsalted butter, cut into 8 pieces

⅔ cup heavy whipping cream

ICING

3 cups confectioners' sugar

¼ cup water

3 or 4 cookie sheets or jelly-roll pans lined with parchment or foil

1. Set racks in the upper and lower thirds of the oven and preheat to 350 degrees.
2. For the dough, mix the flour with the baking soda and spices in a large bowl and set aside.
3. Bring the honey, brown sugar, and butter to a boil over medium heat, stirring occasionally. Remove from the heat and stir in the cream, then let the mixture cool for 10 minutes.
4. Make a well in the center of the flour mixture, add the cooled liquid, and thoroughly stir it in. Scrape the dough onto a lightly floured work surface and knead it briefly until smooth.

5. Use a knife or bench scraper to divide the dough into 4 pieces. Roll each piece of dough about ¼ inch thick, flouring the dough and surface lightly to prevent sticking. Use fancy cutters to cut out the cookies and place them on the prepared pans about 1 inch apart in all directions. Repeat with the remaining dough. If you don't have more than 2 cookie sheets, cut out the cookies and leave them on sheets of parchment or foil until the pans are ready to reuse. Moisten the scraps from cutting out the cookies with a few drops of water, press them firmly together, and reroll once to make more cookies.

6. Bake the cookies until they are puffed and firm (their color doesn't change much), about 15 minutes. Change the position of the pans from upper to lower rack and vice versa, also turning them back to front at least once during baking. If your oven gives strong bottom heat, stack 2 pans together for baking on the lower rack, to provide extra insulation.

7. Slide the papers from the pans to racks to cool the cookies.

8. For the icing, combine the confectioners' sugar and water in a medium saucepan and stir with a wooden spoon until well combined. Place the pan over low heat, stirring constantly, until the icing is just lukewarm. If the icing is too thick, add 1 additional teaspoon of water.

9. Quickly brush the icing on the cookies. If the icing begins to harden, add a few drops of water and reheat, stirring constantly, until the icing is smooth and liquid again.

STORAGE: Keep the cookies between sheets of parchment or wax paper in a tin or plastic container with a tight-fitting cover.

PORTUGAL

Cinnamon Butter Cookies
Raivas

2 cups unbleached all-purpose flour
1 teaspoon cinnamon
5 tablespoons unsalted butter, softened
½ cup sugar
3 large eggs

2 cookie sheets or jelly-roll pans lined with parchment or foil

These intriguing-looking cookies are a specialty of the Beira Litoral region of Portugal. They are adapted from *Cozinha Tradicional Portuguesa* (*Traditional Portuguese Cooking*) by Maria de Lourdes Modesto (Editorial Verbo, 1982). ***24 cookies***

1. Set racks in the upper and lower thirds of the oven and preheat to 350 degrees.
2. Stir the flour and cinnamon together and set aside.
3. Beat the butter and sugar in the bowl of an electric mixer fitted with the paddle attachment on medium speed until soft and light, about 2 to 3 minutes. Beat in the eggs, one at a time, beating smooth after each addition.
4. Remove the bowl from the mixer and stir in the flour mixture by hand, using a large rubber spatula.
5. Scrape the dough onto a lightly floured work surface and fold the dough over on itself 2 or 3 times until it is smooth.
6. Roll the dough into a cylinder and divide it into 6 equal pieces using a knife or a bench scraper.
7. Cut each of the 6 pieces of dough in half, then in half again, to make 24 pieces of dough total.

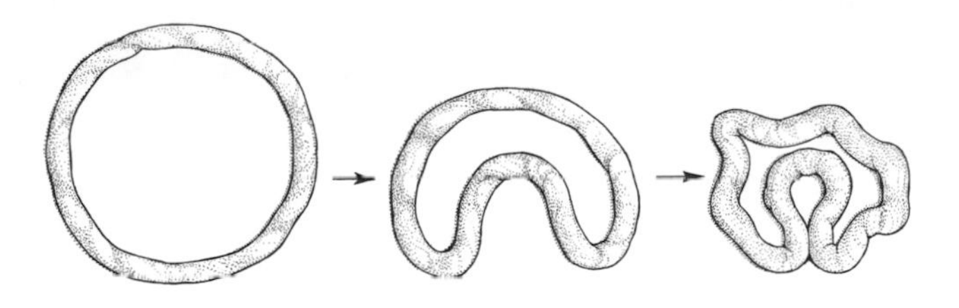

8. Roll one piece of dough to a rope about 20 inches long. Join the ends and place the circle of dough on one of the prepared pans. Push the sides of the circle in toward the center, in an irregular pattern, to crinkle them, as in the illustration above. Continue with the remaining pieces of dough, placing 9 on each pan.

9. Bake the raivas until they are slightly puffed, deep golden, and firm when pressed with a fingertip, about 12 to 15 minutes. Change the position of the pans from upper to lower rack at least once during baking. If your oven gives strong bottom heat, stack 2 pans together for baking on the lower rack, to provide insulation.

10. Slide the papers from the pans to racks to cool the cookies.

STORAGE: Keep the raivas between sheets of parchment or wax paper in a tin or plastic container with a tight-fitting cover for up to a week.

ARMENIA

Sesame Seed Rings
Simit

DOUGH

3½ cups unbleached all-purpose flour (spoon flour into dry-measure cup and level off)

1½ teaspoons baking powder

½ teaspoon salt

16 tablespoons (2 sticks) unsalted butter, melted

½ cup milk

½ cup sugar

1 large egg

FINISHING

2 large eggs well beaten with a pinch of salt

1 cup sesame seeds

3 cookie sheets or jelly-roll pans lined with parchment or foil

These are typical Armenian cookies—crunchy and loaded with sesame seeds. I like to bake them at a low temperature to ensure that they'll be as dry and crisp as they should be. Some people bake them at a higher temperature until done, then return the cookies to the turned-off oven to dry out and crisp. Thanks to my dear friend Sandy Leonard, who lives in the Armenian enclave of Watertown, Massachusetts, for sharing this recipe. ***36 cookies***

1. Set racks in the upper and lower thirds of the oven and preheat to 325 degrees.
2. For the dough, stir the flour with the baking powder and salt and set aside.
3. Pour the melted butter into a large bowl and whisk in the milk, sugar, and egg one at a time. Add the flour mixture and use a large rubber spatula to stir the ingredients together to make a soft dough.
4. Scrape the dough out onto a lightly floured work surface.
5. Roll the dough into an 18-inch cylinder, then cut it every ½ inch to make 36 pieces of dough.

6. Roll each piece of dough under the palms of your hands to make a 4- to 5-inch strand. Connect the ends to make a circle and set aside on the work surface until all the cookies have been formed.

7. Place 1 or 2 tablespoons of the sesame seeds in a small bowl.

8. One at a time, paint the outside of the cookie all over with the egg wash and gently press the top of the cookie into the small bowl of sesame seeds. Arrange the cookie, seeded side up, on the prepared pan, keeping the cookies about 1 inch apart all around.

9. Repeat with the remaining cookies, adding sesame seeds to the bowl a little at a time as you use them up, so that the seeds don't all get sticky from the egg wash.

10. Bake the cookies for about 30 minutes, or until they are golden and dry. Change the position of the pans from upper to lower rack and vice versa, also turning them back to front at least once during baking. If your oven gives strong bottom heat, stack 2 pans together for baking on the lower rack, to provide insulation.

11. Cool on the pans on racks. If the cookies are not completely crisp after they have cooled, return them to the turned-off oven for 20 minutes, then cool.

Storage: Keep the cookies between sheets of parchment or wax paper in a tin or plastic container with a tight-fitting cover.

Torcettini di Saint Vincent (left) and Mamoul (page 95).

ITALY

Twisted Cookies from the Val d'Aosta
Torcettini di Saint Vincent

1 cup warm water, about 110 degrees

2½ teaspoons active dry yeast

3 cups unbleached all-purpose flour (spoon flour into dry-measure cup and level off)

½ teaspoon salt

5 tablespoons unsalted butter, cold

½ cup sugar for rolling the cookies

2 or 3 cookie sheets or jelly-roll pans lined with parchment or foil

This light and delicate yeast-risen cookie is a cross between a buttery bread stick and a caramelized puff pastry palmier. Torcettini were a favorite of Italy's Queen Margherita. In fact, she liked the version in one pastry shop so much that she knighted the owner on the spot. A certificate attesting to this still hangs in the pastry shop in Saint Vincent.

You may have noticed that the name of the town is French, not Italian. Though the Val d'Aosta is not an officially bilingual region, as much French as Italian is spoken there. ***48 cookies***

1. Measure the water into a bowl, then whisk in the yeast. Set aside until needed.

2. In a food processor fitted with the steel blade, pulse the flour and salt a couple of times to mix. Add the butter and pulse until the butter is finely mixed in but the mixture is still powdery, about 15 pulses. Add the yeast mixture all at once, and pulse until the ingredients form a ball.

3. Invert the bowl to remove the dough: Carefully remove the blade first, then put the dough into a buttered bowl, turning the dough over so that the top is buttered. Cover the bowl with plastic wrap and let the dough rise until it is doubled in bulk, about an hour.

4. After the dough has risen, press it down to deflate it. Chill for at least 1 hour and up to 24 hours.

5. When you are ready to form the cookies, remove the dough from the refrigerator and press it into an 8-inch square. Scatter some of the sugar on the work surface if the dough is sticky.

6. Cut the square of dough into eight 1-inch strips. Cut each strip into 6 equal pieces, to make 48 pieces in all.

7. Roll a piece of the dough on a sugared surface under the palms of your hands to make a pencil-thick strand about 4 to 5 inches long. Form a loop by crossing over the ends about 1 inch up from the ends, as in the illustration, right.

8. As the torcettini are formed, place them on the prepared pans, leaving about 1½ inches in all directions around the cookies.

9. Set racks in the upper and lower thirds of the oven and preheat to 325 degrees.

10. Let the cookies stand at room temperature until they puff slightly, about 15 or 20 minutes.

11. Bake the cookies until they are light and the sugar has caramelized to a light golden crust, about 20 to 25 minutes. Change the position of the pans from upper to lower rack and vice versa, also turning them back to front at least once during baking. If your oven gives strong bottom heat, stack 2 pans together for baking on the lower rack, to provide insulation.

12. Slide the papers from the pans to racks to cool the cookies.

Storage: Store the cookies between sheets of parchment or wax paper in a tin or plastic container with a tight-fitting cover.

LEBANON

Pistachio-Filled Butter Cookies
Mamoul

DOUGH

2 cups all-purpose flour (spoon flour into dry-measure cup and level off)

14 tablespoons (1¾ sticks) unsalted butter, cut into 12 or 14 pieces

1 tablespoon rose water

2 tablespoons milk

FILLING

¾ cup unsalted, shelled, very green pistachios, coarsely chopped

⅓ cup sugar

1½ teaspoons rose water

FINISHING

Confectioners' sugar

2 cookie sheets or jelly-roll pans lined with parchment or foil

These cookies are frequently made in carved wooden molds. You can give them the same characteristic marks by using a fork to indent the top and side of each cookie. Not only are the indentations attractive, but they help the confectioners' sugar sprinkled on the cookies stay in place. ***36 cookies***

1. Set racks in the upper and lower thirds of the oven and preheat to 350 degrees.
2. Place the flour in the bowl of a food processor fitted with a steel blade and add the chunks of butter. Pulse to mix the butter in finely, keeping the mixture powdery. Take off the cover and evenly sprinkle the flour and butter mixture with the rose water and the milk. Cover and pulse again until the dough forms a ball. Turn the dough out onto a lightly floured work surface and cover it with plastic wrap while making the filling.
3. For the filling, stir together the pistachios, sugar, and rose water in a small bowl.
4. To form the mamoul, roll the dough into a cylinder about 18 inches long. Use a knife or bench scraper to cut the dough every ½ inch to make 36 pieces of dough.

5. To form one of the cookies, roll one of the pieces of dough between the palms of your hands to make a sphere. Insert a fingertip to make an opening, then use your thumbs to enlarge the opening and make a little cup. Fill the cup with a spoonful of the filling and pinch the opening closed, forming the mamoul into an even sphere. Place the formed mamoul on one of the prepared pans, seam side down. Repeat with the remaining dough and filling, placing the mamoul on the pans about 1 inch apart in all directions.

6. After all the mamoul are formed, use a fork to pierce the sides and tops of the cookies, as in the illustration on page 92.

7. Bake the mamoul until just barely golden (they should remain pale), about 20 to 25 minutes. Change the position of the pans from upper to lower rack and vice versa, also turning them back to front at least once during baking. If your oven gives strong bottom heat, stack 2 pans together for the lower rack, to provide insulation.

8. Cool the mamoul on the pans on racks. When they are completely cooled, dust them heavily with confectioners' sugar.

STORAGE: Keep cookies between sheets of parchment or wax paper in a container with a tight-fitting lid. If you make the cookies in advance, dust with the confectioners' sugar just before serving.

GREECE

Wine Twists
Tsourekakia

2 cups all-purpose flour (spoon flour into dry-measure cup and level off)

⅓ cup sugar

1 teaspoon baking powder

8 tablespoons (1 stick) unsalted butter, cut into 8 or 10 pieces

2 teaspoons Cognac or other brandy

⅓ cup dry white wine

2 cookie sheets or jelly-roll pans lined with parchment or foil

These easy but impressive cookies are moistened with a little dry white wine. Though it's not traditional, you could substitute white vermouth for the wine with excellent results. ***36 cookies***

1. Set racks in the upper and lower thirds of the oven and preheat to 350 degrees.
2. To make the cookie dough, place the flour, sugar, and baking powder in the bowl of a food processor fitted with the steel blade. Pulse several times to mix.
3. Add the butter and pulse until the butter is finely mixed in but the mixture remains cool and powdery.
4. Add the Cognac and wine and pulse until the dough forms a ball. If it resists, add up to 1 additional teaspoon of wine and pulse again.
5. Scrape the dough out onto a floured work surface and form it onto a rough cylinder. Use a knife or bench scraper to cut the dough into 6 pieces. Cut each piece of dough in half to make 12 pieces of dough. Cut each 1/12 of the dough into 3 equal pieces to make a total of 36 pieces of dough.

6. Roll one of the pieces of dough into a 4- to 5-inch strand. Fold the strand in half, pinch the ends together, then give it 3 or 4 twists and place on one of the prepared pans. Repeat with the rest of the dough, placing 18 cookies on each pan.

7. Bake the cookies until they are golden and firm, about 20 minutes. Change the position of the pans from upper to lower rack and vice versa, also turning them back to front at least once during baking. If your oven gives strong bottom heat, stack 2 pans together for baking on the lower rack, to provide insulation.

8. Cool the cookies on the pans on racks.

SERVING: These are a good cookie with coffee, tea, or sweet wine. Think of them as the Greek version of biscotti. Though they are not prepared in the same way, they have a similar texture.

STORAGE: Keep the cookies between sheets of parchment or wax paper in a tin or plastic container with a tight-fitting cover.

Tsourekakia and Simit (page 90).

SWITZERLAND

Little Sugared Cookies
Zuckerbroetli

4 large eggs

2 egg yolks

1½ cups sugar

3 cups all-purpose flour

More sugar for sprinkling the cookies

2 cookie sheets or jelly-roll pans lined with parchment or foil

These are a Swiss and Alsatian classic. A sponge batter is piped out in flat disks, which are then covered with sugar and allowed to dry, making a sparkling crust on the outside of the cookies after they are baked. ***About one hundred 2-inch cookies***

1. Half-fill a medium saucepan with water and bring it to a boil over medium heat.
2. Meanwhile, whisk the eggs, yolks, and sugar together by hand in the bowl of an electric mixer. When the water is boiling, place the bowl over the pan of boiling water and whisk gently to warm the egg mixture to about 110 degrees. It should feel just lukewarm if you plunge in your fingertip.
3. Place the bowl on the mixer with the whisk attachment and whip the egg foam for about 3 or 4 minutes on high speed, or until it is completely cooled, has lightened in color, and has increased in volume.
4. Remove the bowl from the mixer. Sift about a third of the flour over the egg foam and gently fold it in with a rubber spatula. Repeat with the next third and then the final third of the flour.
5. Scrape half the batter into a pastry bag fitted with a ½-inch plain tip (Ateco #806) and pipe the batter onto the prepared pans. Hold the bag at a right angle to the pan and about ½ inch above it. Squeeze out a sphere of the batter about 1 inch in

diameter; this will flatten naturally to about 1½ to 2 inches in diameter. Pipe cookies on both pans, keeping them about 2 inches apart in all directions. Repeat with remaining batter.

6. After all the cookies are piped, sprinkle one row of piped cookies heavily with sugar. Shake the sugar toward you until all the cookies are coated, as in the illustration, right. Remember to hold down the corners of the paper with your thumbs, or the paper with the cookies attached will slide off the pan. Shake the excess sugar off the pan onto a sheet of wax paper and reuse for the next batch. Repeat with the other pan.

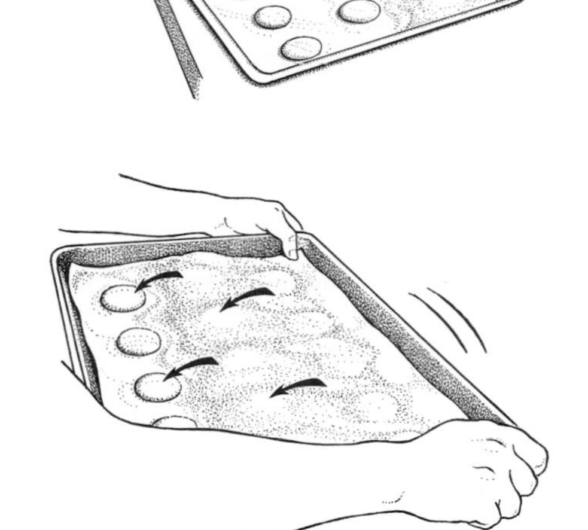

7. Let the cookies dry, uncovered, at room temperature for 3 to 4 hours.

8. About 15 minutes before you are ready to bake the cookies, set racks in the upper and lower thirds of the oven and preheat to 350 degrees.

9. Bake the cookies until the bottoms are very light golden but the sugared tops remain white, about 12 minutes. Change the positions of the pans from upper to lower rack and vice versa, also turning them back to front, at least once during baking. If your oven gives strong bottom heat, stack 2 pans together for baking on the lower rack, to prevent the cookies from burning on the bottom.

10. Slide the papers from the pans to racks to cool the cookies.

Storage: Keep the cookies between sheets of parchment or wax paper in a tin or plastic container with a tight-fitting cover.

ARGENTINA

Crisp Sandwich Cookies Filled with Milk Caramel

Alfajores

DOUGH

1¼ cups unbleached all-purpose flour (spoon flour into dry-measure cup and level off)

1⅔ cups cornstarch

1 teaspoon baking powder

10 tablespoons (1¼ sticks) unsalted butter, softened

⅔ cup sugar

1 teaspoon grated lemon zest

1 tablespoon cognac or brandy

4 large egg yolks

FILLING

One 14-ounce can sweetened condensed milk

One 12-ounce can evaporated milk

Water or milk as needed

FINISHING

1 cup sweetened shredded coconut, ground medium fine in the food processor

2 cookie sheets or jelly-roll pans lined with parchment or foil

This recipe comes from my Argentine connection, Ana Rambaldi (see her heavenly empanadas on page 300). It makes crunchy cookies sandwiched with a filling of dulce de leche—caramelized sweetened condensed milk. The filling is easy to prepare, but canned dulce de leche can sometimes be found in Hispanic grocery stores. ***About fifteen 2- to 3-inch sandwich cookies***

1. Set racks in the upper and lower thirds of the oven and preheat to 350 degrees.

2. For the dough, stir the flour, cornstarch, and baking powder together in a small bowl and set aside.

3. Beat the butter and sugar in an electric mixer fitted with the paddle attachment on medium speed until soft and light, about 2 to 3 minutes. Beat in the lemon zest and cognac.

4. Add the egg yolks one at a time, beating smooth after each addition.

5. Remove the bowl from the mixer and stir in the flour mixture with a large rubber spatula.

6. Scrape the dough from the bowl to a lightly floured work surface and fold it over on itself 2 or 3 times to make it smooth.

7. Use a knife or bench scraper to divide the dough into 3 pieces.

8. Place 1 piece of the dough on a lightly floured work surface and lightly flour the dough. Roll the dough about ¼ inch thick, moving it often to prevent sticking.

9. Cut out the cookies with a 2½-inch-diameter plain cutter. Place the cookies on the prepared pans 1 inch apart in all directions.

10. Gently knead to incorporate the scraps into the next piece of dough and repeat rolling and cutting. Repeat incorporating scraps and rolling and cutting the last piece of dough. Roll the remaining scraps once more, but discard the scraps after rerolling twice. The cookies will be tough if the dough is rolled too much.

11. Bake the cookies until they are evenly golden, about 15 minutes. Change the position of the pans from upper to lower rack and vice versa, also turning them back to front, at least once during baking. If your oven gives strong bottom heat, stack 2 pans together for baking on the lower rack to provide extra insulation and avoid burning the cookies.

12. Slide the papers from the pans to racks to cool the cookies.

13. To make the dulce de leche filling, set a rack in the middle level of the oven and keep it at 350 degrees.

14. Heat the sweetened condensed milk and the evaporated milk in a medium saucepan over low heat, stirring occasionally, until it comes to a boil. Pour the hot milk into a 9 × 13-inch glass or enameled pan and bake it, stirring often, until it is thick and caramel-colored, about 20 to 30 minutes. Scrape the dulce de leche into a glass or stainless steel bowl. Stir in a couple of tablespoons of water or milk to bring the filling to a spreading consistency. Press plastic wrap against the surface and chill it until you are ready to assemble the cookies.

15. To assemble the alfajores, turn half the cookies upside down so that the flat bottom sides are upward. Spoon or pipe about 1 teaspoon of the dulce de leche onto each. Place the other cookies on the filling, flat side down, gently pressing to adhere.

16. To finish the alfajores, spread some of the dulce de leche on the outside of each cookie, then roll the cookies in the coconut.

Storage: Keep the alfajores in a tin or plastic container with a tight-fitting cover between sheets of wax paper.

Sandwich Cookies from Bad Ischl

Ischler Toertchen

DOUGH

16 tablespoons (2 sticks) unsalted butter, softened

1 cup confectioners' sugar

1 cup (about 4 ounces) walnut pieces, finely ground in the food processor

2½ cups all-purpose flour

FILLING

⅔ cup seedless raspberry preserves

CHOCOLATE GLAZE

¼ cup water

¼ cup light corn syrup

⅔ cup sugar

6 ounces semisweet chocolate, cut into ¼-inch pieces

About 24 whole blanched almonds (one for each sandwich cookie)

2 cookie sheets or jelly-roll pans lined with parchment or foil

A famous small resort just outside the city of Vienna, Bad Ischl was a favorite gathering place for members of the imperial court of Vienna during the nineteenth century. Of course, for Viennese aristocrats vacation meant strolling around and enjoying sweets. This was one of their favorites: walnut butter cookies, sandwiched with raspberry preserves, streaked with chocolate icing, and topped with whole blanched almonds. ***About twenty-four 2½-inch sandwich cookies***

1. Set racks in the upper and lower thirds of the oven and preheat to 350 degrees.
2. For the dough, beat the butter and confectioners' sugar with an electric mixer fitted with the paddle attachment on medium speed until soft and light, 2 or 3 minutes. Beat in the ground walnuts.
3. Remove the bowl from the mixer and stir in the flour with a large rubber spatula, mixing until the dough is smooth.

4. Scrape the dough out onto a lightly floured work surface and divide it into 3 parts.

5. Flour the surface and the dough and gently roll the dough to about ¼ inch thick. Use a plain cutter to cut out 2- to 2½-inch cookies. Place the cookies on the prepared pans 1 inch apart in all directions.

6. Incorporate the scraps from the first piece of dough into the second and roll and cut more cookie bases.

7. Repeat step 6 with the last piece of dough. Reroll any remaining scraps once more, then discard the rest. (Leftovers will make tough cookies.)

8. Bake the cookie bases until they are very light golden in color, about 15 to 20 minutes. Change the position of the pans from upper to lower rack and vice versa, also turning them back to front at least once during baking. If your oven gives strong bottom heat, stack 2 pans together for baking on the lower rack, to provide insulation against burning the cookies. Cool the cookies on the pans on racks.

9. Meanwhile, place the preserves in a medium saucepan and bring them to a boil over low to medium heat, stirring occasionally. After the preserves boil, lower to a steady simmer and allow them to reduce for about 5 minutes, or until slightly sticky and no longer watery.

10. Turn half the cookies upside down so that the flat bottom sides face upward. Put about ½ teaspoon of the reduced jam on one of the cookies and top it with another cookie, flat side down. Continue until all the cookies have been sandwiched with the preserves.

11. For the glaze, stir together the water and corn syrup in a medium saucepan and then stir in the sugar. Bring the syrup to a full rolling boil over medium heat, stirring occasionally. Remove from the heat, add the chocolate, and swirl the pan to submerge it. Let the glaze stand for 3 minutes.

12. Meanwhile, line up all the sandwiched cookies close together on a piece of parchment paper (you can reuse the paper they were baked on).

13. Whisk the glaze smooth, then pour some into a paper cone or a nonpleated plastic bag. Whether you are using the cone or bag, snip the end and generously drizzle the glaze over the cookies in straight lines. Continue until you have used all the glaze.

14. While the glaze is still wet, gently press an almond into the center of each cookie.

Serving: These cookies can be served as a dessert by themselves, although some sorbet or ice cream makes a nice accompaniment.

Storage: Keep the cookies at room temperature after they are glazed. For advance preparation, bake and freeze only the cookie bases, then glaze them on the day you intend to serve them. Store leftovers between sheets of parchment or wax paper in a tin or plastic container with a tight-fitting cover.

4. CAKES

ENGLAND	CHECKERBOARD CAKE COVERED WITH MARZIPAN *Battenberg*
AUSTRIA	BAKING POWDER GUGELHUPF, ALSO CALLED HEALTH CAKE *Backpulvergugelhupf* or *Gesundheitskuchen*
ITALY	HAZELNUT CAKE FROM PIEMONTE *Torta di Nocciole alla Piemontese*
THE NETHERLANDS	APPLE CAKE *Appelgebak*
AUSTRIA	VIENNESE BISHOP'S LOAF CAKE *Bischofsbrot*
ENGLAND	PLUM CAKE
SWITZERLAND	RUSTIC BREAD PUDDING CAKE FROM TICINO *Torta di Pane*
JAMAICA	KINGSTON FRUITCAKE
AUSTRIA	VIENNESE CHOCOLATE NUT CAKE FROM JULIUS MEINL AM GRABEN *Millennium Torte*
ITALY	LEMON-SCENTED WHITE CHOCOLATE ALMOND CAKE FROM ANACAPRI *Torta Caprese Bianca*
SWITZERLAND	ALMOND POUND CAKE FROM MONTREUX *Marguerite*
PORTUGAL	ALMOND AND JAM CAKE FROM THE ALGARVE *Morgado de Amendoas*

Overleaf: Prinsessens Kramkake

GREECE	SEMOLINA CAKE SOAKED WITH LEMON SYRUP *Revani*
BRAZIL	COCONUT CUSTARD CAKE *Quindim*
MEXICO	THREE MILKS CAKE *Pastel de Tres Leches*
AUSTRALIA	PAVLOVA
SOUTH AFRICA	MELISSA'S CHOCOLATE PECAN CAKE
FRANCE	COFFEE CREAM LAYER CAKE *Gâteau Mocca*
ITALY	RICOTTA-FILLED CAKE FROM SICILY *Cassata alla Siciliana*
NORWAY	PRINCESS CREAM CAKE *Prinsessens Kramkake*
FRANCE	LEMON-SCENTED SHELL-SHAPE CAKES *Madeleines*
FRANCE	CHOCOLATE ALMOND CAKES *Pleyels*
SWITZERLAND	CHOCOLATE MERINGUE RING CAKES *Schoggiringli*
AUSTRIA	CARDINAL SLICES *Kardinalschnitten*
HUNGARY	CHOCOLATE RIGO SQUARES *Rigo Jansci*

CAKES MEAN ONE THING: CELEBRATION. That doesn't mean they have to be fancy, however. The occasion being marked can be as simple as inviting a friend for coffee or tea, although cakes are traditionally served for more significant events, such as birthdays and anniversaries. The cakes in this chapter cover a wide range of types. Some—which I like to call "mix-bake-eat" cakes—are very simple and need no further adornment after they are baked. Others call for application of a dressy glaze, but are also fairly quick and easy to prepare.

Other recipes are more challenging; they require you to perform multiple steps. Don't be intimidated by these more complex recipes, but do leave yourself plenty of time. They are best prepared over a span of a couple of days so that you are not spending an entire day in the kitchen with them. And you will find that when you break down a more complex recipe, the individual steps are not terribly difficult.

Remember, cakes are meant to be enjoyed. Have fun preparing and finishing them, as well as eating them.

Here are the types of cakes in this chapter:

1. Plain Cakes: I'm not happy with using this drab name to describe perfectly good, extremely satisfying cakes, but I'm not sure what else to call them. They are plain, but in no way dull or lacking. These are the "mix-bake-eat" cakes referred to above. They may be made in loaf, tube, or round pans, and are usually unadorned, except perhaps for a sprinkling of confectioners' sugar or a simple glaze.

2. Cakes with Fresh or Dried Fruit: These are like the plain cakes, but with the addition of some form of fruit. Obviously, fruitcakes of all types fit into this category, as well as some simple cakes meant to be served with coffee or tea between meals. Like most plain cakes, these are not necessarily meant to be served as dessert, except in the context of a multiple-dessert presentation for a large party. They are homey, but slightly richer than plain cakes.

3. One-Layer Cakes: These are generally rich cakes, but rather than being split into layers and filled before serving (see Layer Cakes, opposite), they are left intact. Often they have multiple-glaze finishes and require just a little more time and trouble than plain cakes.

4. Layer Cakes: These are of two types. Either they are baked as a single layer, which is subsequently cut into two or more layers, or they are baked as separate layers and assembled and covered with filling and frosting (which is less complicated than it sounds, as the filling and frosting are often the same preparation).

5. Individual Cakes: These may fall into any of the categories above. What distinguishes them is that they are either baked in individual pans or are cut and finished as individual pieces. Individual cakes make for elegant presentations and are perfect for parties.

SOME HINTS FOR ACHIEVING GOOD CAKES

No matter what type of cake you intend to prepare, review these hints before starting.

1. Use the correct size pan or pans: The recipes here are very specific about what type of pan to use. If you change the diameter or depth of the pan from the one called for in the recipe, you will not get the same results and baking time may be inaccurate.

2. Get the pan ready: When I bake a cake, the first thing I do after I turn on the oven to preheat is prepare the pan. Soft, not melted, butter gives the best results for greasing the pan. Slice off 2 pats of butter, put them in the pan, and they will soften almost immediately. If you don't feel like dirtying a brush to spread the butter in the pan, use a crumpled piece of plastic wrap (a paper towel absorbs the butter, but plastic wrap doesn't). Make sure that both the bottom and the sides of the pan are well coated.

3. Measure the ingredients: Measure accurately. I can't stress this enough. Inaccurate measurement can result in cakes that sink or dome unattractively in the center. Also, take out all the ingredients and measure them before you start mixing. It's too easy to forget to add something if it's still sitting on the cupboard shelf.

4. Mix according to recipe instructions. Undermixing and overmixing can both result in unattractive cakes.

5. Use the baking time in the recipe as a guide: Ovens work at different speeds. Learn to use the description of doneness in the recipe, rather than just setting a timer and taking the cake out when the time has elapsed. Always check the cake for doneness

after about two-thirds of the baking time has elapsed. You may find that your oven is fast (hot) and that the cake is almost done before the time suggested in the recipe has elapsed.

6. Alternate: As in baking cookies, change the position of cake layers in the oven if you are using more than one rack. Move the layer or layers from the lower rack to the upper and vice versa. Also, turn them back to front, since the back of the oven always gives off slightly higher heat than the front.

7. Cool thoroughly: Butter-based cakes should cool in the pan for a few minutes before being inverted onto a rack. Sponge-type cakes must come out of the pan immediately, or they will shrink and fall. Loosen the cake from the side of the pan with a paring knife (scrape against the pan, not the cake) and invert it onto a rack.

8. Divide up the work: If you want to attempt a cake that has multiple subrecipes, plan on baking the cake layer or layers on one day, then wrap and refrigerate them for a day or two. During the intervening time you can prepare moistening syrup or other components. On the day you intend to serve the cake, you'll just need to prepare the filling and frosting and proceed with assembling and finishing the cake. I don't like to prepare butter cream in advance, however, as it spreads better and is less likely to separate when freshly made and used right away.

9. Above all, keep calm and focused: Don't try to answer the phone while you are holding a cake and pressing chocolate shavings against the side. Cake finishing requires concentration and is not meant to be done at the same time as other work. This is one situation where multitasking is definitely out.

ENGLAND

Checkerboard Cake Covered with Marzipan
Battenberg

CAKE BATTER

16 tablespoons (2 sticks) unsalted butter, softened

1 cup sugar

3 large eggs

2 teaspoons vanilla extract

2 cups cake flour (spoon flour into dry-measure cup and level off)

1 teaspoon baking powder

3 tablespoons alkalized (Dutch-process) cocoa, sifted after measuring

3 tablespoons milk

MARZIPAN

8 ounces almond paste

3 cups confectioners' sugar

¼ cup light corn syrup

RASPBERRY GLAZE

1 cup seedless raspberry jam

Two 9 × 5 × 3-inch loaf pans, buttered and the bottoms lined with rectangles of parchment paper

This chocolate-and-vanilla version of a very British cake bears the original German name of the family now known in Britain as Mountbatten. The cake batter is divided in half, and cocoa is added to one portion of it. (Some versions just use food coloring in half the batter.) After baking, the two cakes are cut into even bars and stacked up checkerboard-style. A covering of marzipan finishes off the cake. Thanks to my friend Kyra Effren for sharing her expert knowledge of British baking.

One 8 × 5 × 5-inch loaf cake

1. Set a rack in the middle level of the oven and preheat to 350 degrees.
2. Combine the butter and sugar in the bowl of an electric mixer and beat with the paddle on medium speed until very light and smooth, about 5 minutes.
3. Beat in the eggs, one at a time. Beat in the vanilla.

4. Sift the cake flour into a bowl and stir in the baking powder.

5. Stop the mixer and add a third of the flour mixture to the batter. Mix on lowest speed until the flour is absorbed. Repeat with the remaining second and last third of the flour. After all the flour has been added, let the batter beat on lowest speed for 2 additional minutes.

6. Remove the bowl from the mixer and put half the batter into another bowl.

7. Mix the cocoa and milk together and stir the cocoa mixture into one of the batters. Scrape each batter into a separate pan and bake until well risen and a toothpick inserted in the center of each cake emerges clean, about 20 to 25 minutes.

8. Unmold the cakes to racks to cool completely.

9. To make the marzipan, cut the almond paste into ½-inch pieces and combine in the bowl of an electric mixer with about half the confectioners' sugar. Place on the mixer fitted with the paddle attachment and beat on lowest speed until the almond paste absorbs the sugar, about 3 to 4 minutes. Add the remaining sugar in a stream and continue mixing until the marzipan looks like very fine crumbs. Add the corn syrup to the bowl and continue mixing until the marzipan begins to form larger crumbs. Remove the bowl from the mixer and pour the marzipan out onto a work surface. Knead the crumbs together until they form a firm dough, adding a drop or two of water if the mixture seems too dry. Wrap the marzipan in plastic wrap.

10. After the cakes have cooled, trim the sides straight and cut each cake into a 9 × 5 × 2½-inch slab. Cut one cake down the middle to make two 9 × 2½ × 2½-inch bars. Repeat with the other cake.

11. To make the glaze, place the jam in a medium saucepan and heat it over medium heat until it is slightly reduced and no longer sticky, about 3 to 4 minutes.

12. Assemble the cake on a piece of parchment paper. First brush some of the glaze on the side of one of the plain cake bars and press a bar of the chocolate cake against it so that you have one white bar and one chocolate bar, side by side.

13. Paint the top of the white bar with the glaze and place the second bar of chocolate cake on top of it. Paint the side of that second bar of chocolate cake and the top of the bar of chocolate cake on the bottom layer with the glaze and place the last bar of white cake in place. Now you should have two layers of alternating colors, like a checkerboard.

14. Roll out the marzipan to a 10 × 22-inch rectangle, dusting the marzipan and the work surface with a little cornstarch to keep it from sticking. Brush the glaze on one side of the cake and invert the cake so that the glaze is on the bottom. Position the cake so that it is 1 inch from one of the 10-inch sides of the marzipan. Paint the remainder of the outside of the cake with the glaze and wrap the marzipan around to cover the whole cake, trimming it evenly where it meets the other end of the marzipan.

15. Trim the ends of the cake flat.

Serving: Serve this rich cake in thin slices, with tea, of course.

Storage: The cake will keep for a few days in plastic wrap at room temperature. Wrap tightly and freeze for longer storage.

AUSTRIA

Baking Powder Gugelhupf, Also Called Health Cake
Backpulvergugelhupf or Gesundheitskuchen

1 cup all-purpose flour (spoon flour into dry-measure cup and level off)

1 teaspoon baking powder

16 tablespoons (2 sticks) unsalted butter, softened

1 cup sugar

5 large eggs, separated

½ cup cornstarch

¼ cup milk

2 teaspoons finely grated lemon zest

1 teaspoon vanilla extract

One 10- or 12-cup gugelhupf or Bundt pan, buttered and the buttered surface sprinkled with fine, dry breadcrumbs

Like a pound cake, this cake with a funny name is both delicious and easy to prepare. When we used to bake this in classes, students referred to it as "sneeze cake" because gesundheit is part of its name. Actually, *Gesundheit* means "health" in German, and here it probably referred to the fact that this plain cake is easy to digest. Unfortunately, nowadays we no longer consider cake health food—changing times even change our attitudes toward cake! ***One 8- to 10-inch tube cake, depending on the size of the mold used; about 16 servings***

1. Set a rack in the lower third of the oven and preheat to 350 degrees.
2. Stir the flour and baking powder together and set aside.
3. Combine the butter and ½ cup of the sugar in the bowl of an electric mixer. Beat the mixture with the paddle attachment on medium speed until it is soft and light, about 3 to 4 minutes.
4. Add the egg yolks, one at a time, beating smooth after each addition.

5. Beat in the cornstarch, milk, lemon zest, and vanilla, one at a time, beating smooth after each addition.

6. Scrape the batter into a large mixing bowl. If you only have one bowl for your mixer, clean and thoroughly dry it.

7. Pour the egg whites into a clean mixer bowl and place on the mixer fitted with the whisk attachment, then whip the egg whites until they are very white, opaque, and beginning to hold a very soft peak. Increase the speed to medium-high and whip in the remaining ½ cup sugar in a slow stream, continuing to whip the egg whites until they hold a soft, glossy peak.

8. Fold about a third of the egg whites into the butter and egg mixture, followed by about half the flour. Fold in another third of the egg whites, then the remaining flour. Finally, fold in the remaining egg whites.

9. Scrape the batter into the prepared pan and smooth the top.

10. Bake the cake until it is well risen and deep golden, and until a toothpick inserted midway between the side of the pan and the central tube emerges dry, about 45 to 50 minutes.

11. Cool the cake in the pan on a rack for 10 minutes, then invert the cake to the rack to cool completely.

Serving: This is good snacking cake and perfect with tea or coffee. If you want to dress it up, serve a few berries and a little unsweetened (Viennese-style) whipped cream with it.

Storage: Wrap the cake in plastic and keep it at room temperature. It will stay fresh for several days. Freeze for longer storage.

ITALY

HAZELNUT CAKE FROM PIEMONTE
Torta di Nocciole alla Piemontese

3 large eggs

¼ teaspoon salt

1⅓ cups sugar

20 tablespoons (2½ sticks) unsalted butter, melted and slightly cooled

2½ cups whole hazelnuts (about 12 ounces) with or without skins, finely ground in the food processor

2 cups all-purpose flour (spoon flour into dry-measure cup and level off)

One 9-inch round pan, 2 inches deep, buttered and the bottom lined with a disk of buttered parchment

Some of the world's most flavorful hazelnuts grow in the Langa Hills (*Le Langhe*, in Italian), a fairly small area roughly between the towns of Alba and Asti in Italy's Piemonte region. This area offers seriously good food—to my mind, the most carefully prepared in all of Italy. It's also the terrain where the rare, exquisitely perfumed white truffle is found, its presence inspiring the local cooking to even greater heights. I've been fortunate to visit the Langhe on several occasions, enjoying the excellent food in many of the region's fine restaurants. Desserts are simple there—nothing more than a slightly sweet note on which to end the meal with the real dessert of Piemonte, the delicately perfumed and sometimes slightly bubbly moscato wine.

This hazelnut cake might seem dry if you compare it with a moist American-style cake. But its dense and slightly dry quality makes it marry well with a glass of sweet wine, whether it is a moscato from Piemonte or another favorite of yours. Remember, this is also meant to be a very casual cake, something you put on the table at the end of the meal so that the guests can nibble on it between sips of wine, which might carry them along to a cup of espresso to finish. ***One 9-inch cake, about 12 small servings***

1. Set a rack in the middle level of the oven and preheat to 350 degrees.
2. In the bowl of an electric mixer, whisk the eggs and salt by hand. Whisk in the sugar in a stream. Place the bowl on the mixer and whip on high speed with the whisk attachment until the mixture is very light and has increased about 3 times in volume, about 3 minutes.
3. Remove the bowl from the mixer and fold in the butter, followed by the ground hazelnuts.
4. Sift the flour over the batter and fold it in with a large rubber spatula.
5. Scrape the batter into the prepared pan and smooth the top.
6. Bake the cake until it is firm and deep golden and a toothpick inserted in the center emerges clean, about 50 to 60 minutes.
7. Cool the cake in the pan on a rack for 10 minutes, then unmold it onto another rack. Remove the paper and replace it with another rack. Grasping the cake between the two racks, turn the cake right side up and remove the top rack. Cool the cake completely.

SERVING: Cut the cake into wedges or squares to serve. See the headnote for accompaniments.

STORAGE: Keep the cake in plastic wrap to prevent it from drying out.

Apple Cake
Appelgebak

CAKE

2 cups all-purpose flour (spoon flour into dry-measure cup and level off)

1½ teaspoons baking powder

½ teaspoon salt

12 tablespoons (1½ sticks) unsalted butter, softened

¾ cup sugar plus 2 tablespoons sugar for sprinkling on the apples

3 large eggs

1 teaspoon vanilla extract

1 teaspoon finely grated lemon zest

3 Golden Delicious apples, peeled, quartered, and cored

GLAZE

½ cup apricot preserves

2 tablespoons water

One 10-inch round pan, 2 inches deep, buttered and lined with a disk of buttered parchment

Several years ago I stopped in to see my friend the cookbook dealer Bonnie Slotnick at her shop in Greenwich Village and found this cake and its maker, Dirk-Jan Zonneveld, sitting on the floor. He was busy cutting thick wedges of appelgebak and fortunately I was immediately given a wedge, and then given the recipe. This is a typically homey cake: nothing fancy, but very good. ***One 10-inch cake, about 12 servings***

1. Set a rack in the middle level of the oven and preheat to 350 degrees.
2. Stir together the flour, baking powder, and salt in a bowl and set aside.
3. Place the butter and ¾ cup sugar in the bowl of an electric mixer and beat with the paddle on medium speed until soft and light, about 3 to 4 minutes.
4. Beat in 1 egg until smooth. Beat in the vanilla and lemon zest.

5. Beat in about a third of the flour mixture until smooth, and then beat in another egg.
6. Beat in another third of the flour mixture and then beat in the remaining egg.
7. Stop and scrape the bowl and paddle, and then beat in the remaining flour mixture.
8. Scrape the batter into the prepared pan and smooth the top. Arrange 11 of the apple quarters, core side down, on the batter, in a circle near the edges of the pan. Place the last apple quarter in the center of the batter. Sprinkle the apples with the 2 tablespoons sugar.
9. Bake the cake until the apples have softened, about 1 hour. The batter will definitely be baked through in this amount of time.
10. Cool the cake on a rack in the pan, then unmold it onto another rack and lift away the first rack and replace it with a platter. Invert the cake again and lift off the top rack.
11. For the apricot glaze, stir the preserves and water together in a small saucepan. Cook over medium heat, stirring occasionally, until the glaze comes to a simmer. Strain the glaze into another pan and place it back on the heat. Allow the glaze to reduce until it is slightly sticky and no longer watery, about 2 minutes.
12. Immediately paint the hot glaze onto the apple quarters, using a brush. Let the glaze cool and set before serving the cake.

SERVING: Cut the cake into wedges. A little whipped cream would be good with this cake.

STORAGE: Keep the cake under a dome or loosely covered with plastic wrap at room temperature. For longer storage, wrap and refrigerate the cake before applying the glaze. Bring the cake to room temperature and paint the apples with the glaze before serving.

AUSTRIA

Viennese Bishop's Loaf Cake
Bischofsbrot

24 tablespoons (3 sticks) unsalted butter, softened

1½ cups confectioners' sugar

2 teaspoons vanilla extract

2 teaspoons finely grated lemon zest

1 tablespoon dark rum

7 large eggs, separated

Pinch of salt

½ cup granulated sugar

3 cups all-purpose flour (spoon flour into dry-measure cup and level off)

½ cup (about 2½ ounces) dark raisins

1 cup (about 7 ounces) mixed candied fruit or candied orange peel, cut into ¼-inch dice

1 cup (about 4 ounces) walnut pieces

2 ounces semisweet chocolate, cut into ¼-inch pieces and sifted to remove the tiniest particles

Two 8½ × 4½ × 2¾-inch loaf pans buttered and the bottoms lined with rectangles of buttered parchment or wax paper

One of the most popular Viennese coffee cakes aside from gugelhupf (see page 47 for a recipe for the classic yeast-risen gugelhupf and page 118 in this chapter for a version made with baking powder), bishop's loaf is a rich pound cake studded with raisins, candied fruit, walnuts, and chocolate. ***Two 8½ × 4½ × 2¾-inch loaf cakes***

1. Set a rack in the middle level of the oven and preheat to 350 degrees.

2. Beat the butter with the paddle attachment on medium speed until it is very soft and light. Decrease the speed to lowest and beat in the confectioners' sugar. Increase the speed to medium and beat until the mixture is light and whitened, about 3 to 4 minutes. Beat in the vanilla, lemon zest, and rum. Add the egg yolks, one at a time, beating smooth after each addition.

3. Scrape the batter into a large mixing bowl. If you only have one bowl for your mixer, clean and thoroughly dry it.

4. Clean and thoroughly dry the mixer bowl. Combine the egg whites and salt in the bowl and place on the mixer fitted with the whisk attachment. Whip the egg whites until they are very white, opaque, and beginning to hold a very soft peak. Increase the speed to medium-high and whip in the granulated sugar in a slow stream, continuing to whip the egg whites until they hold a soft, glossy peak.

5. Fold about a quarter of the egg whites into the butter and yolk mixture. Sift over and fold in about a third of the flour. Fold in another quarter of the whipped egg whites, then another third of the flour. Fold in another quarter of the whipped egg whites.

6. Remove 2 tablespoons from the remaining flour and toss it with the remaining ingredients. Fold the remaining flour into the batter, followed by the remaining egg whites.

7. Gently fold in the floured fruit, nut, and chocolate mixture.

8. Divide the batter between the prepared pans. Bake the cakes until they are well risen and deep golden and a toothpick inserted in the center of each cake emerges clean, about 1 hour.

9. Cool the cakes in the pans for about 5 minutes, then invert onto racks to cool right side up.

Serving: Cut into ½-inch slices to serve. This cake is better in texture the next day.

Storage: Keep the cakes in plastic wrap at room temperature for up to several days.

ENGLAND

Plum Cake

FRUIT AND NUT MIXTURE

2 cups (about 10 ounces) dried currants

2 cups (about 10 ounces) dark raisins

1 cup (about 5 ounces) golden raisins

¾ cup (about 5 ounces) candied cherries, halved

¾ cup (about 4 ounces) pitted dried plums (prunes), cut into ½-inch pieces

1 cup (about 6 ounces) candied citron, cut into ¼-inch dice

¾ cup (about 3 ounces) slivered almonds

CAKE BATTER

16 tablespoons (2 sticks) unsalted butter, softened

1 cup sugar

5 large eggs

½ teaspoon salt

2 cups all-purpose flour (spoon flour into dry-measure cup and level off)

1 pound almond paste, preferably canned

One 10-inch springform pan lined with buttered foil

This is an example of the type of fruitcake that the British excel in baking. It is chock-full of dried and candied fruit and further enriched with a layer of almond paste in the center, which, despite the added richness it provides, actually makes the cake lighter and perfumes it with delicate almond flavor. Most British bakers use a pan that is fairly narrow in diameter and very tall for this type of cake, resulting in a very long baking time and the risk that some of the fruit will become heavily caramelized and taste slightly burned. I use a wider, shallower pan, which helps the cake to bake more quickly and virtually eliminates the risk of a burned flavor. ***One 10-inch cake, about forty 5 × ½-inch slices***

1. Set a rack in the middle level of the oven and preheat to 325 degrees.
2. Combine all the fruit and almonds in a large bowl and stir well to mix.

3. In the bowl of an electric mixer fitted with the paddle attachment, beat the butter and sugar on medium speed until soft and light, about 5 minutes. Add 3 of the eggs, one at a time, beating smooth after each addition. Beat in the salt and 1 cup of the flour.

4. Beat in the remaining eggs, one at a time, scraping the bowl and paddle well after each addition. Finally, beat in the remaining flour.

5. Scrape the batter over the fruit and almond mixture and fold it in with a large rubber spatula, making sure that the fruit and batter are evenly distributed throughout.

6. Scrape half the batter into the prepared pan and smooth the top.

7. Knead the almond paste to make it pliable and, on a surface lightly dusted with granulated sugar, roll it out into a 10-inch disk. Arrange the disk of almond paste on the batter in the pan, gently pressing it into place. Scrape the remaining batter over the almond paste.

8. Bake the cake until a toothpick inserted in the center emerges dry, about 1 hour and 45 minutes.

9. Cool the cake in the pan for 10 minutes and unmold it onto a rack to cool completely.

Serving: I like to cut this cake in half, down the middle, then into ½-inch slices. As far as I am concerned, this is the ultimate tea cake.

Storage: Double-wrap the cake in plastic wrap, then a tight layer of aluminum foil to keep it from drying out. Keep it in a cool place, though it doesn't need to be refrigerated.

SWITZERLAND

Rustic Bread Pudding Cake from Ticino
Torta di Pane

One 1-pound loaf of French or Italian bread, slightly stale, cut into ½-inch cubes

1 tablespoon finely grated lemon zest

1 quart milk

6 large eggs

1¼ cups sugar

1 teaspoon ground cinnamon

1 teaspoon alkalized (Dutch-process) cocoa powder, sifted after measuring

½ teaspoon freshly grated nutmeg

2 teaspoons vanilla extract

1 cup (about 4 ounces) whole almonds, skinned or not, finely ground in a food processor

2 cups (about 10 ounces) dark raisins

Whole blanched almonds and pine nuts for topping

2 tablespoons unsalted butter

Confectioners' sugar for finishing

One 10-inch round cake pan, 2 inches deep, buttered and the bottom lined with a disk of buttered parchment or wax paper

Switzerland's southernmost canton, Ticino, abounds in traditional recipes. This bread-based cake is a common offering in a *grotto*, a type of rustic mountainside restaurant, usually outdoors, that serves only the old specialties of the region—sliced cured meats, polenta with a variety of homey toppings, and of course torta di pane for dessert. My version is based on one I have tasted many times at my favorite *grotto*, Da Pierino, in Cureggia in the mountains above Lugano. ***One 10-inch cake, about 16 servings***

1. Set a rack in the middle level of the oven and preheat to 400 degrees.

2. Place the bread cubes in a food processor fitted with the steel blade and pulse to make ⅛-inch crumbs. Place the crumbs in a large mixing bowl and scatter the lemon zest over them. In a small saucepan, bring the milk to a simmer over medium heat and pour over the bread to cover it entirely. Let the mixture stand for 10 minutes so that the bread absorbs the milk.

3. In a large mixing bowl, whisk the eggs until they are broken up and whisk in the sugar in a stream. Whisk in the cinnamon, cocoa, nutmeg, and vanilla. Stir in the soaked bread mixture and then stir in the ground almonds and raisins.

4. Scrape the batter into the prepared pan and smooth the top. Decorate with the almonds and pine nuts in a symmetrical pattern. Dot the top of the batter with the butter.

5. Place the pan in the oven and immediately lower the heat to 350 degrees. Bake the cake until it is deep golden and a toothpick inserted in the center emerges dry, about 1 hour.

6. Cool the cake in the pan on a rack.

7. Invert the cake onto the rack and remove the pan and paper. Place a platter on the cake and invert onto the platter, firmly grasping both the rack and the platter to keep the cake from sliding out. Remove the rack.

8. Dust the cake with confectioners' sugar immediately before serving.

SERVING: At a *grotto*, this cake is always served in squares, but you can also cut it into slices.

STORAGE: Keep the cake loosely covered with plastic wrap and at a cool room temperature on the day you prepare it. Wrap in plastic and refrigerate for longer storage. Bring the cake to room temperature before serving.

JAMAICA

Kingston Fruitcake

FRUIT MIXTURE

3¼ cups (about 1 pound) currants

4 cups (about 1¼ pounds) dark raisins

1½ cups (about 9 ounces) candied citron, cut into ¼-inch dice

1¼ cups (about ½ pound) dried figs, stemmed and diced

1¼ cups (about ½ pound) pitted dried plums (prunes) snipped into ½-inch pieces

1 cup (about 6 ounces) seedless dates, snipped into ½-inch pieces

1 cup (about 6 ounces) candied cherries, quartered

1 cup (about 6 ounces) candied orange peel, cut into ¼-inch dice

2 cups (about ½ pound) blanched whole almonds, lightly toasted and coarsely chopped

3 cups dark Jamaica rum (I like Meyer's)

CAKE BATTER

2 cups all-purpose flour (spoon flour into dry-measure cup and level off)

2 teaspoons baking powder

½ teaspoon salt

1½ teaspoons ground cinnamon

1½ teaspoons ground allspice

1½ teaspoons freshly grated nutmeg

16 tablespoons (2 sticks) unsalted butter, softened

2 cups dark brown sugar, firmly packed

5 large eggs, at room temperature

More rum for aging the fruitcake and soaking the cloth wrapping

Two 9 × 5 × 3-inch loaf pans lined with buttered foil, plus a roasting pan for water

This cake always brings back fond memories. I first made it as a teenager when my mother and I went on a fruitcake-baking spree before the holidays one year. We made such an enormous batch that we used a large plastic bin for soaking the fruit and rum together. We aged the fruitcakes in rum-soaked cheesecloth and kept them in our cool, dark storage cellar, where the walls were lined with jars of preserves, pickles, and all the tomato preparations that we put up every year. With so many fruitcakes left over after the holidays, we even tried our hand at preserving them. Nowadays I live in a Manhattan apartment and age my fruitcakes in the refrigerator, alongside the mincemeat I made in 1992. One taste of the cake brings me back to the carefree days of my youth and the love and comfort of family life around the holidays.

The recipe comes from a wonderful book by Avanelle Day and Lillie Stuckey called *The Spice Cookbook* (David White, 1964). I have made minor adjustments over the years, but it still remains one of my favorite fruitcakes. Remember to bake the cake about 3 or 4 weeks before you intend to serve it, to give it time to age. ***Two 9 × 5 × 3-inch cakes, about 36 thin servings***

1. At least a week before you intend to bake the cake, combine all the fruit and almonds with the rum in a large mixing bowl or another nonreactive container and stir well to mix. Cover with plastic wrap, store in a cool place, and stir once a day for a week while the fruit is soaking.

2. On the day you are going to bake the cake, set racks in the lowest level and middle level of the oven and preheat to 275 degrees.

3. Stir the flour, baking powder, salt, and spices together and set aside.

4. Put the butter and brown sugar in the bowl of an electric mixer and place on the mixer fitted with the paddle attachment. Beat the butter and sugar until they are soft and light, about 3 to 4 minutes. Beat in 2 of the eggs, one at a time, beating smooth after each addition. Beat in about a third of the flour and spice mixture. Beat in another 2 eggs, one at a time, and then beat in another third of the flour and spice mixture. Stop and scrape the bowl and paddle. Beat in the remaining egg, followed by the remaining flour mixture.

5. Scrape the batter over the fruit and rum mixture and fold it in thoroughly with a large rubber spatula.

6. Pack the batter into the prepared pans and smooth the tops.

7. Place the pans on the middle rack of the oven. Place a roasting pan on the lowest rack of the oven, and half-fill the roasting pan with warm water, which will evaporate during baking and keep the cakes moist to prevent them from drying out and burning.

8. Bake the cakes until a toothpick inserted in the center emerges clean, about 3 to 3¼ hours. Check every 45 minutes or so and add water to the roasting pan as necessary to keep the water from evaporating completely.

9. Cool the cakes in the pans on a rack. Unmold the cakes and peel away the foil.

10. To age the cakes, sprinkle them with more rum. Wet 2 pieces of cheesecloth or 2 flat-weave towels with more rum and wrap the cakes in them. Double-wrap the cakes in plastic wrap and a layer of aluminum foil. Age the cakes in a cool, dark place, or in the refrigerator, for a month before serving. To preserve the cakes longer, repeat the procedure above and store them in tins.

SERVING: Serve the fruitcake in very thin slices. Fruitcake is good with a selection of other holiday desserts, or as a petit four with coffee after dinner and dessert.

STORAGE: After serving some of the fruitcake, rewrap it as in step 10, above.

AUSTRIA

Viennese Chocolate Nut Cake from Julius Meinl am Graben

Millennium Torte

CAKE BATTER

12 tablespoons (1½ sticks) unsalted butter, softened

⅔ cup sugar

7 ounces semisweet chocolate, melted and cooled

7 large eggs, separated

1⅓ cups (about 5½ ounces) ground hazelnuts or walnuts

⅔ cup dry breadcrumbs

Pinch salt

CURRANT GLAZE

1 cup currant jelly

CHOCOLATE GLAZE

⅓ cup water

⅓ cup light corn syrup

1 cup sugar

8 ounces semisweet chocolate, cut into ¼-inch pieces

Gold leaf for decorating

One 10-inch round cake pan, 2 inches deep, buttered and the bottom lined with a disk of buttered parchment or wax paper

This cake was created by the pastry chef Josef Haslinger of Vienna's fanciest fancy food store, Julius Meinl am Graben (also now in Chicago), in honor of the beginning of the twenty-first century. It is a rich chocolate nut cake with a chocolate glaze, decorated with gold leaf. This is my version of the cake, not the official recipe from Meinl. See Sources on page 363 for purchasing gold leaf. ***One 10-inch round cake, about 12 servings***

1. Set a rack in the middle level of the oven and preheat to 350 degrees.
2. In an electric mixer fitted with the paddle attachment, beat the butter with half the sugar on medium speed until light, about 5 minutes. Beat in the chocolate and scrape down the bowl and paddle with a large rubber spatula.
3. Add the egg yolks, one at a time, beating smooth after each addition. Beat in the ground nuts and breadcrumbs. Remove the bowl

from the mixer and give the batter a good stir with a large rubber spatula. If you have only one mixer bowl, scrape the butter and yolk mixture into a medium bowl and wash the mixer bowl with hot soapy water, then rinse and dry it.

4. In the clean, dry mixer bowl, whip the egg whites and salt with the whisk attachment on medium speed, until the egg whites are white, opaque, and beginning to hold their shape. Increase the mixer speed to medium-high and whip in the remaining sugar in a stream, continuing to whip until the egg whites hold a soft, glossy peak.

5. Stir a quarter of the egg whites into the batter, and then fold in the rest—gently, to avoid deflating the egg whites and losing air in the batter.

6. Scrape the batter into the prepared pan and smooth the top. Bake the cake until it is well risen and a toothpick inserted in the center of the cake emerges dry, about 35 to 40 minutes. Cool the cake in the pan on a rack for 5 minutes, then invert it onto the rack and lift off the pan. Cool the cake completely on the rack.

7. To finish the cake, turn it right side up and trim the top of the cake straight if it has sunk slightly in the center. Turn the cake over again onto a cardboard so that the smooth bottom of the cake is now facing up.

8. For the currant glaze, place the jelly in a small saucepan over low heat. Bring to a boil and reduce until it is no longer watery, about 5 minutes. Use a small pastry brush to paint the glaze all over the outside of the cake. Position the cake on a rack over a clean jelly-roll pan before preparing the chocolate glaze.

9. For the chocolate glaze, stir together the water, corn syrup, and sugar in a medium saucepan. Place over medium heat and bring the syrup to a full rolling boil, stirring occasionally to make sure that all the sugar crystals dissolve. Remove the pan from the heat and add the chocolate. Gently shake the pan to make sure that all the chocolate is submerged in the syrup. Let the glaze stand for 2 minutes to melt the chocolate. Whisk the glaze smooth and immediately pour the glaze over the cake, starting in the center of the cake and making a spiral with the stream of glaze, ending with a final pour on the top edge of the cake. Quickly patch up any bare spots on the side of the

cake with a small spatula, using the glaze that has dripped onto the pan under the cake. Let the cake stay in place on the rack for at least 30 minutes to set the glaze.

10. Use a small paring knife to detach the bottom edge of the cake from the rack before trying to move it. Place the cake on a platter and decorate with shreds of gold leaf.

Serving: In Vienna it would be obligatory to serve unsweetened whipped cream with this type of cake.

Storage: The cake will keep well under a dome or loosely covered in plastic wrap at room temperature for a few days.

Lemon-Scented White Chocolate Almond Cake from Anacapri

Torta Caprese Bianca

8 tablespoons (1 stick) unsalted butter, softened

½ cup sugar, divided

8 ounces Guittard or Lindt white chocolate, melted and cooled

7 large eggs, separated

3 tablespoons lemon juice, strained

1 tablespoon finely grated lemon zest

1½ cups (about 7 ounces) blanched whole almonds, finely ground in the food processor

⅓ cup all-purpose flour

Confectioners' sugar and cocoa powder for finishing

One 10-inch round cake pan, 2 inches deep, buttered and bottom lined with a disk of buttered parchment or wax paper

My friend Gary Peese from Austin, Texas, discovered this cake when he was vacationing at Anacapri in the Bay of Naples. It is similar to the popular torta caprese (a chocolate walnut cake that I gave a recipe for in *Chocolate*), but uses white chocolate, almonds, and a lemon flavoring. It is a specialty of the restaurant Materita on the island.

A note of caution about melting white chocolate: Melt it over hot, not simmering, water, stirring often, or the milk solids and sugar in the chocolate will lump up and result in a gritty mess.

One 10-inch cake, about 12 generous servings

1. Set a rack in the middle level of the oven and preheat to 350 degrees.

2. Place the butter in the bowl of an electric mixer and beat with the paddle attachment on medium speed until soft and light, about 2 minutes. Beat in ¼ cup of the sugar and continue beating until the mixture whitens somewhat.

3. Beat in the white chocolate. Then beat in the yolks, one at a time, beating smooth after each addition. Beat in the lemon juice and zest.

4. Remove the bowl from the mixer and fold in the ground almonds, followed by the flour. If you only have one mixer bowl, scrape the mixture into a medium bowl and wash the mixer bowl with hot soapy water, then rinse and dry it.

5. In the clean, dry mixer bowl, whip the egg whites with the whisk attachment on medium speed until they are very white, opaque, and beginning to hold a very soft peak. Increase the speed to medium high and whip in the remaining ¼ cup of sugar in a slow stream, continuing to whip the egg whites until they hold a soft glossy peak.

6. Stir a quarter of the egg whites into the batter to soften it, then gently fold in the remaining egg whites.

7. Scrape the batter into the prepared pan and smooth the top.

8. Bake the cake for about 35 to 40 minutes, or until it is well risen and deep golden and a toothpick inserted in the center of the cake emerges clean.

9. Invert the cake onto a rack to cool, and lift off the pan. Cool the cake completely.

SERVING: Slide the cake onto a platter and dust it with the confectioners' sugar. Dust just a tiny amount of cocoa over the confectioners' sugar for contrast.

STORAGE: Keep under a cake dome at room temperature for a day or two. For advance preparation, wrap in plastic and freeze. Defrost the cake and bring it back to room temperature before serving. If you bake the cake in advance, dust it with the confectioners' sugar and cocoa just before serving.

SWITZERLAND

Almond Pound Cake from Montreux
Marguerite

CAKE BATTER

4 ounces canned almond paste, about 1/3 cup

2 tablespoons water

3/4 cup sugar

6 large eggs, separated

2 teaspoons finely grated lemon zest

1 2/3 cups all-purpose flour

6 tablespoons (3/4 stick) unsalted butter, melted and slightly cooled

APRICOT GLAZE

3/4 cup apricot preserves

2 tablespoons water

WATER ICING

2 cups confectioners' sugar

1/4 cup water

One 8-cup tube or Bundt pan, buttered and coated with fine dry breadcrumbs

The name of this lovely cake from the Confiserie Zurcher, the best pastry shop in Montreux, on Lake Geneva, means "daisy" and refers more to its delicacy than to its shape. The pastry chef at Zurcher, Max Muller, gave it to me during a recipe-finding trip I made to western Switzerland in 1996. Do try the chocolate version of this cake, listed as a variation at the end of the recipe.

One 9-inch tube cake, about 12 servings

1. Set a rack in the middle level of the oven and preheat to 350 degrees.
2. Cut the almond paste into 1/2-inch cubes and place it in the bowl of an electric mixer fitted with the paddle attachment. Add the water and about half the sugar. Beat on medium speed until smooth, about 2 minutes.
3. Beat in the egg yolks one at a time, beating smooth after each addition. Add the lemon zest. Scrape the bowl and paddle well with a rubber spatula and beat 1 additional minute.
4. Remove the bowl from the mixer and fold in the flour with a large rubber spatula.
5. Stir the melted butter into the batter.

6. In a clean, dry mixer bowl, whip the egg whites with the whisk attachment on medium speed until they are very white, opaque, and beginning to hold a very soft peak. Increase the speed to medium high and add the sugar in a stream, continuing to whip the whites until they hold a soft glossy peak. Fold the egg whites into the batter with a large rubber spatula.

7. Scrape the batter into the prepared pan and smooth the top. Bake the cake for about 40 minutes, or until it is well risen and deep golden and a toothpick inserted midway between the side of the pan and the central tube emerges dry.

8. Cool the cake in the pan on a rack for 5 minutes, then invert it onto the rack, lift off the pan, and cool the cake completely.

9. To make the glaze, combine the preserves and water in a saucepan and bring to a boil over medium heat, stirring occasionally. Strain the glaze into a pan and return it to a boil until it is sticky and no longer watery, about 2 minutes.

10. Paint the glaze all over the top of the cooled cake. Let the glaze dry for 30 minutes.

11. For the water icing, combine the confectioners' sugar and water in a saucepan and stir well to mix. Cook over medium heat, stirring constantly, until the glaze is hot, about 140 degrees. Immediately pour the hot glaze over the cake. There might be some dribbles on the side, but pay no attention to them—any attempt to smooth them out will make a sticky mess with the apricot glaze underneath and the crust of the cake.

12. Let the cake sit on the rack for 1 hour to set the glaze.

13. Detach the edge of the cake from the rack with the point of a small paring knife, and slide a large spatula underneath to move it to a platter.

Serving: Serve wedges of the cake garnished with some berries, if you like.

Storage: Keep under a cake dome at room temperature.

VARIATION: *Marguerite au Chocolat*

Substitute 1¼ cups flour and ⅓ cup alkalized (Dutch-process) cocoa powder, sifted after measuring, for the flour in the recipe above. Substitute the chocolate icing from the millennium torte, on page 133, for the water icing.

Almond and Jam Cake from the Algarve
Morgado de Amendoas

ALMOND CAKE MIXTURE

1½ cups (about 7 ounces) blanched almonds

2 tablespoons water

¾ cup sugar

½ pound canned almond paste

3 large egg yolks

¼ cup all-purpose flour

FILLING

1 cup Spaghetti Squash Jam (see the variation) or unstrained apricot preserves

ICING

3 cups confectioners' sugar

¼ cup water

Silver or multicolored dragées for decorating

One 9-inch round cake pan, 2 inches deep, lined with buttered foil

I would never have known about this sweet, delicious cake if it had not been for my friend Marta Curro, who brought one back for me after a trip to Portugal. Many Portuguese sweets are made with almonds, and this cake is no exception—it is basically a baked almond paste made with a little bit of egg and flour, similar in spirit to many Sicilian convent sweets. The filling is usually made from a rustic Portuguese squash jam called doce de chila, all but unobtainable outside Portugal. Chila is similar to spaghetti squash, but not exactly the same. You may make your own jam using spaghetti squash (see Note), or substitute apricot preserves, a little different in flavor from the original, but no less good.

Though the pastry shop where Marta bought the cake would not provide the recipe, I managed to find a version in Maria de Lourdes Modesto's monumental book *Traditional Portuguese Cooking* or *Cozinha Tradicional Portuguesa* (Editorial Verbo, 1982). Her recipe, coupled with my lingering memory of the cake my friend had so generously given me, was the inspiration for this recipe. One word of caution: This is a very sweet cake, and it is meant to be served in tiny slivers, preferably with espresso. ***One 9-inch cake, about 24 small servings***

1. Set a rack in the middle level of the oven and preheat to 325 degrees.
2. Place the almonds in the bowl of a food processor fitted with the steel blade, and pulse at 3-second intervals to grind them to a paste. As soon as the almonds begin to clump up and form a paste, add the water in 4 additions, pulsing after each addition. Scrape down the inside of the bowl and add the sugar. Pulse to form a sticky paste.
3. Cut the almond paste into 1-inch cubes and place in the bowl of an electric mixer. Beat with the paddle on low speed, then beat in the almond and sugar mixture in 4 separate additions, beating smooth after each addition.
4. Beat in the egg yolks one at a time, and then beat in the flour.
5. Spread half the almond mixture in the prepared pan, using a metal spatula. Top with the jam, spreading it to within ½ inch of the side of the pan.
6. Scrape the remaining almond mixture out onto a floured work surface and pat and press it into a 9-inch disk, using the palms of your hands to keep the top as flat as possible. Slide a cake cardboard or a thin flexible cookie sheet under the disk of almond mixture and transfer it to the pan, easing it off the cardboard onto the filling. Use the back of a spoon to gently press the top and bottom layers of almond mixture together at the inside edge of the pan, then use the bowl of the spoon to smooth the top of the cake.
7. Bake the cake for 30 to 35 minutes, or until it puffs slightly and feels slightly firm. Because of the high sugar content in the almond mixture, the cake will not firm up completely until it has cooled.
8. Cool the cake in the pan on a rack.
9. To finish the cake, once it is cool, invert it onto a 9-inch cardboard round and remove the pan and the foil. Place the cake on a rack over a jelly-roll pan.
10. For the icing, combine the confectioners' sugar and water in a medium saucepan and stir well to mix. Cook the icing over medium heat, stirring constantly, until it is just lukewarm, about 105 degrees.

11. Quickly pour the icing over the cake. Spread it with an offset metal spatula and make sure the sides of the cake are also covered. If necessary, touch up the sides with icing that drips onto the pan under the rack.

12. Quickly, before the icing dries, decorate the top of the cake with 20 or so dragées, arranged symmetrically all over the top of the cake.

SERVING: Slide the cake onto a platter and cut it into very thin slices.

STORAGE: On the day it is made, keep the cake at a cool room temperature. Refrigerate in plastic wrap for longer storage. The icing may become sticky, but the cake will remain fresher in the refrigerator. Bring to room temperature before serving again.

VARIATION: SPAGHETTI SQUASH JAM (*DOCE DE CHILA*)

You can make a substitute for doce de chila with spaghetti squash. It won't be exactly the same, but it's closer in flavor and texture than apricot preserves. This is based on information from Jean Anderson's *The Food of Portugal* (Morrow, 1986) and used with her kind permission. If you don't want leftover jam, make half a batch. ***About 2 cups jam, enough to make the cake two times***

2 spaghetti squash, about 5 pounds total

Approximately 4 cups sugar

2 cinnamon sticks

1. Use a stainless steel knife to halve the squash. Use a spoon to scrape away the seeds and long filaments, then cut the squash into 2-inch chunks.

2. Bring a large pan of water to a boil and salt it. Drop the squash chunks into the boiling water and let them return to a boil. Boil 1 minute, then drain in a colander.

3. Cool the chunks of squash and scrape the spaghetti-like filaments away from the skin. Collect all the filaments in a bowl, then weigh them. Place them in a large pan with an equal weight of sugar. Bring to a boil, stirring occasionally so that the sugar dissolves in the water clinging to the squash filaments. Boil 1 minute, then lift out the filaments with a skimmer or slotted spoon and transfer to a bowl.

4. Add the cinnamon sticks to the syrup and cook the syrup to about 235 degrees on a candy thermometer. At that point, skim out the cinnamon sticks and return the filaments to the concentrated syrup. Bring back to a boil.

5. Pack the hot jam into two 1-pint glass or plastic containers and store them in the refrigerator.

6. When you use the jam in the above recipe, drain away excess syrup if necessary.

GREECE

Semolina Cake Soaked with Lemon Syrup
Revani

CAKE BATTER

3 large eggs

1 cup sugar

1½ cups coarse semolina or cream of wheat

1 cup sour cream

½ teaspoon baking soda

1 tablespoon Metaxa Greek brandy or other brandy

1 tablespoon finely grated orange zest

5 tablespoons butter, melted and cooled slightly

SYRUP

1 cup water

1½ cups sugar

½ lemon

One 9 × 9 × 2-inch Pyrex pan, buttered and coated with fine dry breadcrumbs

This delicious, easy-to-prepare Greek cake comes from my friend and colleague of many years Michelle Tampakis. Both her family and her husband's are from Greece, where cakes of this type are popular. The recipe originated with a friend of Michelle's who was born in Sparta. Michelle also helped me with some of the filo pastries that appear in Chapter 7.

Because this cake is served from the pan in which it baked, it is good for a casual occasion. Use a glass pan so that the lemony syrup doesn't react with metal.

One 9 × 9-inch cake, about sixteen 2-inch servings

1. Set a rack in the middle of the oven and preheat to 350 degrees.

2. Whisk the eggs and ½ cup of the sugar by hand in the bowl of an electric mixer. Place the bowl on the mixer fitted with the whisk attachment and whip the mixture on medium high speed until pale and thickened, about 4 minutes.

3. While the eggs are whipping, stir the semolina and remaining ½ cup sugar together in a medium mixing bowl. Stir in the sour cream.

4. Dissolve the baking soda in the brandy in a small cup and stir into the semolina mixture. Add the orange zest and butter and stir to combine thoroughly.

5. When the egg mixture is ready, fold it into the semolina batter with a large rubber spatula.

6. Scrape the cake batter into the prepared pan and smooth the top. Bake the cake for about 30 minutes, or until it is well risen and deep golden and a toothpick inserted in the center emerges dry.

7. Cool the cake on a rack for 10 minutes.

8. While the cake is cooling, prepare the syrup. Stir together all the ingredients in a medium saucepan and bring to a boil over medium heat. Let the syrup boil gently for 5 minutes.

9. While the syrup is cooking, score the cake into 2-inch diamonds or rectangles with the point of a sharp knife, cutting about 1 inch into the cake.

10. After the syrup is cooked, remove the lemon half from the syrup and slowly pour the syrup all over the top of the cake so that it is evenly absorbed. Cool completely.

Serving: Cut through the scoring marks completely with a sharp knife. Use a flexible spatula to first loosen each piece of cake, then remove it from the pan. Only the first piece is difficult to remove and may break slightly; the rest should come out easily.

Storage: Keep the cake pan covered with plastic wrap at a cool room temperature.

BRAZIL

Coconut Custard Cake
Quindim

1 fresh coconut (about 1½ pounds)

7 large egg yolks

½ cup sugar

1 tablespoon unsalted butter, softened to the consistency of mayonnaise

⅔ cup milk, or a combination of equal parts milk and canned coconut milk

One 8-inch round pan, 2 inches deep, buttered and dusted with sugar, set in a small roasting pan

A classic Brazilian dessert, quindim is a cross between a cake and a coconut-laced baked custard. The whole coconuts you buy in supermarkets or fruit stores can sometimes be rather old and dried out. Taste the coconut before you make the recipe: if it seems drab, replace half of the milk with canned coconut milk, which is easy to find in specialty stores or ordinary grocery stores.

I have a special affection for quindim because it was one of the desserts we made at the Sporting Club and Hotel de Paris in Monte Carlo when I worked there in the 1970s. Quindim was served not in the main dining room but in Le Maona, the restaurant of the disco diva Regine in the Sporting Club. ***One 8-inch cake, about 8 servings***

1. Set a rack in the middle level of the oven and preheat to 325 degrees.
2. Use a large nail or ice pick to puncture one of the three eyes in the coconut (only one can be punctured, so you will need to try each until you find it). Pour the liquid out over a bowl and reserve it for a drink or another use.
3. Place the coconut in the oven and bake it until it cracks, about 15 minutes. Remove the coconut from the oven and let it cool slightly. Remove the shell. (It should come away easily.) Then cut the coconut meat into 8 to 10 pieces. Remove the brown skin with a vegetable peeler. Finely grate about half the coconut, using a food processor outfitted with the fine grating blade. Alternatively, grate the coconut by hand on the

largest holes of a box grater, and then pulse it in a food processor fitted with a metal blade to grind it finely. Measure the coconut with any juice resulting from grating it. It should be 1½ cups. Set aside any coconut in excess of 1½ cups for another use.

4. In a medium mixing bowl, whisk the egg yolks, then whisk in the sugar in a stream. Whisk until the mixture lightens, about 1 minute. Whisk in the butter until smooth.

5. Whisk in the milk, then stir in the grated coconut with a large rubber spatula.

6. Pour the batter into the prepared pan. Place the round pan, set inside the roasting pan, in the preheated oven. After placing the pan on the oven rack, pour 2 cups of warm water into the roasting pan under the cake pan.

7. Bake the cake until it is firm and set, about 40 minutes. While the quindim is baking, the coconut will rise to the top. This is normal.

8. On a rack, cool the quindim to room temperature, then cover it with plastic wrap. Refrigerate it until it is cold, about 6 hours or overnight.

9. To unmold the quindim, run a small paring knife between the pan and the cake. Invert a platter onto the pan and invert the pan and platter. Give the pan a sharp rap, and the cake should unmold easily. If it does not, invert again and place the pan on a low burner for a few seconds to melt the butter under the cake. Then repeat this step.

10. Cover the cake loosely with plastic wrap and refrigerate it until serving time.

Serving: Cut the quindim into wedges and serve with a little sweetened whipped cream if you like. You may also garnish it with fruit or berries.

Storage: Wrap and refrigerate leftovers.

MEXICO

Three Milks Cake
Pastel de Tres Leches

CAKE BATTER

1½ cups cake flour (spoon flour into dry-measure cup and level off)

1 cup sugar

2 teaspoons baking powder

3 large egg yolks

⅓ cup vegetable oil, such as corn or canola

½ cup water

2 teaspoons vanilla extract

⅔ cup (about 5 large) egg whites

Pinch of salt

MILK MIXTURE

One 12-ounce can evaporated milk

One 14-ounce can sweetened condensed milk

1 cup heavy whipping cream

1 cinnamon stick

Three 3-inch strips of orange zest, removed with a vegetable peeler

Three 2-inch strips of lime zest, removed with a vegetable peeler

WHIPPED CREAM

1 cup heavy whipping cream

2 tablespoons sugar

1 teaspoon grated orange zest

½ teaspoon grated lime zest

One 9 × 13 × 2-inch Pyrex pan, ungreased, plus 4 cups or glasses for inverting the cake pan after baking

This dessert—a light, spongy cake soaked with a citrus-perfumed mixture of evaporated milk, sweetened condensed milk, and cream—has a convoluted and conflicting history. Mexico, Nicaragua, Venezuela, and other countries in South and Central America all claim it as their own. In some areas it is topped with meringue; in other places it is finished with a layer of whipped cream. According to my friend Roberto Santibanez, culinary director of the Rosa Mexicano restaurant group in New York, during the late nineteenth century there appeared several written recipes for a cake called pastel de leche (milk cake) in the state of Tabasco in southern Mexico. This was a cake cooked in a lidded iron pan in which a sponge cake batter was poured into heated milk scented with cinnamon and lime zest, and baked in hot coals. The resulting cake absorbed most of the milk and had a creamy, puddinglike texture. Mexican cooks who cling to old-fashioned and classic cooking traditions still make a similar cake. The present version of the cake probably evolved in the 1940s, when canned milk first became available in Mexico. Roberto suggested that the cake's popularity might be due at least in part to the fact that the recipe was printed in a pamphlet by one of the first companies to market evaporated milk in Mexico. This is a commonly held belief throughout Mexico, but it may be apocryphal: Roberto also pointed out that no one has ever been able to locate a copy of the pamphlet.

In any case, the version of the cake I give here is thoroughly up-to-date, requiring no burning coals. At Roberto's suggestion, I baked a traditional American chiffon cake, cooled it, and then soaked it with the hot milk mixture. This technique works perfectly. This version may not be as strictly authentic as a classic Mexican torta de leche, but it's the best version I have encountered in many tastes of this elusive dessert. Besides, I don't have a fireplace. ***One 9 × 13 × 2-inch cake, about twenty-four 2-inch squares***

1. Set a rack in the middle level of the oven and preheat to 325 degrees.

2. Sift the cake flour into the bowl of an electric mixer. Stir in ¾ cup of the sugar and the baking powder.

3. In a medium bowl, whisk the egg yolks to break them up. Whisk in first the oil, then the water, and then the vanilla. Thoroughly fold this mixture into the flour and sugar mixture. Place the bowl on the mixer and beat the batter with the paddle attachment on medium speed to aerate it slightly, about 1 minute. If you have only one mixer bowl, scrape the mixture into a medium bowl and wash the mixer bowl with hot soapy water, then rinse and dry it.

4. In the clean, dry mixer bowl combine the egg whites and salt. Place on the mixer with the whisk attachment and whip the egg whites on medium speed until they are white, opaque, and beginning to hold a very soft peak. Increase the speed to medium high and add the remaining ¼ cup of sugar in a slow stream. Continue whipping the egg whites until they hold a firm peak.

5. Using a large rubber spatula, fold the egg whites into the batter.

6. Scrape the batter into the prepared pan and smooth the top. Bake the cake about 35 minutes, or until it is well risen and deep golden and a toothpick inserted in the center emerges dry.

7. Invert the cups or glasses on a work surface and invert the cake pan onto them, positioning one in each corner of the pan. Like an angel food cake, a chiffon cake needs to hang upside down to cool, or it may collapse and fall.

8. After the cake has cooled, prepare the milk soaking liquid. Combine all the ingredients in a large saucepan and stir very well to mix thoroughly. (If the mixture is not well combined, the sweetened condensed milk will fall to the bottom and burn.) Place the saucepan over medium heat and bring to a simmer, about 180 degrees.

9. Turn the cake right side up and use a flexible metal spatula (a pancake turner is perfect for this) to loosen it, sides and bottom, from the pan. Poke holes in the cake with a skewer or the point of a paring knife at ½-inch intervals. Strain the hot milk mixture evenly all over the top of the cooled cake. Allow it to soak in and cool for at least 1 hour at room temperature. Refrigerate the cake and chill it well before serving.

10. To make the whipped cream, combine all ingredients and whip by machine with the whisk attachment on medium speed until soft peaks form.

Serving: Cut the cake into 2- to 3-inch squares and serve each square with a spoonful of whipped cream on top.

Storage: Cover the cake with plastic wrap and keep it in the refrigerator before and after serving it.

AUSTRALIA

Pavlova

MERINGUE LAYER

1 cup (about 7 or 8 large) egg whites, at room temperature

Pinch of salt

1 teaspoon distilled white vinegar

1 teaspoon vanilla extract

2½ cups sugar, divided

1 tablespoon cornstarch

TOPPING

2 cups heavy whipping cream

About 1½ to 2 cups fruit: passion fruit pulp, or other fruit (see headnote)

1 cookie sheet or jelly-roll pan lined with parchment

This delicate meringue cake honors the famous Russian ballerina Anna Pavlova (1882–1931). Pavlova performed in Perth for only one season, in 1929, to stellar reviews. A few years later the pastry chef at the hotel where she had stayed, the Esplanade, created this meringue and cream cake and named it after her, both because it is light and because it resembles a tutu. Today a "Pav," as it is generally referred to in Australia, is that country's national dessert par excellence. I tasted many versions in Australia, though none were as good as the one below made by my dear friend in Melbourne, the food stylist Maureen McKeon.

In Australia, the fruit for topping is usually passion fruit pulp, or a combination of passion fruit pulp and bananas. Maureen also suggests using sliced strawberries or mixed berries in summer. A Pavlova makes a great Passover dessert if you substitute potato starch for the cornstarch. ***One 10-inch cake, about 16 servings***

1. Set a rack in the middle level of the oven and preheat to 325 degrees. Trace a 10-inch circle with dark pencil on the parchment paper and turn it over. Lightly butter the paper and sprinkle with a thin coating of cornstarch. You should still be able to see the traced circle.

2. Pour the egg whites, salt, vinegar, and vanilla into the bowl of an electric mixer. Whip on medium speed with the whisk attachment until the egg whites are white, opaque, and beginning to hold a very soft peak. Increase the speed to medium high and whip in 2 cups of the sugar, 1 tablespoon at a time, whipping for 20 to 30 seconds after each addition.

3. After all the sugar has been added, the meringue should stand in very stiff peaks.

4. Remove the bowl from the mixer and quickly mix the remaining ½ cup of sugar with the cornstarch. Fold the mixture into the meringue.

5. Scrape the meringue onto the prepared pan and spread it with a medium offset spatula, using the traced circle as your guide, into a straight-sided, straight-topped disk about 2 inches tall. Try to spread the meringue as evenly and symmetrically as possible; there is no opportunity to trim it after it has baked.

6. Bake the meringue disk for 15 minutes, then lower the oven temperature to 225 degrees and bake an additional 1½ hours. Turn off the oven and open the door. Cool the meringue disk in the turned-off oven. For advance preparation, keep the meringue disk loosely covered with plastic wrap at a dry room temperature. Humid weather will soften it to a gooey mess.

7. To finish the Pavlova, slide the cooled meringue disk from the paper to a platter. Whip the cream and spread it evenly on the top of the meringue disk. Neatly top the whipped cream with the chosen fruit. Some of the fruit will invariably drip down the side.

SERVING: Use a sharp serrated knife to cut the Pavlova into wedges.

STORAGE: As you might suspect, this doesn't keep well. Don't throw away leftovers, but keeping them in the refrigerator will soften the meringue. If you are going to prepare the meringue disk in advance, top it with the cream and fruit at the last minute, just before you are going to serve it.

SOUTH AFRICA

Melissa's Chocolate Pecan Cake

CHOCOLATE CAKE

3 cups sugar

2 1/4 cups all-purpose flour (spoon flour into dry-measure cup and level off)

1/2 teaspoon salt

1 teaspoon baking soda

6 ounces unsweetened chocolate, cut into 1/4-inch pieces

1 1/2 cups boiling water

3 large eggs

12 tablespoons (1 1/2 sticks) salted butter, melted

1 1/2 teaspoons vanilla extract

3/4 cup sour cream

CHOCOLATE FILLING

1 1/2 cups heavy whipping cream

1/3 cup sugar

12 tablespoons (1 1/2 sticks) salted butter

1 1/2 pounds (24 ounces) semisweet chocolate cut into 1/4-inch pieces

2 teaspoons vanilla extract

3/4 cup (about 3 ounces) pecan pieces, lightly toasted and coarsely chopped

Chocolate shavings for finishing

Three 9-inch round pans, 2 inches deep, buttered and the bottoms lined with disks of buttered parchment or wax paper

I first heard about this rich cake from my friend Gary Peese, an inveterate traveler. He had tasted the cake in Cape Town and was intrigued by it. So I sent my deputy cake sleuth, my friend Kyra Effren, to Melissa's, a lovely prepared food store a little outside the center of Cape Town. Unfortunately, neither Gary nor Kyra was able to extract the recipe from the store, so I made it my business to go right to Melissa's on my first visit to Cape Town in June 2004. I was thrilled to finally have a taste of the now-legendary cake, and I immediately realized that the intriguing butterscotch taste of the chocolate filling came from South Africa's highly salted butter. ***One tall 9-inch cake, about 16 servings***

1. Set racks in the upper and lower thirds of the oven and preheat to 350 degrees.

2. For the cake batter, stir together the sugar, flour, salt, and baking soda and set aside.

3. Place the chocolate in a heatproof mixing bowl and pour the boiling water over it. Let stand for 2 minutes to melt the chocolate, then whisk smooth.

4. In another large mixing bowl, whisk the eggs to break them up and whisk in the melted butter, vanilla, and sour cream. Whisk in the chocolate mixture.

5. Gently whisk the flour and sugar mixture into the batter a third at a time, whisking smooth between additions, and whisking more vigorously if you see lumps.

6. Divide the batter equally among the prepared pans and smooth the tops. Bake the cake layers until they are well risen and a toothpick inserted in the center of each layer emerges clean, about 40 minutes. While the layers are baking, change the position of the pans once, moving those from the lower rack to the upper one and vice versa.

7. Cool the cake layers in the pans for 5 minutes, then invert them onto racks and remove the pans. Invert onto other racks so that they are right side up, then cool the layers completely. Remember to remove the papers under the layers before assembling the cake. (Leaving the papers under the layers after they are baked makes them easier to move around without crumbling.)

8. To prepare the filling, bring the cream and sugar to a boil over medium heat in a large saucepan, stirring occasionally to make sure the sugar dissolves.

9. Remove the pan from the heat and add the butter and chocolate. Shake the pan slightly so that the butter and chocolate are completely submerged in the hot cream, and let the mixture stand for 2 minutes to melt the chocolate. Whisk smooth and whisk in the vanilla.

10. Cool the filling in the refrigerator just until it reaches spreading consistency, about 1 hour.

11. Before beginning to assemble the cake, remove about two-thirds of the filling and combine with the chopped pecans. Reserve the remaining third of plain filling.

12. To assemble the cake, place a dab of the filling on a cardboard and press one of the layers onto it, right side up. Spread with about half of the pecan-enriched filling. Place another cake layer on the filling and spread with the remaining pecan filling. Place the last cake layer on the filling upside down, so that the smooth bottom of that layer is uppermost.

13. Use the rest of the filling without the pecans to cover the entire outside of the cake.

14. Use a metal spatula to press the chocolate shavings against the side of the cake. Refrigerate the finished cake for 1 hour to set the filling.

SERVING: Bring the cake to room temperature before cutting into thin wedges. (This is a very rich cake.)

STORAGE: Keep the cake loosely covered with plastic wrap at a cool room temperature. Wrap and refrigerate leftovers, but bring to room temperature before serving again.

FRANCE

Coffee Cream Layer Cake
Gâteau Mocca

VANILLA GENOISE

3 large eggs

3 large egg yolks

Pinch of salt

1 teaspoon vanilla extract

3/4 cup sugar

1/2 cup cake flour (spoon flour into dry-measure cup and level off)

1/4 cup cornstarch

RUM SYRUP

1/2 cup water

1/2 cup sugar

1/3 cup dark rum

COFFEE BUTTERCREAM

2 tablespoons instant espresso coffee

2 tablespoons brewed coffee or dark rum

4 large egg whites

1 cup sugar

24 tablespoons (3 sticks) unsalted butter, softened

Toasted sliced almonds for finishing

One 9-inch round pan, 2 inches deep, buttered and the bottom lined with a disk of buttered parchment or wax paper

This is a modern version of one of the very first French cream-filled layer cakes. In the early days of elaborate French baking, toward the end of the eighteenth century, French pastry chefs made crème mocca (coffee cream) by whisking sweetened coffee into very soft butter. This simple preparation was cited as the glory of several fancy Parisian pastry shops at the time. Nowadays the cream is made with a more stable and much more delicate meringue base, but the cake remains just as good as the original.

Many Americans think that the term *mocca* (or *moka*) refers to a combination of coffee and chocolate. Some American bakers of the early twentieth century did add chocolate to coffee buttercream, but only to make it darker in color, not to flavor it. ***One 9-inch layer cake, about 12 servings***

1. Set a rack in the middle level of the oven and preheat to 350 degrees.

2. To make the genoise, half-fill a medium saucepan with water and bring it to a simmer over medium

heat. In the bowl of an electric mixer whisk the eggs, yolks, salt, vanilla, and sugar by hand. Place the bowl over the pan of simmering water and whisk constantly until the egg mixture is just lukewarm, about 110 degrees. Remove the bowl from the pan of water and place on the mixer fitted with the whisk attachment. Whip the egg mixture about 4 minutes on medium-high speed until it is light in color, is very much risen in volume, and forms a slowly dissolving ribbon when the whisk is lifted from the eggs.

3. While the egg mixture is whipping, stir together the flour and cornstarch and place the flour mixture in a sifter or strainer.

4. When the egg mixture is fully whipped, remove the bowl from the mixer and sift about a third of the flour mixture over the egg foam, folding it in with a large rubber spatula. Repeat with the second and third portions of the flour mixture, folding in between additions.

5. Scrape the batter into the prepared pan and smooth the top of the batter. Bake the cake for about 30 minutes, or until it is well risen and deep golden and a toothpick inserted in the center emerges dry.

6. Immediately invert the cake onto a rack and remove the pan. Cool the cake layer completely. For advance preparation, at this point the cake may be wrapped and refrigerated for a few days or frozen for a month.

7. For the syrup, combine the water and sugar in a small saucepan and bring to a boil over medium heat, stirring occasionally to make sure that all the sugar dissolves. Cool to room temperature and stir in the rum.

8. For the buttercream, dissolve the instant espresso into the coffee or rum and set aside.

9. Bring a pan of water to a simmer, as for the genoise. Combine the egg whites and sugar in the bowl of an electric mixer and whisk by hand to mix. Place over the pan of simmering water and whisk gently but constantly until the egg whites are hot (about 130 degrees) and the sugar is completely dissolved. Remove the bowl from the pan of water and place it on the mixer fitted with the whisk attachment. Whip

the meringue until it is completely cooled, first on high speed, then on medium speed after the meringue has become stiff. Touch the bowl with the palm of your hand to make sure that it has cooled completely before continuing.

10. Switch to the paddle attachment and beat in the butter, a couple of tablespoons at a time, on medium speed. After all the butter has been added, increase the speed to medium-high and continue beating the buttercream until it has become thick and smooth, about 5 minutes. If the buttercream separates during the process and looks scrambled, just continue beating and eventually it will smooth out.

11. Stir up the coffee mixture to make sure all the granules have dissolved completely. Then beat it into the buttercream in about 5 or 6 additions, making sure that it is completely absorbed before adding more.

12. To assemble the cake, use a long, sharp serrated knife to cut the cake into three equal horizontal layers. Invert the layer that was the top of the cake onto a cardboard and moisten with about a third of the syrup, using a brush. Spread with about a third of the buttercream, using an offset cake-icing spatula. Place the middle layer on the buttercream and moisten with another third of the syrup. Spread with another third of the buttercream. Finally, place the last layer on the buttercream so that what was the smooth bottom of the cake is uppermost. Moisten the top layer with the remaining syrup. Spread the outside of the cake smoothly with the remaining buttercream.

13. Press the sliced almonds against the side of the cake, using the palm of your hand. If you wish you may cover the entire cake, side and top, with almonds.

SERVING: Cut this rich cake into small wedges. It is the ideal adult birthday cake.

STORAGE: Keep the cake at a cool room temperature until it is served. Wrap leftovers in plastic and refrigerate. Bring the cake to room temperature before serving again.

VARIATION: PRALINE CREAM LAYER CAKE (*GÂTEAU PRALINÉ*)
Omit the instant and brewed coffees from the buttercream. Beat in ⅔ cup praline paste (see Sources, page 363) after the butter.

ITALY

Ricotta-Filled Cake from Sicily
Cassata alla Siciliana

PAN DI SPAGNA

⅔ cup all-purpose flour (spoon flour into dry-measure cup and level off)

½ cup cornstarch

5 large eggs, separated

1 cup sugar

2 teaspoons vanilla extract

Pinch salt

RUM SYRUP

⅓ cup water

⅓ cup sugar

¼ cup white rum

RICOTTA FILLING

2½ pounds whole-milk ricotta

2 cups confectioners' sugar

1 teaspoon vanilla extract

½ teaspoon ground cinnamon

4 ounces semisweet chocolate, cut into ⅛-inch pieces

ALMOND PASTE DECORATION (PASTA REALE)

8 ounces almond paste

3 cups confectioners' sugar

Green food coloring

5 tablespoons light corn syrup

Candied citron and cherries for decorating

One 10-inch round pan, 2 inches deep, buttered and the bottom lined with a disk of buttered parchment or wax paper

One 10-inch sloping-sided pie pan lined with plastic wrap

This is the most lavish and wonderful of all Sicilian desserts—a rum-sprinkled pan di Spagna sponge cake with a creamy ricotta filling, just like the type used to fill cannoli (see page 358). The outside is covered with a sheet of pale green almond paste, giving the cake a tailored, delicious finish. In Sicily, a sugar icing is often poured over the almond paste covering. I have omitted this final step, since most Americans would find it excessively sweet. Though cassata alla siciliana originated as an Easter cake, it is now available all year in pastry shops in Sicily. ***One 10-inch cake, about 16 servings***

1. To prepare the pan di Spagna, set a rack in the middle level of the oven and preheat to 350 degrees.

2. Stir the flour and cornstarch together in a small bowl and set aside.

3. Place egg yolks in the bowl of an electric mixer with ½ cup sugar and the vanilla, and whisk by hand. Place the bowl on the mixer fitted with the whisk attachment and whip on medium speed until very light in color, about 3 to 4 minutes. If you have only one mixer bowl, scrape the mixture into a medium bowl and wash the mixer bowl with hot soapy water, then rinse and dry it.

4. In the clean, dry mixer bowl combine the egg whites with the salt. Whip by machine with the whisk attachment on medium speed until the egg whites are white, opaque, and beginning to hold their shape. Increase speed to medium-high and add the remaining ½ cup sugar in a slow stream, continuing to whip the egg whites until they hold a firm peak.

5. Use a large rubber spatula to fold the yolks into the whites, then sift about a third of the flour and cornstarch mixture over the egg foam and fold it in. Repeat with the second and last thirds of the flour mixture, folding each time.

6. Scrape the batter into the prepared pan and smooth the top. Bake the pan di Spagna until it is well risen, well colored, and firm, and a toothpick inserted in the center emerges dry, about 30 to 40 minutes.

7. Immediately unmold the cake onto a rack, leaving the paper on the bottom of the cake. Place another rack against the paper and invert. Remove the top rack so that the cake cools right side up. Cool the cake completely.

8. To prepare the rum syrup, place the water and sugar in a small saucepan and bring to a boil, stirring occasionally to dissolve the sugar. Remove from heat and cool. Stir in the rum.

9. For the ricotta filling, gently stir the ricotta in a large mixing bowl with a rubber spatula, just until it is smooth. Gently stir in the confectioners' sugar. Do not beat the mixture, or it will liquefy. Stir in the vanilla and cinnamon. Remove about ½ cup of the ricotta mixture and set aside for finishing.

10. Put the chopped chocolate in a small strainer and shake to sift away any very fine pieces of chocolate, which would color the filling. Stir the larger pieces of chocolate remaining in the strainer into the large bowl of ricotta filling (not the ½ cup).

11. To assemble the cassata, use a long serrated knife to cut the pan di Spagna into ¼-inch-wide vertical slices. Line the prepared pie pan completely—bottom and sides—with cake. Sprinkle the cake slices with about a third of the rum syrup and spread about half the ricotta filling with the chocolate bits in the lined pan. Arrange a layer of cake slices over the filling and sprinkle with another third of the syrup, then spread the remaining filling over the cake slices. Top with more slices of cake, but don't moisten them. (Once the cassata is inverted, this will be the bottom.)

12. Give a good press to the top layer of cake with the palm of your hand and wrap the cassata in plastic wrap. Refrigerate at least 8 hours or overnight to set.

13. While the cassata is chilling, make the almond paste. Combine the almond paste and sugar in a food processor fitted with the metal blade. Add 1 or 2 drops of the food coloring, and pulse until the mixture resembles fine crumbs. Add the corn syrup and pulse until the mixture is about to form a ball. Scrape the almond paste from the food processor to a surface lightly dusted with confectioners' sugar and knead it smooth, making sure that the coloring is evenly distributed throughout. Wrap in plastic wrap and store at room temperature until needed.

14. To finish the cassata, unwrap it and place a platter over the pie pan. Invert the whole stack onto the platter and lift off the pie pan, leaving the cassata on the platter. Use a brush to moisten the outside of the cassata with the remaining syrup. Spread the reserved ricotta mixture without the chocolate bits over the outside.

15. Roll the almond paste thinly on a surface dusted with cornstarch and drape it over the cassata. Trim away any excess almond paste at the base of the cake. Use the scraps of almond paste to make a twisted rope to finish the bottom of the cake. Decorate the top with candied fruit in a symmetrical pattern.

SERVING: Cut thin wedges of this rich cake.

STORAGE: Cover and refrigerate until serving time. Wrap and refrigerate leftovers.

NORWAY

Princess Cream Cake
Prinsessens Kramkake

SPONGE CAKE LAYER

4 large eggs

½ cup sugar

1 teaspoon baking powder

1 cup all-purpose flour (spoon flour into dry-measure cup and level off)

PASTRY CREAM FILLING

1½ cups milk

⅓ cup sugar

5 large egg yolks

¼ cup all-purpose flour

2 tablespoons unsalted butter

1 teaspoon vanilla extract

MARZIPAN

6 ounces canned almond paste, cut into 1-inch cubes

2 cups confectioners' sugar, plus more for kneading marzipan

Pink food coloring

4 tablespoons light corn syrup

Cornstarch for rolling the marzipan

WHIPPED CREAM

1½ cups heavy whipping cream

3 tablespoons sugar

One 9-inch round pan, 2 inches deep, buttered and the bottom lined with a disk of buttered parchment or wax paper

This is by far the most popular layer cake in all of Norway. It consists of layers of a light sponge cake alternating with layers of custard cream and whipped cream, then covered with a sheet of green or pink almond paste. It's a wonderful dessert cake because it is both light and extremely delicate in flavor and texture. ***One 9-inch cake, about 12 servings***

1. Set a rack in the middle level of the oven and preheat to 350 degrees.
2. For the cake layer, place the eggs in the bowl of an electric mixer and whisk by hand, then whisk in the sugar in a stream. Place the bowl on the mixer fitted with the whisk attachment and whip the mixture on high speed until it is lightened in color and increased 3 to 4 times in volume, about 5 minutes.

3. While the eggs and sugar are whipping, combine the baking powder and flour in a small bowl.

4. When the egg mixture is ready, remove the bowl from the mixer and sift the flour and baking powder over the egg mixture in 3 additions, folding it in with a large rubber spatula.

5. Scrape the batter into the prepared pan and smooth the top. Bake the cake until it is well risen and deep golden and a toothpick inserted in the center of the cake emerges dry, about 30 minutes.

6. Immediately unmold the cake onto a rack to cool completely. For advance preparation, wrap and refrigerate or freeze the cake at this point.

7. To prepare the pastry cream, combine the milk with about half the sugar in a nonreactive saucepan. Bring to a boil over medium heat, whisking occasionally to make sure the sugar dissolves.

8. In a medium mixing bowl, whisk the egg yolks, then whisk in the remaining sugar. Sift and whisk in the flour.

9. When the milk boils, whisk a third of the boiling milk into the yolk mixture. Return the remaining milk to a boil over low heat, then whisk the yolk and milk mixture into the milk in the saucepan, continuing to whisk constantly until the pastry cream thickens and returns to a boil. Let the cream boil for about 15 seconds, whisking constantly, then remove the pan from the heat.

10. Whisk in the butter and vanilla, then scrape the cream into a glass or stainless steel bowl. Press plastic wrap against the surface of the cream to prevent a skin from forming, and chill the cream until it is completely cold. The pastry cream can be prepared the day before you intend to assemble the cake.

11. To prepare the marzipan, place the almond paste and confectioners' sugar in the bowl of a food processor fitted with the steel blade. Pulse the mixture until it is reduced to fine crumbs. Add a drop or two of the food coloring (you can always add more later if the color is not vivid enough) and the corn syrup and pulse again

repeatedly until the marzipan begins to form large clumps. Turn the marzipan out onto a surface lightly dusted with confectioners' sugar and knead it smooth, adding more drops of food coloring as necessary. Keep the marzipan in plastic wrap at room temperature until you intend to use it.

12. When you are ready to assemble the cake, whip the cream with the sugar on medium speed with the whisk attachment until it holds a firm peak.

13. To assemble the cake, use a sharp serrated knife to cut the cake layer into 3 thin horizontal layers. Place one of the cake layers on a cardboard round the same diameter as the cake.

14. Spread the cooled pastry cream on the layer, doming it in the center.

15. Place the second cake layer on the pastry cream and spread it with about half the whipped cream, doming it again as for the pastry cream.

16. Place the last cake layer on the whipped cream, easing the layer to conform to the domed shape of the cake. Spread the outside of the cake completely with a thin layer of the remaining whipped cream.

17. To roll out the marzipan, form it into a thick disk and place it on a work surface lightly dusted with cornstarch. Dust the marzipan with a little cornstarch and roll it out to a disk about 14 inches in diameter. Roll the marzipan up onto the rolling pin without pressing (it will stick if you press it) and quickly unroll it onto the cake to cover the cake completely. Use the palms of your hands to gently press and smooth the marzipan against the sides of the cake. Neatly trim away any excess marzipan at the bottom of the cake. (Excess marzipan may be kneaded together, wrapped, and frozen for a later use.)

Serving: Place the cake on a platter and lightly dust it with confectioners' sugar. Cut the cake into thin wedges.

Storage: Keep the cake refrigerated until you intend to serve it, or the pastry cream may spoil and the whipped cream melt.

FRANCE

Lemon-Scented Shell-Shape Cakes
Madeleines

3/4 cup all-purpose flour (spoon flour into dry-measure cup and level off)

1/2 teaspoon baking powder

2 large eggs

1/2 cup sugar

2 teaspoons finely grated lemon zest

2 teaspoons vanilla extract

5 tablespoons unsalted butter, melted and cooled

1 madeleine pan with 12 cavities, buttered and floured.

The story of madeleines, little shell-shape cakes, is riddled with literary reference and legend. The famous early twentieth-century French novelist Marcel Proust refers to them at the beginning of the first book of his multivolume autobiographical novel, *Searching for Lost Time.* In the first novel of the series, *Swann's Way*, Proust writes of eating a bit of madeleine soaked in linden flower tea, given to him by his mother. The taste provokes a rush of memories from his early life that eventually forms the plot of *Swann's Way.*

Another interesting reference to madeleines was made by Eduard de Pomiane, a Polish-born French scientist and radio food personality of the 1940s and 1950s. It occurs in a translation of transcriptions of some of his radio shows, in a British book by Peggy Benton called *Cooking with Pomiane* (Roy, 1961). The story goes like this: In 1551, a baker decides to embark on a pilgrimage and leaves his young, pretty wife in charge of the bakery. After a little while, a handsome young man happens into the bakery and the wife asks him to stay—and not necessarily to bake cakes! The baker returns unexpectedly, finds his wife with the young man, and threatens to kill them both if they can't produce 18 cakes in an hour. Fearing for his life, the young man prays to Saint Mary Magdalen (la Madeleine in French), who, Pomiane explains, is believed to understand those who have sinned. The saint miraculously appears and creates 18 shell-shape cakes (the shape echoes the pilgrim's alms container). Before leaving she enjoins the young man to mend his ways. The baker returns, everyone lives happily ever after, and the cakes are named madeleines, in honor of their maker. Pomiane states that the story comes from a book called *Le Pâtissier de Bellone*, written by another scientist, Charles Nicolle, a Nobel laureate in medicine.

The profusion of madeleine recipes available is almost as miraculous as the saint's appearance, but the version here is the best I've tried. It comes from a well-known and unfortunately now-defunct Parisian pastry shop called Lerch, which was owned and operated by André Lerch, an Alsatian pastry chef. Thanks to my dear friend Dorie Greenspan for sharing the recipe from her book *Paris Sweets* (Broadway, 2002).

About a dozen 3-inch shell-shape cakes

1. In a small bowl, combine the flour and baking powder. Set aside.
2. In the bowl of an electric mixer, whisk the eggs by hand. Whisk in the sugar in a stream. Whisk in the lemon zest and vanilla.
3. Place the bowl on the mixer fitted with the whisk attachment and whip the mixture on medium-high speed until it is light and fluffy, about 2 to 3 minutes.
4. Remove the bowl from the mixer and fold in the flour mixture. After the flour has been absorbed, fold in the butter.
5. Cover the bowl and chill the batter for 3 hours or overnight. (Chilling the batter helps the madeleines to develop the characteristic humps or bumps on their undersides, though you can proceed immediately to the baking if you don't mind flat madeleines.)
6. When you are ready to bake the madeleines, set a rack in the middle level of the oven and preheat to 400 degrees.
7. Use a spoon to fill each of the cavities in the pan about three-quarters full.
8. Bake the madeleines until they are light golden and feel firm when pressed with a fingertip, about 10 to 12 minutes.

9. Invert the pan onto the work surface and gently bang one of the sides of the pan to encourage the madeleines to fall out. Immediately transfer them to a rack, grooved side up, to cool completely. If some of the madeleines stick to the pan, use the point of a paring knife to loosen them around the edges.

Serving: Serve the madeleines with tea, in homage to Proust, and also because they complement tea so well.

Storage: On the day they are baked, keep them loosely covered with plastic wrap. Place in a tin or plastic container with a tight-fitting cover for longer storage, but madeleines are best on the day they are baked.

VARIATION

Substitute grated orange zest for the lemon zest and add 2 teaspoons orange flower water in addition to the vanilla.

FRANCE

Chocolate Almond Cakes
Pleyels

10 tablespoons (1¼ sticks) unsalted butter

8 ounces semisweet chocolate, cut into ¼-inch pieces

½ cup blanched almonds, finely ground in the food processor

1 cup confectioners' sugar

4 large eggs, separated

1 teaspoon vanilla extract

½ teaspoon almond extract

¾ cup all-purpose flour (spoon flour into dry-measure cup and level off)

Pinch of salt

2 tablespoons granulated sugar

One 12-cavity muffin pan, lined with paper liners

These are named in honor of the Austrian composer Ignaz Pleyel, whose works were extremely popular in nineteenth-century France, to the extent that the Salle Pleyel, a theater where orchestral music is performed, was named for him. The recipe comes from Robert Linxe, master chocolatier and proprietor of La Maison du Chocolat, one of the best chocolate stores in the world, with branches in New York and Paris. Linxe is an opera lover, and many of his creations bear names with operatic allusions. I got the recipe from him years ago, when I interviewed him for an article I was writing for the *New York Daily News* about the opening of his New York store.

Pleyels are rich, light little cakes, like cupcakes with a French pedigree. I like to bake them in cupcake pans, although they are much more elegant than the standard cupcake. ***12 individual cakes***

1. Set a rack in the middle level of the oven and preheat to 400 degrees.
2. Put the butter in a medium saucepan and place it over medium heat. Cook until the butter is melted and foams a little. Remove the pan from the heat and add the chocolate. Swirl the pan to make sure all the chocolate is submerged, and wait for

the chocolate to melt, which should only take 1 minute. Whisk smooth. Scrape the mixture into a mixing bowl.

3. Whisk in the ground almonds and the confectioners' sugar. Whisk in the yolks, one at a time, followed by the vanilla and almond extracts. Fold in the flour.

4. Put the egg whites and salt in a clean, dry mixer bowl and place the bowl on the mixer fitted with the whisk attachment. Whip the egg whites on medium speed until they are white, opaque, and beginning to hold a very soft peak. Increase the speed to medium high and whip in the granulated sugar in a stream, continuing to whip the egg whites until they hold a soft, glossy peak.

5. With a large rubber spatula, fold the egg whites into the chocolate batter.

6. With a large spoon, scoop the batter into the prepared pans, dividing it equally among the cavities.

7. Bake the cakes for 10 minutes. Lower the heat to 350 degrees and bake until the cakes are well risen (they are meant to remain moist in the center), about 7 to 8 minutes.

8. Cool the cakes in the pan on a rack.

Serving: Arrange the Pleyels on a platter. Serve them alone or as part of a more elaborate dessert with some whipped cream or ice cream and, if you are really in an indulgent mood, some chocolate sauce.

Storage: Keep the Pleyels loosely covered at room temperature on the day they are made. For longer storage, wrap in plastic and refrigerate. Bring to room temperature before serving.

SWITZERLAND

Chocolate Meringue Ring Cakes
Schoggiringli

These Swiss chocolate rings are a delicious variation on the standard nut meringue. The addition of unsweetened chocolate makes them a little less sweet, and the crumbly meringue is a perfect complement to the creamy chocolate buttercream filling.

About 20 individual cakes

CHOCOLATE ALMOND MERINGUE

1 cup egg whites (from about 7 large eggs)

Pinch of salt

1¼ cups sugar

2 cups (about 8 ounces) blanched almonds, finely ground in the food processor

3½ ounces unsweetened chocolate, melted and cooled

CHOCOLATE BUTTERCREAM

4 large egg whites

1 cup sugar

20 tablespoons (2½ sticks) unsalted butter, softened

5 ounces bittersweet or semisweet chocolate, melted with ¼ cup water and cooled

2 to 3 cookie sheets or jelly-roll pans lined with parchment

1. Set racks in the upper and lower thirds of the oven and preheat to 300 degrees.

2. Use a cup or glass that is 3 inches in diameter as a pattern to draw fifteen to twenty 3-inch circles on each piece of parchment paper with a dark pencil. Turn the papers over on the pans.

3. Put the egg whites and salt in the bowl of an electric mixer fitted with the whisk attachment. Whip the egg whites on medium speed until they are very white, opaque, and beginning to hold a very soft peak. Increase the speed to medium high and whip in the sugar 1 tablespoon at a time, continuing to whip until the egg whites are stiff, but not dry.

4. Remove the bowl from the mixer and use a large rubber spatula to fold in the almonds. Once the almonds are incorporated, fold in the chocolate.

5. Use a pastry bag fitted with a ½-inch plain tube (Ateco #806) to pipe the meringue onto the traced circles. Hold the bag perpendicular to the pan and 1 inch above it; follow the outline to pipe 3-inch rings. When you complete the circle, stop squeezing and pull the tube away parallel to the pan to avoid leaving a point. If you do get a point, flatten it with a fingertip.

6. Bake the meringue rings until they are crisp and still a little moist in the center, about 30 to 40 minutes. While the meringues are baking, move the pans from the lower rack to the upper one and vice versa, turning the pans back to front at the same time. Press one lightly to check the texture.

7. Cool the meringues on the pans on racks.

8. While the meringues are baking, prepare the filling. Half-fill a medium saucepan with water and bring it to a boil over medium heat. Put the egg whites and sugar in the clean, dry bowl of an electric mixer and stir them together with a whisk. Place the bowl over the pan of boiling water and whisk gently but constantly until the egg whites are hot, about 130 degrees, and the sugar is dissolved. Place the bowl on the mixer fitted with the whisk attachment and whip the meringue on medium high until it is cooled and stiff.

9. Change to the paddle attachment and beat in the butter, 2 tablespoons at a time. Continue beating the buttercream until it is thick and smooth. If the buttercream separates during mixing, just continue beating until it is smooth. (This happens sometimes when the butter is too cold.) Beat in the chocolate mixture and continue beating until it is completely incorporated and the buttercream is very smooth and light.

10. To assemble the cakes, turn half the meringue rings over so that their flat bottom sides are uppermost. Use a pastry bag fitted with a medium star tube (Ateco #846) to pipe a thick circle of buttercream on each meringue base. Top the buttercream with another meringue base, flat side down.

SERVING: These need to be served on a plate with a fork; they are too messy to eat from the hand.

STORAGE: Keep the cakes at a cool room temperature until serving time. Refrigerate leftovers and bring back to room temperature before serving again.

VARIATIONS

CHOCOLATE TRUFFLES (*SCHOGGI TRUFFELN*): Pipe the chocolate almond meringue into 2½-inch half spheres, using the same technique for holding the bag, but not moving it while piping. Bake as above. Pipe or spread a layer of the buttercream on the flat side of half the meringues, then top with the remaining meringues to make complete spheres. Spread a thin layer of the buttercream on the outside of each sphere and roll the spheres in chocolate shavings.

CHOCOLATE STICKS (*SCHOGGISTAENGELI*): Pipe the chocolate almond meringue into 3½-inch sticks, about ¾ inch wide. Sprinkle them with finely crushed sliced almonds. Bake as above. Pipe a layer of the buttercream or the chocolate filling on page 173 onto the flat side of half the meringues. Sandwich them and stand them on their sides so that the meringue sticks form the sides of the cake. Use a small star tube to pipe a series of overlapping shell shapes over the filling between the meringues.

Schoggiringli (left) and Pleyels (page 170).

AUSTRIA

Cardinal Slices
Kardinalschnitten

MERINGUE BATTER

1 cup egg whites (from about 7 large eggs)

Pinch salt

1 cup sugar

LADYFINGER BATTER

2 large eggs

3 large egg yolks

¼ cup sugar

1 teaspoon vanilla extract

½ cup all-purpose flour (spoon flour into dry-measure cup and level off)

Confectioners' sugar for dusting

COFFEE CREAM FILLING

1¼ cups heavy whipping cream

2 tablespoons sugar

2 tablespoons instant espresso dissolved in 2 tablespoons boiling water and cooled

Confectioners' sugar for finishing

2 cookie sheets or jelly-roll pans lined with parchment

This elaborate cake is one of the glories of Viennese pastry. The cake layers are made of alternating meringue and ladyfinger batters, and the filling is a luscious coffee-flavored whipped cream. All my attempts to find out about the origins of the name have met with failure—though it isn't too far-fetched to imagine a jolly, rotund Austrian prince of the church enjoying these.

This is a recipe in which organization is important. Have all the ingredients for the ladyfinger batter ready before you start mixing the meringue. Prepare the ladyfinger batter as quickly as possible, or the meringue will fall and liquefy before you have a chance to pipe the ladyfinger batter between the piped meringue layers. You'll also need 2 pastry bags with a 1-inch opening at the ends, but no tubes.

About ten 1½-inch-wide slices

1. Set racks in the upper and lower thirds of the oven and preheat to 350 degrees.

2. In the middle of each piece of parchment paper, draw 2 parallel lines 5 inches apart with dark pencil. Turn the papers over on the pans.

3. For the meringue batter, put the egg whites and salt in the bowl of an electric mixer fitted with the whisk attachment. Whip the egg whites until they are very white, opaque, and beginning to hold a very soft peak. Increase the speed to medium high and whip in the sugar in a slow stream, continuing to whip the egg whites until they hold a soft peak. Scrape the meringue batter into a pastry bag with a 1-inch opening at the end, but no tube. Pipe the meringue in three lines: one at each side along and inside the pencil marks, and a third line in the middle between the two. Repeat with the second pan. Set aside.

4. For the ladyfinger batter, put the eggs and yolks in the same bowl in which you whipped the meringue. (It's not necessary to wash the bowl between uses here.) Whisk in the sugar and vanilla. Place on the mixer fitted with the whisk attachment and whip on medium-high speed until the mixture is very light and thickened, about 3 to 4 minutes. Remove the bowl from the mixer and sift and fold in the flour. Scrape the batter into the second pastry bag and pipe lines of ladyfinger batter between the lines of meringue, piping two lines of batter on each pan. The ladyfinger and meringue strips should be touching.

5. Lightly dust the cake layers with confectioners' sugar and bake them until the ladyfinger batter is light golden and firm, about 20 minutes. The meringue will color slightly but remain quite soft. Cool the layers on the pans on racks.

6. Before you assemble the cake, whip the cream with the sugar and dissolved coffee by machine with the whisk attachment on medium speed until firm, not stiff, peaks form. Refrigerate the cream.

7. To assemble the cake, loosen the layers from the papers with a long, sharp knife or spatula. Carefully invert one of the layers onto a cutting board so that the smooth side, which was on the bottom, faces up. Trim the edges of the remaining layer and cut it into about 10 vertical slices 1½ inches wide, leaving them in place on the paper.

8. Remove the whipped cream from the refrigerator and rewhip it by hand if it has softened. With a medium offset spatula, evenly spread it on the inverted cake layer on the cutting board.

9. Carefully place the slices of the second layer on the cream, right side up and close together. Trim the ends of the bottom layer and cut through between slices to separate the filling and bottom layer, making sure to wipe the knife after each cut. Lightly dust the tops of the cakes with confectioners' sugar.

SERVING: Use an offset cake server or spatula to move the slices to a platter.

STORAGE: Keep the slices at a cool room temperature for up to 2 hours. If you need to wait longer to serve them, refrigerate the slices, or the whipped cream filling will melt. Cover and refrigerate leftovers.

HUNGARY

Chocolate Rigo Squares

Rigo Jansci

CHOCOLATE CAKE

6 ounces semisweet chocolate

6 large eggs, separated

Pinch of salt

½ cup sugar

¼ cup all-purpose flour (spoon flour into dry-measure cup and level off)

CHOCOLATE FILLING

1½ cups heavy whipping cream

2 tablespoons light corn syrup

2 tablespoons butter

16 ounces semisweet chocolate, cut into ¼-inch pieces

CHOCOLATE GLAZE

½ cup heavy whipping cream

2 tablespoons light corn syrup

6 ounces semisweet chocolate, cut into ¼-inch pieces

One 12 × 18-inch jelly-roll pan, bottom and sides buttered and lined with buttered parchment or foil

I know this originally Hungarian cake only in its Viennese form. In Vienna, it is made from two thin layers of chocolate cake with a whipped chocolate cream filling and a shiny chocolate glaze—definitely a dessert for an important party. The good news is that it can be made entirely in advance. Do wait to cut it until right before serving, however, or the cake layers will dry out. ***Twenty to twenty-four 2-inch squares***

1. Set a rack in the middle level of the oven and preheat to 350 degrees.

2. Bring a small pan of water to a boil and turn off the heat. Combine the chocolate and ¼ cup water in a heatproof bowl and place over the pot of water. Stir until chocolate is melted and smooth.

3. For the cake batter, put the 6 yolks in the bowl of an electric mixer and whisk in ¼ cup of the sugar by hand. Place the bowl on the mixer fitted with the whisk attachment and whip the mixture on medium-high speed until the yolks and sugar are light and thickened. If you have only one mixer bowl and one whisk, scrape the yolk mixture into a medium mixing bowl. Wash the bowl and whisk in hot, soapy water, then rinse and dry them.

4. Put the 6 egg whites and salt in the clean, dry mixer bowl. Place on the mixer fitted with the whisk attachment, and whip the whites on medium speed until they are white, opaque, and beginning to hold a very soft peak. Increase the speed to medium high and whip in the remaining ¼ cup sugar in a stream. Continue whipping the whites until they hold a firm peak.

5. Stir the melted chocolate into the yolk mixture, immediately followed by about a fourth of the whipped egg whites. Sift and fold in the flour, and then fold in the remaining egg whites.

6. Scrape the batter onto the prepared pan and use a medium offset spatula to spread the batter evenly.

7. Bake the cake layer until it is risen (it will not rise very high) and firm when pressed with a fingertip, about 15 to 20 minutes. Slide the paper from the pan to a rack to cool the cake.

8. For the filling, bring the cream and corn syrup to a boil in a large saucepan, stirring occasionally to make sure that the corn syrup doesn't fall to the bottom and burn. Remove the pan from the heat and add the butter and chocolate. Gently shake the pan to make sure that the butter and chocolate are completely submerged, then wait 2 minutes for them to melt. Whisk the filling smooth and pour it into a bowl. Refrigerate the filling until it is about 80 degrees, or until it is of spreading consistency. Don't leave the filling in the refrigerator too long, or it will become too hard to whip.

9. To assemble the cake, slide the paper with the cake still stuck to it onto a cutting board. Cut through both the paper and the cake with a sharp serrated knife to make two 12 × 9-inch rectangles. Slide one off the cutting board. Run a long, thin knife or spatula between the paper and the cake that remains on the cutting board to loosen it, but leave the paper under the cake. (This will make the cubes of finished cake easier to remove later on.)

10. Scrape the cooled filling into the bowl of an electric mixer and beat it with the paddle on medium speed until it is lightened to a milk chocolate color. Don't overbeat, or the filling will separate.

11. Immediately use a medium offset spatula to spread the whipped filling evenly over the cake layer on the cutting board.

12. Invert the remaining cake layer, still stuck to the paper for easy handling, to a cookie sheet with no sides or to a stiff rectangular piece of cardboard. Gently slide the cake layer into place over the filling. Carefully peel off the paper.

13. Place a stiff cardboard or cookie sheet on the cake and gently press to make sure the top layer of cake adheres well to the filling.

14. Refrigerate the cake while preparing the glaze.

15. For the glaze, bring the cream and corn syrup to a simmer in a medium saucepan, stirring occasionally. Remove the pan from the heat and add the chocolate. Gently shake the pan to make sure that all the chocolate is submerged, then wait 2 minutes for it to melt. Whisk the glaze just until smooth. Avoid whisking too much, or the glaze will be riddled with bubbles. Let the glaze cool until it is just slightly warm to the touch, about 100 to 105 degrees.

16. After the glaze has cooled, remove the cake from the refrigerator and pour the glaze over it. Quickly spread the glaze evenly with a medium offset spatula. Don't worry about any glaze that drips down the sides of the cake; it will be trimmed away later.

17. Refrigerate the cake again for at least 1 hour, or up to 24 hours, to set the glaze.

18. Rinse a long, sharp serrated knife in hot water, then wipe it dry with a cloth. Use the knife to trim the sides of the cake evenly, rinsing and wiping after each cut. Cut the cake into 2-inch squares.

SERVING: Lift the cubes of cake off the paper with an offset cake server or spatula and line them up symmetrically on a platter. Serve alone or with a little unsweetened whipped cream.

STORAGE: Keep the cake refrigerated, but bring it to room temperature for an hour or so before serving. Cover leftovers with plastic wrap and refrigerate. Bring to room temperature again before serving.

5. PIES AND TARTS

CANADA	MAPLE SYRUP TART *Tarte au Sirop d'Erable*
FRANCE	LEMON TART FROM NICE *Tarte au Citron à la Niçoise*
AUSTRIA	VIENNESE CHEESECAKE *Topfentorte*
SWITZERLAND	PRUNE PLUM TART WITH CUSTARD FILLING *Zwetschkenwaie*
AUSTRALIA	STEPHANIE ALEXANDER'S QUINCE TART
ITALY	ROMAN LATTICE-TOPPED APPLE TART *Crostata di Mele alla Romana*
FRANCE	MODERN RASPBERRY TART *Tarte Moderne aux Framboises*
SWITZERLAND	CHOCOLATE PASTRY RASPBERRY JAM TART FROM ST. GALLEN *St. Gallen Klostertorte*
FRANCE	APRICOT CUSTARD TART *Tarte Bergère aux Abricots*
ENGLAND	BLACKBERRY AND APPLE PIE
THE NETHERLANDS	SWEET-CRUST APPLE PIE *Appeltaart*

Overleaf: Engadiner Nusstorte

ITALY	SICILIAN BAKED CASSATA *Cassata al Forno*
SWITZERLAND	CARAMELIZED WALNUT PIE FROM THE ENGADIN *Engadiner Nusstorte*
FRANCE	BASQUE CUSTARD PIE *Gâteau Basque*
SWITZERLAND	CHOCOLATE CREAM TARTLETS *Guayaquils*
ITALY	CUSTARD-FILLED TARTLETS *Bocconotti di Crema*
FRANCE	RASPBERRY TARTLETS *Tartelettes aux Framboises*
CANADA	BUTTER TARTS
PORTUGAL	CUSTARD CREAM TARTLETS *Pasteis de Nata*
AUSTRIA	VIENNESE APPLE SLICES *Muerbteig-Apfelschnitten*
SWITZERLAND	LINZER SLICES *Linzerschnitten*
FRANCE	PEAR SLICES *Tranches aux Poires*

PIES AND TARTS used to be among the most popular baked goods made at home. Nowadays, while a lot of people will attempt a cake or cookies, they shy away from desserts made with pastry doughs because they think these doughs are difficult to make and even more difficult to roll and form. Nothing could be farther from the truth. The problem lies in the fact that most people have never learned to work with pastry doughs at home, so they reach adulthood with no experience in handling them. Also, the difficulty of working with pastry doughs has been greatly exaggerated. Endless precautions about not overhandling doughs can paralyze the novice. It's true that you need to be careful when mixing and rolling doughs, but really no more careful than you need to be with any other culinary procedure. With good, accurate instructions to help you, you'll discover that pastry doughs needn't intimidate.

I, for one, hate recipes that aren't clear about the amount of liquid to add to a dough. Inexperienced bakers will never learn the correct amount to add unless it is carefully specified in the recipe. Therefore, the recipes in this chapter are very specific about how to assemble every dough needed to bake the tarts and pies. You might even find that you can adapt the dough recipes and crust forms here and use them with other fillings. There is absolutely no mystery to preparing a light, tender crust, so set aside your fear of handling dough and roll up your sleeves. After a few tries you'll wonder why you ever thought making or rolling dough was difficult.

BAKING POWDER IN DOUGH

I use a little baking powder in almost all pastry doughs. It helps the dough bake through to a light, tender texture and also saves the work of having to prebake crusts before adding a filling and baking again—something I consider an enormous waste of time. When you add a raw filling to a raw crust containing baking powder, the crust can't puff upward during baking. Instead it presses well against the bottom of the pan, weighed down by the filling above. This expansion and good contact with the hot pan bottom during baking help the bottom of the crust to bake through efficiently, yielding a bottom crust that is both appetizingly well-colored and dry. This works for both flaky and sweet doughs.

CHILLING DOUGHS

Whenever you mix a dough for a pastry crust, the butter softens somewhat, making the whole dough somewhat soft. Chilling the dough for a few hours or a few days hardens the butter again and firms up the entire dough. There's only one problem: it's impossible to roll out a thoroughly chilled dough. The dough just breaks apart into many little pieces. With sweet dough the solution is easy: you just have to knead the dough gently until it is slightly softened and malleable. The dough will not be nearly as soft as when you initially prepared it, and it will roll out easily. With flaky doughs, things are a little more complicated. You can't knead the dough without making it too elastic to roll (this doesn't happen with sweet doughs, because the presence of the sugar makes the dough less elastic). To soften a flaky dough enough to roll it easily, gently press it with a rolling pin in close parallel strokes. Gently fold over a corner of the dough. If the folded corner doesn't break off, the dough is ready to roll. If the corner does break off, soften the dough a little more before rolling by pressing again at a right angle to the first press.

GETTING READY TO ROLL

Once you soften your dough, ease it into the correct shape for your pan. If you have a round pan, start with a disk of dough. If you need to roll the dough into a square or rectangle to cut strips for a lattice top crust, form it into a square or rectangle. Never roll dough into an arbitrary shape or roll it larger than the diameter of the pan including the sides, or the dough will be too thin (the quantity of dough in every recipe is calculated with the size of the pan in mind). It may then be impossible to move your dough to the pan without its disintegrating.

DUSTING THE DOUGH WITH FLOUR

Before you begin to roll any dough, you must flour the work surface. Use several large pinches of flour and place the dough on it. Do the same to the top of the dough. When you use pinches of flour, you may add more pinches as necessary, but be cautious about adding too much flour to the dough. Causing the dough to absorb too much flour during rolling is the equivalent of using too much flour to mix the dough and will result in dry, heavy dough.

To roll the dough into a large, flat disk, position the rolling pin at the point closest to you on the dough and gently roll away from you to the other end of the dough without rolling over the end. (Rolling over the end can cause the dough to stick and also makes it uneven, two things you want to avoid.) Check under the dough to see if you need to add a few more pinches of flour, and move the top edge of the dough (the edge farther from you) about 30 degrees. Add more pinches of flour to the top of the dough, if necessary, and repeat the rolling as before, moving the pin away and back toward you. Repeat the 30-degree turn, flour under and on the dough if necessary, and roll again. In most instances you'll need to roll over the dough only 3 or 4 times to get it to the size you need.

OFF THE SURFACE AND INTO THE PAN

Be sure to position the pan close to the work surface, rather than move the dough a long distance to the pan. You don't want to carry your delicate dough across the room. Usually I fold the dough in half to move it to the pan. In the case of deep pans, it's good to fold the dough into quarters, as this helps the dough drape against the sides of the pan more efficiently. In any case, carefully unfold the dough into the pan. If a sweet dough tears while you are doing this, don't worry; just press it together at the point where it's ripped and proceed. If a flaky dough tears, moisten one of the torn edges with a little water and press the other torn edge over it, overlapping them by about ¼ inch. Use your fingertips to seal the tear and press that spot back to the dough's original thickness.

THE TOP EDGE

Even if you are an expert at rolling, it's best to roll your crust a tiny bit larger and trim the top edge of the crust even. Use a bench scraper or the back of a knife for this, scraping outward from the inside of the crust at the top rim of the pan. Or you can roll over the top of the pan with your rolling pin to sever excess dough at the top. I like to even off the top edge of the crust by pressing down with the index finger of one hand while pressing in on the inside of the crust with my thumb. This results in a perfectly straight, flat top for your pastry crust.

GIVE IT A REST

If you can, refrigerate the rolled-out crust for a while before filling and baking it. This helps the elastic strands of gluten formed during rolling to relax a little, helping to prevent excessive shrinkage. If this rest doesn't fit into your schedule, don't worry about it. But if you can do it, so much the better.

I hope that the tart and pie recipes here will become some of your favorites. Aside from a few that are more elaborate, they are easy to prepare and even easier to serve.

WHERE TO BAKE

In some of the following recipes, I have specified baking a tart, especially an open-faced tart, on the lowest rack in the oven. The strong bottom heat in that part of the oven helps the bottom of the crust to color and bake through efficiently. In other recipes I specify setting the rack in the lower third—a little higher up. These are cases in which the bottom crust benefits from strong bottom heat and the top is also a little farther up in the oven, especially useful when there is a top crust that needs to bake through.

INDIVIDUAL TARTS

These fall into two categories. In the first category are small tarts baked in small, sloping-sided tartlet pans. The ones I use are about 2½ inches in diameter at the top and about ½ inch deep. When you buy new ones, butter them the first few times you use them, but instead of washing them with soap and water, simply wipe them off afterward with a dry cloth or paper towels. Washing them will cause the pores in the metal to open up again, perhaps encouraging the next tartlets you bake to stick. See the general introduction about equipment (page xxi) for instructions on seasoning pans before their first use.

In the second category are pastry slices, like the cake slices in Chapter 4. These are baked in a deep pan, unmolded, cut into bars, and then cut into individual slices after any finishing necessary. They differ from bar cookies in that they have richer and more plentiful fillings. Such slices are called *tranches* in French and *Schnitten* in German.

CANADA

Maple Syrup Tart
Tarte au Sirop d'Erable

How can we think of Canada without thinking of maple syrup? There is even a maple leaf on the country's flag. The recipe here comes from Martin Picard, chef-owner of a delightful and popular restaurant in Montreal called Au Pied de Cochon (At the Pig's Foot). The menu abounds with hearty specialties, like the restaurant's namesake dish, plus plenty of other pork dishes, foie gras, duck breasts, and even a fish or two for the abstemious. The maple syrup tart here is another of the restaurant's specialties. Picard sent me a recipe that called for preparing individual tarts, but I have modified it to make one large tart, which is easier to prepare and serve.

One 11- or 12-inch tart, about 12 servings

PASTRY DOUGH

1½ cups all-purpose flour (spoon flour into dry-measure cup and level off)

½ teaspoon baking powder

½ teaspoon salt

8 tablespoons (1 stick) unsalted butter, cut into 8 pieces

3 tablespoons water

MAPLE SYRUP FILLING

2 cups pure maple syrup, grade B (see Note)

2 tablespoons all-purpose flour

⅔ cup heavy whipping cream

5 tablespoons unsalted butter, melted

4 large eggs

One 11- or 12-inch tart pan with removable bottom

1. To prepare the dough, combine the dry ingredients in the bowl of a food processor fitted with the metal blade. Pulse several times to mix. Add the butter and pulse several times until the butter pieces are the size of peas. Add the water and pulse only 2 times. The dough will not form a ball. Invert the dough onto a floured work surface and carefully remove the blade. Gently squeeze the dough together and form it into a disk. Chill the dough in plastic wrap while preparing the filling. You may leave the dough refrigerated for up to 2 days before baking the tart.

2. To prepare the filling, bring the maple syrup to a simmer in a medium saucepan over low heat. Ignore any foam that accumulates on the surface of the syrup.

3. Put the flour in a medium mixing bowl and add ⅓ cup of the cream to it. Whisk the cream and flour together to avoid lumps. Whisk in the rest of the cream until smooth. Whisk in the melted butter. Then whisk in the eggs, one at a time. Whisk in the hot maple syrup in a slow stream. Let the filling cool to room temperature.

4. When you are ready to bake the tart, set a rack in the lowest level of the oven and preheat to 350 degrees.

5. Remove the dough from the refrigerator and place it on a floured work surface. Flour the dough and gently press down on it with a rolling pin in regular, parallel strokes, to soften it enough to roll. Roll the dough to a 14-inch disk.

6. Fold the dough in half and transfer it to the pan, lining up the fold with the diameter of the pan. Unfold the dough into the pan and press it well into the bottom and sides of the pan. Use a bench scraper or the back of a knife to sever the excess dough at the rim of the pan.

7. Pour the cooled filling into the crust and bake the tart until the crust is baked through and the filling is set, about 40 minutes.

8. Cool the tart on a rack.

Note: If you can find it, always use grade B maple syrup, which is a little less refined but has a stronger maple flavor.

Serving: Unmold the tart from the outside of the pan and slide it from the metal pan base to a platter. You may need to loosen the bottom of the tart from the pan base with a long, thin spatula or knife. Serve the tart warm or at room temperature with a little whipped cream.

Storage: Keep the tart at room temperature on the day it is baked. Wrap and refrigerate leftovers and bring them to room temperature or warm up for 10 minutes at 350 degrees before serving again.

FRANCE

Lemon Tart from Nice
Tarte au Citron à la Niçoise

SWEET PASTRY DOUGH

2 cups all-purpose flour (spoon flour into dry-measure cup and level off)

1/3 cup sugar

1 teaspoon baking powder

1/2 teaspoon salt

8 tablespoons (1 stick) unsalted butter, cold, and cut into 10 pieces

2 large eggs

LEMON FILLING

1 cup sugar

1/3 cup all-purpose flour

8 large eggs

1 tablespoon finely grated lemon zest

2/3 cup strained lemon juice

2 cups heavy whipping cream

One 10-inch round pan, 2 inches deep, buttered

The Côte d'Azur, the seaside area of southern France that stretches from Cassis in the west to Menton at the Italian border, abounds in excellent citrus fruit. Lemon tarts of all kinds are made in the area, but to me the best one is from Nice. One of my favorite haunts in Nice's old town is the Rue Peyrolière, a narrow, winding way that is filled with food stores such as bakeries and fish markets (it's not unusual to see a half-ton tuna lying on the ground in front of a fish market). One of the best places to taste authentic Niçoise specialties is Chez René, a socca palace on a corner on the Rue Peyrolière. (Socca is Nice's traditional chickpea pancake. I give a recipe for it in *How to Bake.*) Chez René also makes a wonderful lemon tart, probably about 2 feet in diameter and baked in the same wood-burning oven as the socca. The tart blackens completely on top because of the oven's high heat, a feature that, though picturesque, I have never found particularly appealing.

You'll notice that the dough for the tart is rather thick—this is typical and not a mistake. And do use regular lemons in this tart. I tried it once with Meyer lemons, and the filling lacked the characteristic bite that it should have. ***One 10-inch tart, about 12 large servings***

1. For the dough, combine the dry ingredients in the bowl of a food processor fitted with the metal blade. Pulse several times to mix. Add the butter and pulse about 10 times to finely mix in the butter. Add the eggs and pulse again until the dough forms a ball. Invert the dough onto a floured work surface and carefully remove the blade. Form the dough into a disk and chill it in plastic wrap while preparing the filling. You may prepare the dough up to 2 days before assembling and baking the tart.

2. When you are ready to bake the tart, set a rack in the lower third of the oven and preheat to 350 degrees.

3. Remove the dough from the refrigerator and knead it lightly on a floured work surface until it is smooth, malleable, and no longer hard. Shape the dough into a disk, flour it, and roll it to a 14-inch disk. Fold the dough in quarters and drape it into the pan, lining up the point with the center of the pan. Unfold the dough into the pan and press it well into the bottom and sides of the pan. Trim away the excess dough at the top edge with a bench scraper or the back of a knife. Chill the crust while preparing the filling.

4. In a large mixing bowl combine the sugar and flour and stir with a whisk to mix. Whisk in the eggs, 2 at a time, whisking smooth after each addition. Whisk in the lemon zest and juice, followed by the cream.

5. Pour the filling into the prepared crust. Bake the tart until the filling is set and the crust is golden, about 50 to 60 minutes. Cool the tart on a rack, then chill it.

6. To unmold the tart, warm the bottom of the pan over low heat for a few seconds. Place a flat plate or cardboard round on the tart and invert. Remove the pan and replace it with a platter. Invert again with the tart between the 2 plates and remove the top plate. Cover the tart loosely with plastic wrap and refrigerate it until serving.

Serving: Serve the tart in wedges with a little sweetened whipped cream and maybe a few strawberries or raspberries to dress it up.

Storage: Keep the tart covered with plastic wrap in the refrigerator.

AUSTRIA

Viennese Cheesecake
Topfentorte

VIENNESE SWEET DOUGH (MUERBTEIG)

8 tablespoons (1 stick) unsalted butter, softened

½ cup confectioners' sugar

1 teaspoon vanilla extract

2 teaspoons finely grated lemon zest

Pinch of salt

1 large egg yolk

1¼ cups all-purpose flour (spoon flour into dry-measure cup and level off)

CHEESECAKE BATTER

1 cup sugar

⅓ cup all-purpose flour

⅓ cup (1½ ounces) nonfat dry milk

1 pound (or one 15-ounce container) part–skim milk ricotta

One 16-ounce container sour cream

2 teaspoons vanilla extract

1 tablespoon finely grated lemon zest

3 large eggs, separated

3 large egg whites

Pinch of salt

Confectioners' sugar for finishing

One 10-inch springform pan, buttered only on the bottom

I've grouped this cheesecake with pies and tarts because it has a pastry dough base, which is rolled out to fit the pan in which the cake is baked. The typical cheese used in Vienna is topfen, a kind of pot cheese. Part–skim milk ricotta makes an adequate substitute, though this is by no means a low-fat recipe. You may be surprised to see nonfat dry milk as one of the ingredients, but it is commonly used in preparations such as this one to boost the proportion of solids in the batter. This makes it less likely that the cheese filling will weep whey after it is baked. ***One 10-inch cheesecake, about 16 servings***

1. For the pastry dough, combine the butter and confectioners' sugar in the bowl of an electric mixer. Place on the mixer fitted with the paddle attachment and beat on low speed until smoothly mixed. Increase the speed to medium and beat until lightened, about 3 minutes. Beat in the vanilla, lemon zest, and salt.

Beat in the egg yolk and continue beating until the mixture is smooth. Stop the mixer and scrape the bowl and beater with a large rubber spatula. On lowest speed, beat in the flour. Scrape the dough onto a floured work surface and form it into a disk. Wrap the dough in plastic and chill it until it is firm, about 1 hour. You may leave the dough in the refrigerator for up to 2 days before continuing.

2. When you are ready to bake the cheesecake, set a rack in the middle level of the oven and preheat to 325 degrees.

3. Remove the dough from the refrigerator and place it on a floured surface. Flour the dough and gently press it with a rolling pin in close parallel strokes to soften it. Roll the dough to a 10-inch disk and slide it into the prepared pan. Pierce the dough all over at 1-inch intervals with a fork. Bake the crust until it is golden and baked through, about 20 minutes. Cool on a rack. Once the pan has cooled, butter the sides of the pan. Increase the oven heat to 375 degrees.

4. For the cheesecake batter, combine ½ cup of the sugar, the flour, and the milk powder in a large mixing bowl. Whisk briefly to mix. Add the ricotta and beat it with the sugar mixture until well combined, using a large rubber spatula. Beat in the sour cream, vanilla, and lemon zest smoothly, followed by the egg yolks, one at a time.

5. Place the egg whites and salt in a clean, dry mixer bowl and place on the mixer fitted with the whisk attachment. Whip the egg whites on medium speed until they are white and opaque and are beginning to hold a very soft peak. Increase the mixer speed to medium high and whip in the remaining ½ cup sugar in a slow stream, continuing to whip the egg whites until they hold a soft, glossy peak. Carefully fold the egg whites into the cheese batter.

6. Pour the batter over the baked crust in the pan and bake for 20 minutes.

7. Open the oven and run a small paring knife between the side of the pan and the batter, about ½ inch down the side of the pan, to loosen it. Decrease the oven heat to 325 degrees. Continue baking the cake until it is golden and firm in the center, about 60 to 70 additional minutes.

8. Turn off the oven, open the door, and leave the cheesecake in the oven to cool.

9. After the cheesecake has cooled completely, run a knife between the side of the pan and the pie to loosen it and remove the pan, but leave the pie on the metal base. Cover the pie loosely with plastic wrap and refrigerate it.

SERVING: Serve the cake on a platter, still on the springform base. Berries or sliced fruit are great with this.

STORAGE: Keep the cheesecake refrigerated until about an hour before you intend to serve it. Wrap and refrigerate leftovers and bring them to room temperature before serving again.

SWITZERLAND

Prune Plum Tart with Custard Filling
Zwetschgewaie

PASTRY DOUGH

1½ cups all-purpose flour (spoon flour into dry-measure cup and level off)

3 tablespoons sugar

1 teaspoon baking powder

½ teaspoon salt

6 tablespoons (¾ stick) unsalted butter, cold, cut into 8 pieces

1 large egg

2 tablespoons cold water

FILLING

15 medium (about 1½ pounds) prune plums, rinsed, halved, and pitted but not peeled

¼ cup sugar

2 tablespoons all-purpose flour

⅔ cup heavy whipping cream or half and half

1 large egg

3 large egg yolks

1 tablespoon Kirsch

One 10-inch tart pan with removable bottom

A *Waie* (*Waehe* in high German) is a classic Swiss tart in which fruit is covered with an uncooked custard cream before it is baked. Prune plums are traditional, and tarts of this type are seen all over Switzerland as soon as the plums come into season in late summer. Apples, poached pears, apricots, rhubarb, and sour cherries also make their appearance in *Waien* (the plural form) as the seasons progress. Back in the days when people ate more sweets, a *Waie* was sometimes the main course of the noon or evening meal, especially in the German-speaking part of Switzerland.

When I recently had lunch at a simple outdoor restaurant, Remise, in the countryside near Chur, the capital of canton Graubuenden, the owner of the restaurant came to our table after the meal and announced that she had this tart for dessert. We happily ordered some and she asked, "Half or whole?" Since we had eaten plenty, I asked for half, thinking she meant half a portion. A few minutes later half of a 9-inch tart arrived before me on a plate! Of course I had to eat it—how could I insult our hosts by not finishing my piece of tart? ***One 10-inch tart, about 8 large servings***

1. For the dough, combine the dry ingredients in the bowl of a food processor fitted with the metal blade. Pulse several times to mix. Add the butter and pulse about 10 times to mix in finely. Add the egg and water and pulse repeatedly until the dough forms a ball. Invert the dough onto a floured work surface and carefully remove the blade. Form the dough into a disk and chill it in plastic wrap for 1 hour or up to 2 days before continuing.

2. When you are ready to bake the tart, set a rack in the lowest level of the oven and preheat to 350 degrees.

3. Remove the dough from the refrigerator, place it on a floured work surface, and gently knead it until it is smooth and malleable. Flour the dough and roll the dough to a 12-inch disk. Fold the dough in half and transfer it to the pan, lining up the fold with the diameter of the pan. Unfold the dough into the pan and press it well into the bottom and sides of the pan. Cut away the excess dough at the top edge of the pan with a bench scraper or the back of a knife.

4. To assemble the tart, arrange the plums, cut side up, in concentric circles on the prepared crust. Make 2 rows and fill in the center with a few more plum halves.

5. In a medium mixing bowl, combine the sugar and flour and stir with a whisk to combine. Whisk in the cream, then add the egg and yolks, one at a time, whisking smooth after each addition. Whisk in the Kirsch.

6. Pour the custard cream over the plums in the crust and carefully place the tart on the oven rack.

7. Bake the tart until the pastry is baked through and golden and the custard cream has set and puffed slightly, about 40 minutes.

8. Cool the tart on a rack and serve it at room temperature.

Serving: Remove the outside of the tart pan and slide the tart off the metal pan base onto a platter. You may need to loosen the tart from the pan base with a long, thin spatula or knife first. Serve a wedge of the tart with a little whipped cream, if you like.

Storage: Keep the tart at room temperature on the day it is baked. Wrap and refrigerate leftovers. Bring them to room temperature before serving again.

AUSTRALIA

Stephanie Alexander's Quince Tart

POACHED QUINCE

6 cups water

3 cups sugar

6 large apple quinces, peeled, halved, and cored, with each half cut into 3 pieces (see Note)

1 vanilla bean, split

2 tablespoons lemon juice

SHORT CRUST PASTRY

1¼ cups all-purpose flour (spoon flour into dry-measure cup and level off)

½ teaspoon baking powder

¼ teaspoon salt

8 tablespoons (1 stick) unsalted butter, cold, cut into 8 pieces

3 tablespoons water

BROWN BUTTER FILLING

8 tablespoons (1 stick) unsalted butter

2 large eggs

½ cup sugar

2 tablespoons all-purpose flour

One 10-inch tart pan with removable bottom

When I visited Australia for the first time in May 2002, I was privileged to meet Stephanie Alexander, the country's most widely acclaimed food writer. A veteran of many cookbooks and the former chef-owner of Stephanie's Restaurant, she is the author of the impressive tome *The Cook's Companion: The Complete Book of Ingredients and Recipes for the Australian Kitchen* (Viking, 1996), from which this recipe is adapted. At present she runs the Richmond Hill Café and Larder, one of Melbourne's most popular restaurants and food stores.

Quinces appear in the fall. You're more likely to find them in a farmers' market than in a supermarket. Plan on cooking the quinces a day or two before you intend to prepare the tart because cooking them can easily become an all-day job. It doesn't require your constant attention, but make sure to be nearby to test them for tenderness and not overcook them. There are several varieties of quince, including apple, pear, and pineapple. You want to choose the ones that look like large apples. This recipe would make an ideal Thanksgiving dessert. ***One 10-inch tart, about 10 servings***

1. One day (or up to several days) before you intend to prepare the tart, poach the quinces. Set a rack in the lower third of the oven and preheat to 325 degrees.

2. Bring the water and sugar to a boil over medium heat in a large enameled iron casserole that has a lid. Stir occasionally, to make sure all the sugar dissolves. Add the quinces, vanilla bean, and lemon juice and return to a boil. Invert a small ovenproof plate on top of the quinces to keep them submerged, cover the pan, and bake them for about 1½ hours. Test the quinces by plunging the point of a small knife into one of the pieces. The fruit should be tender and red. If the fruit is not yet tender, bake until it is, testing it every 30 minutes. Don't stir the quinces while they are cooking, or they may break. Cool the quinces in the syrup and refrigerate until you intend to prepare the tart.

3. For the dough, combine the dry ingredients in a food processor fitted with the metal blade. Pulse several times to mix. Add the butter and pulse 3 or 4 times, until the butter is in pea-size pieces. Add the water and pulse 2 or 3 times, until the dough forms clumps, but not a ball. Invert the dough onto a floured work surface and carefully remove the blade. Form the dough into a disk and wrap it in plastic. Refrigerate the dough for 1 hour, or up to 2 days.

4. To bake the tart, set a rack in the lowest level of the oven and preheat to 350 degrees.

5. Remove the dough from the refrigerator and place it on a floured work surface. Flour the dough and gently press it with a rolling pin in close parallel strokes to soften it. Roll the dough to a 12-inch disk. Fold the dough in half and transfer it to the pan, lining up the fold with the diameter of the pan. Unfold the dough and press it well into the bottom and sides of the pan. Use a bench scraper or the back of a knife to sever any excess dough at the rim of the pan. Chill the crust while preparing the filling.

6. With a slotted spoon, carefully remove the wedges of quince from the syrup and place them on a pan lined with several thicknesses of paper towels to drain.

7. For the brown butter filling, melt the butter in a small saucepan over medium heat. Cook the butter until it is foamy and turns light brown. Immediately pour the butter into a heatproof bowl to cool slightly. In a medium mixing bowl, whisk the eggs to break them up, then whisk in the sugar. Sift and whisk in the flour, followed by the cooled butter.

8. Arrange the wedges of quince on the tart crust, close together and perpendicular to the edge of the crust. Fill in the center with more wedges. Pour the filling over the quince wedges. Bake until the pastry is baked through and the filling is well colored, about 40 minutes.

9. Cool the tart on a rack. The filling will fall as the tart cools.

NOTE: Be careful when peeling and paring the quinces: their tough flesh can make the knife slip and cut you.

SERVING: Remove the side of the pan and slide the tart from the metal pan base to a platter. You may need to loosen the bottom of the tart from the pan base with a long, thin spatula or knife.

STORAGE: Keep the tart at room temperature on the day it is baked. Wrap and refrigerate leftovers. Bring them to room temperature before serving again.

Roman Lattice-Topped Apple Tart
Crostata di Mele alla Romana

PASTA FROLLA

3 1/4 cups all-purpose flour

1/2 cup sugar

1 1/2 teaspoons baking powder

3/4 teaspoon salt

12 tablespoons (1 1/2 sticks) unsalted butter, cold, but into 12 pieces

2 teaspoons finely grated lemon zest

2 large eggs

3 large egg yolks

APPLE FILLING

3 pounds Granny Smith or other tart apples, peeled, halved, cored, and sliced

1/2 cup sugar

2 tablespoons butter

2 tablespoons dark rum

1/2 teaspoon ground cinnamon

Egg wash: 1 egg well beaten with a pinch of salt

1 large cookie sheet lined with parchment or foil

In Italy, a crostata is a fairly thin tart, usually with a lattice top crust. This one, as is typical, is assembled entirely free-form on a cookie sheet, eliminating the need for a special pan to bake it in.

I first noticed tarts like this one in Rome when I was traveling there in the late 1980s. It was early May, and all the pastry shops were filled with a sour cherry version called *crostata di visciole*, the name applied to a local tangy sour cherry. I gave a recipe for that tart in my book *Great Italian Desserts.* This apple version appears in the fall, and I like to make it with a cooked apple filling. Cooking the apples in advance makes for a less watery tart and really concentrates the flavor of the apples. ***One 12-inch-diameter tart, about 16 servings***

1. For the dough, combine the dry ingredients in the bowl of a food processor fitted with the metal blade. Pulse several times to mix. Add the butter and pulse 10 times to mix in

finely. Add the lemon zest, eggs, and yolks and pulse repeatedly until the dough forms a ball. Invert the dough onto a floured work surface and carefully remove the blade. Form the dough into a rough cylinder. Refrigerate it in plastic wrap. The dough may be kept refrigerated for up to 2 days before you continue with the recipe.

2. For the apple filling, combine the apples, sugar, butter, rum, and cinnamon in a large enameled iron Dutch oven or another pan with a tight-fitting lid. Stir well to mix. Place over medium heat until the apples start to sizzle. Cover the pan and cook the apples, uncovering the pan and stirring 3 or 4 times, until the apples are swimming in water, about 15 minutes. Uncover the pan and let the water evaporate, stirring occasionally—but not too often, or the apple slices will break up too much. By the time the apples have cooked down, about half will have disintegrated and half the slices should remain intact, yielding a sliced apple filling bound with apple puree. Scrape the filling into a bowl and let it cool to room temperature. Cover the bowl with plastic wrap and refrigerate the filling for up to 2 days if you do not intend to bake the tart immediately.

3. When you are ready to bake the tart, set a rack in the lower third of the oven and preheat to 350 degrees.

4. Remove the dough from the refrigerator and gently knead it on a floured surface until it is smooth and malleable. Use a bench scraper or a knife to cut the dough in half.

5. Form one of the pieces of dough into a disk and place it on a floured surface. Flour the dough and roll it to a little larger than 12 inches in diameter. Slide the dough onto the prepared pan. Place a 12-inch cake cardboard on the dough and use a pizza wheel to cut the dough into an even 12-inch disk. Reserve scraps. Spread the cooled filling on the dough to within ½ inch of the edge.

6. Cut off two-thirds of the remaining dough and roll it to a rectangle about 7 × 12 inches. Use a pizza wheel to trim the 12-inch edges of the dough straight and cut it into fourteen ½-inch strips. Brush egg wash on the strips of dough.

7. To make the lattice top for the tart, transfer 1 strip of dough to the top of the filling and arrange it down the middle of the tart. Place 3 more strips on either side of the first one, equidistant from the first (diameter) strip and the edge of the filling, a little more than an inch apart. Apply 1 strip down the middle of the tart at a 45-degree angle to the first one. Repeat with 3 more strips on either side of it.

8. Trim away any overhanging strips with a pizza wheel at the edge of the tart. Gently knead the scraps into the remaining dough, and with the palms of your hands, roll the remaining dough into a 36-inch-long cylinder. (It will be very thin.) Egg-wash the dough at the edge of the tart and apply the cylinder of dough there. Use floured fingertips to press gently and flatten the cylinder of dough. Use the back of a knife to make diagonal indentations in the strip of dough at the edge of the tart. Egg-wash the edge of the tart.

9. Bake the tart until the crust is baked through and the filling is gently bubbling, about 45 minutes.

10. Slide the tart from the pan to a rack to cool.

SERVING: Slide the tart from the rack to a platter. Cut it in wedges and serve slightly warm or at room temperature. A small scoop of vanilla ice cream is nice with it.

STORAGE: Keep the tart at room temperature on the day it is baked. Wrap leftovers in plastic and keep them at room temperature.

VARIATION: ROMAN JAM TART (*CROSTATA DI MARMELLATA*)

This is a specialty of my friend Natalie Danford, who has spent much time traveling in Italy. It is an excellent alternative to the apple filling in the tart above. However, because jam is more likely to melt and become runny during baking, this tart must be baked in a tart pan with a removable bottom.

Use half the dough to line a 12-inch tart pan. Spread the crust with about 2 cups of your favorite jam or preserves (Natalie uses an imported Italian mixed-berry jam). Use the remaining dough to fashion a lattice top crust, as in the instructions above, but don't finish the edge with the cylinder of dough. You'll have a little dough leftover, which you can save and use for individual tartlets. Bake, cool, and serve the tart as above.

FRANCE

Modern Raspberry Tart
Tarte Moderne aux Framboises

CRUMBLY PASTRY DOUGH (PÂTE SABLÉE)

2 cups all-purpose flour (spoon flour into dry-measure cup and level off)

1½ teaspoons baking powder

12 tablespoons (1½ sticks) unsalted butter, softened

¾ cup sugar

4 large egg yolks

RASPBERRY CREAM FILLING (CRÈME AUX FRAMBOISES)

1 10-ounce package frozen raspberries, defrosted

⅓ cup sugar

3 large egg yolks

1 large egg

1½ teaspoons unflavored gelatin

3 tablespoons cold water

6 tablespoons unsalted butter, softened to the consistency of mayonnaise

FINISHING

Three ½-pint baskets fresh raspberries

3 tablespoons very green pistachios, skinned, halved, and dried out in the oven (not toasted)

Confectioners' sugar

One 10-inch spring form pan, buttered

This recipe is modeled on a tart made by Frédéric Bau, the research chef for Valrhona Chocolate in France. It is based on a recipe in his book *Au Coeur des Saveurs* (*At the Heart of Flavors*) (Montagud, 1998). Though this recipe is rather complicated, it's actually one of the simplest in Bau's book, which is filled with multilayered confections embodying many different flavors and textures. A rich, ½-inch-thick crumbly pastry base holds an emphatically flavored raspberry cream, set with just a bit of gelatin, topped by fresh raspberries and a sprinkling of pistachios for color and crunch. The best way to approach this is to prepare the crust the day before you intend to serve the tart. Save this for a special occasion—it is incredibly elegant.

One note of caution about preparing the filling: Make sure the butter is very soft, or it will not incorporate smoothly into the raspberry cream. ***One 10-inch tart, about 10 servings***

1. For the dough, in a small bowl stir the flour and baking powder together and set aside. Combine the butter and sugar in the bowl of an electric mixer. Place on the mixer fitted with the paddle attachment and beat on medium speed until very light, about 5 minutes. Beat in the egg yolks, one at a time, beating smooth after each addition. Stop the mixer and use a large rubber spatula to scrape down the bowl and paddle. Add the flour and baking powder mixture and beat on lowest speed until the flour is just absorbed. Scrape the dough out onto a floured surface and form it into a disk. Wrap the dough in plastic and refrigerate it until firm, about 1 to 2 hours.

2. To form the tart crust, place the dough on a floured surface and dust it with flour. Gently roll the dough to an 11-inch disk. Place a plate or cardboard cake circle that is 10 inches in diameter on the dough and use a pizza wheel to cut around it, leaving a strip of dough 1 inch wide all around it. Cut through the 1-inch strip again with a paring knife and ease and slide it away from the 10-inch disk. Use a cookie sheet or tart pan bottom to transfer the disk of dough to the prepared pan. Moisten a 1-inch-wide strip around the perimeter of the dough and place the 1-inch strip of dough on it, to make the sides of the tart crust. If the dough breaks, just patch it together. Gently press the strip of dough in place without making indentations in it. Chill the unbaked crust in the pan, in plastic wrap, until the day you intend to serve the tart. It may remain in the refrigerator for up to 2 days.

3. When you intend to bake and assemble the tart, set a rack in the middle level of the oven and preheat to 350 degrees. Bake the tart crust for about 30 minutes, or until it is golden and firm. Cool the crust on a rack.

4. While the crust is baking, prepare the raspberry cream. Combine the defrosted raspberries and sugar in a medium saucepan and bring to a boil over medium heat, stirring occasionally. Decrease heat to low and simmer the mixture until it is slightly thickened, about 5 to 6 minutes. Puree the sweetened raspberries in a blender. Force the puree through a fine-meshed strainer to remove the seeds. There should be about ¾ cup seedless raspberry puree.

5. Pour the raspberry puree into a small heavy saucepan and bring it to a simmer over low heat. In a small bowl, whisk the yolks and egg together. Whisk about a third of the boiling raspberry puree into the egg mixture. Return the remaining raspberry puree to a boil, then reduce the heat and whisk the egg mixture into the boiling raspberry puree, continuing to whisk constantly until the mixture thickens slightly, about 30 seconds. (It will not become very thick.) Don't let the mixture come to a boil, or the eggs will scramble. Remove from the heat and strain into a medium bowl.

6. In a small bowl whisk the gelatin and water together. Set aside until the gelatin has evenly absorbed the water and swelled slightly, about 5 minutes. Whisk the soaked gelatin into the hot raspberry cream. Cool to room temperature and whisk in the butter 1 tablespoon at a time.

7. Remove the side of the springform pan and use a spatula to ease the cooled tart crust off the pan base onto a platter. Spread the raspberry cream evenly in the tart crust. Then refrigerate for 1 hour to begin to set the cream.

8. Before the raspberry cream has completely set, arrange concentric rows of raspberries on the cream, covering the entire surface.

9. Immediately before serving, sprinkle with the pistachios and a light coat of confectioners' sugar.

SERVING: Cut this tart with a very sharp knife, or you will maul it.

STORAGE: Keep the tart refrigerated until about 1 hour before you intend to serve it, or the raspberry cream will melt. Wrap and refrigerate leftovers and bring to room temperature before serving again.

SWITZERLAND

Chocolate Pastry Raspberry Jam Tart from St. Gallen
St. Gallen Klostertorte

COCOA-ALMOND DOUGH

2¼ cups all-purpose flour (spoon flour into dry-measure cup and level off)

1 cup (about 4 ounces) whole blanched almonds, finely ground in the food processor

½ cup sugar

¼ cup alkalized (Dutch-process) cocoa powder, sifted after measuring

2 teaspoons baking powder

12 tablespoons (1½ sticks) unsalted butter, cold and cut into 12 pieces

¼ cup milk

FILLING

1 cup seedless raspberry jam

Confectioners' sugar for finishing

1 10-inch tart pan with removable bottom, lightly buttered

St. Gallen is a lovely small city in eastern Switzerland, well known for its great architectural monument, the Benedictine monastery of Saint Gall. An enterprising baker must have invented this specialty in honor of the monastery. Klostertorte is like a chocolate version of a linzertorte, with a cocoa-and-nut dough that encloses a filling of raspberry jam. You'll have some scraps of dough left over after you prepare the Klostertorte. Roll them to a square and cut them into square or diamond-shaped cookies. Bake them for about 12 minutes, after you have baked the Klostertorte.

One 10-inch tart, about 8 to 10 servings

1. Set a rack in the middle level of the oven and preheat to 350 degrees.

2. For the dough, combine the dry ingredients in the bowl of a food processor and pulse several times to mix. Add the butter and pulse until the butter is finely mixed in, about 10 times. Add the milk and pulse until the dough starts to form large clumps but does not form a ball. Invert the dough onto a floured surface and carefully remove the blade. Gently squeeze and press the dough together and cut off about two-thirds of it using a bench scraper or a knife.

3. Form the larger piece of dough into a disk and place it on a floured surface. Flour the dough and roll it to a 12-inch disk. Slide a thin cookie sheet or tart pan bottom under the dough and transfer it to the prepared pan, sliding it off into the pan. (This dough is much too soft and fragile to be folded in half the way other doughs are.) Press the dough well into the bottom and sides of the pan and cut away the excess dough at the top of the pan.

4. Stir the jam to soften it, and use a spoon to spread it evenly on the prepared crust.

5. Gently knead the scraps of dough into the remaining smaller piece and form it into a rough square. Place the dough on a floured surface and lightly flour the dough. Roll it to a 10-inch square. Use a pizza wheel to cut the dough into 10 strips, each 1 inch wide.

6. Place 5 of the strips about 1 inch apart on the tart, letting the ends overlap the edge of the pan. Place the remaining strips at a 45-degree angle to the first ones to form a lattice. Press the edges of the strips with your fingertips to sever the ends at the rim of the pan.

7. Bake the Klostertorte until the dough is firm and dry-looking and the jam bubbles very gently, about 40 minutes. Cool in the pan on a rack.

SERVING: Remove the side of the tart pan and slide the Klostertorte off the metal pan base onto a platter. You may need to use a long spatula or knife to loosen it before sliding it off. Dust lightly with confectioners' sugar immediately before serving.

STORAGE: Keep the Klostertorte loosely covered at room temperature before and after serving.

FRANCE

Apricot Custard Tart
Tarte Bergère aux Abricots

SWEET PASTRY DOUGH

3 cups all-purpose flour (spoon flour into dry-measure cup and level off)

½ cup sugar

1½ teaspoons baking powder

½ teaspoon salt

12 tablespoons (1½ sticks) unsalted butter, cold, cut into 12 pieces

3 large eggs

FILLING

¾ cup sugar

6 tablespoons all-purpose flour

Pinch of ground cinnamon

6 large eggs

1½ cups heavy whipping cream

2 teaspoons vanilla extract

2 pounds ripe apricots, rinsed, halved, and pits removed, or three 8-ounce cans of apricot halves in syrup

One 10-inch round layer cake pan, 2 inches deep, thickly buttered

This tart is composed of a sweet pastry crust around a creamy custard that encloses the apricots. Apricots can be a problem. Even when fresh ones are available in early summer, they can be unbearably sour. Some years I wait until local ones are available and am disappointed anyway, because they lack the sweetness I expect. I have to confess that I sometimes use well-drained canned apricot halves for this recipe—about the only solution I can recommend for procuring sweet apricots. Many other fruits can be substituted for apricots, however.

I have never managed to find out why this tart is called *bergère*, or shepherdess.

One 10-inch pie, about 12 servings

1. For the dough, combine the dry ingredients in the bowl of a food processor fitted with the metal blade. Pulse several times to mix. Add the butter and pulse 10 times. Add the eggs and pulse repeatedly until the dough forms a ball. Invert the dough onto a floured surface and carefully remove the blade. Form the dough into a rough cylinder and refrigerate it in plastic wrap until you are ready to bake the tart, up to 2 days.

2. To bake the tart, set a rack in the lower third of the oven and preheat to 350 degrees.

3. To make the filling, combine the sugar, flour, and cinnamon in a large mixing bowl. Whisk by hand to mix. Then whisk in the eggs, 2 at a time, whisking smooth after each addition. Whisk in the cream and the vanilla. Set the filling aside.

4. Remove the dough from the refrigerator and place it on a lightly floured surface. Gently knead the dough until it is smooth and malleable. Cut off two-thirds of the dough.

5. Form the larger piece of dough into a disk and place it on a floured work surface. Flour the dough and roll it to a 14-inch disk. Fold the dough into quarters and transfer it to the prepared pan, lining up the point with the center of the pan. Unfold the dough into the pan and press it well against the bottom and sides. Use a bench scraper or the back of a knife to sever the excess dough at the rim.

6. Arrange the apricot halves cut side up and close together in 2 layers in the prepared crust, and pour the custard filling over them.

7. Place the remaining piece of dough on a floured surface and flour it. Roll the dough to a 10-inch square. Use a pizza wheel to cut the dough into 10 strips, each 1 inch wide. Place 5 of the strips 1 inch apart on the filling, letting the ends hang over the edge of the pan. Place the remaining 5 strips at a 45-degree angle to the first ones, about 1 inch apart, to create a lattice. Press down with your fingertips to sever the excess dough at the edge of the pan and to press the ends of the strips against the top of the bottom crust.

8. Bake the tart until the crust is baked through and the filling is set, about 1 hour. To check for doneness, plunge the point of a knife between the strips at the center of the pie and see if it emerges fairly clean, with no liquid custard clinging to it.

9. Cool the pie completely on a rack.

Serving: To unmold the pie, place a flat plate or a cooling rack on the pie and invert. Lift off the pan and replace it with a platter. Invert the whole stack of platter, pie, and rack and remove the rack. Serve the pie in wedges; it needs no accompaniment.

Storage: Keep the pie at room temperature for up to a few hours. If you bake it early in the day and intend to serve it in the evening, refrigerate it in plastic wrap. Bring it to room temperature for 1 hour before serving. Wrap and refrigerate leftovers.

VARIATIONS

Pear Custard Tart (*Tarte Bergère aux Poires*)
Substitute 10 poached pear halves, quartered, for the apricots. See the recipe for French pear slices on page 250 to make the poached pears.

Prune Plum Custard Tart (*Tarte Bergère aux Prunes*)
Substitute halved, pitted prune plums for the apricots.

ENGLAND

Blackberry and Apple Pie

CREAM SHORT CRUST PASTRY

2½ cups all-purpose flour

1 teaspoon baking powder

1 teaspoon salt

12 tablespoons (1½ sticks) unsalted butter, cut into 12 pieces

7 tablespoons heavy whipping cream

BLACKBERRY AND APPLE FILLING

2 pounds tart apples, such as Granny Smith, peeled, halved, cored, and sliced (reserve the peels and cores)

2 teaspoons lemon juice

1 pound (about 3 half-pint baskets or one and a half 12-ounce bags frozen) blackberries

1 cup water

1 cup sugar

Egg wash: 1 egg well beaten with a pinch of salt

Additional sugar for sprinkling the dough

One 12-inch-long enameled iron or earthenware gratin dish, about 2½ quarts in capacity

Though most of us think of fruit pies as having both a bottom and a top crust, this recipe is for an old-fashioned British pie, usually baked in a deep oval porcelain pie dish, with only a top crust. This eliminates the risk that the bottom crust may become soaked through with the abundant juices of the filling and remain underbaked, or become soggy after baking.

This recipe is adapted from Jane Grigson's *Fruit Book* (Athaneum, 1982). Jane Grigson was one of Britain's most gifted food writers of the twentieth century, and she has left us an outstanding legacy of excellent food and writing. This particular recipe cleverly calls for cooking half the blackberries with some water and the apple parings to take advantage of the abundant pectin in the apple cores and peels to thicken the juices of the pie. It is a pretty juicy affair, nonetheless.

The dish traditionally used for this pie is not readily available from American sources. I have chosen an oval gratin dish (you can also use a 9 × 13 × 2-inch glass pan). It makes a thinner pie, but it also increases the amount of pastry in relation to the fruit, which I think is best. ***One 12-inch oval pie, about 8 generous servings***

1. For the pastry dough, combine the dry ingredients in the bowl of a food processor fitted with the metal blade. Pulse several times to mix. Add the butter and pulse 4 or 5 times, or until the butter is in pea-sized pieces. Add the cream and pulse 2 or 3 times, but do not allow the dough to form a ball. Invert the dough to a floured work surface and carefully remove the blade. Gently squeeze and press the dough together and form it into an oval. Chill the dough in plastic wrap while preparing the filling.

2. For the filling, in a large bowl toss the apple slices with the lemon juice. Cover with plastic wrap and refrigerate while preparing the rest of the filling.

3. Put half the blackberries and the apple peels and cores in a large saucepan. Stir to combine and add the water. Cook over medium heat until the mixture becomes very juicy and liquid. Continue cooking until the juices are slightly reduced. Strain the mixture to eliminate the peels and seeds and measure it. You should have about ⅔ cup liquid. If you have too much, boil down the mixture. Stir the sugar into the strained juices and set aside.

4. Set a rack in the middle level of the oven and preheat to 375 degrees.

5. Make a layer of about a third of the apple slices in the gratin dish and sprinkle about half of the blackberries over them. Repeat with another third of the apples and the remaining blackberries. Top with a layer of the remaining apples. Pour the cooked, sweetened blackberry juice evenly over the fruit.

6. Remove the dough from the refrigerator and place it on a floured work surface. Flour the dough and press it with the rolling pin in gentle parallel strokes to soften it slightly. Roll the dough to the size of the dish you are using. Slide a cookie sheet or a 12-inch tart pan bottom under the dough and transfer it to the dish, sliding it onto the filling. Brush the egg wash on the dough and sprinkle it with sugar. Cut several 2-inch vent holes in the top crust with the point of a knife.

7. Bake the pie until the pastry is baked through and the apples are tender, about 40 minutes. Push the point of a knife through one of the vent holes to see if the apples have softened. When they are fully cooked they should offer no resistance to the knife.

8. Cool the pie on a rack.

SERVING: Serve the pie warm or at room temperature. Use a large serving spoon to scoop out portions of the pie, first cutting through the crust into a portion-sized piece, then scooping under the filling to lift out a piece of the pie. If you don't manage to get enough of the fruit on the spoon, pile more next to the portion of pie. Serve with thick liquid cream. Grigson says that clotted cream, sometimes available in American supermarkets, is the best. Failing either of these, whipped cream makes an adequate substitute.

STORAGE: Keep the pie at room temperature until you intend to serve it. Cover loosely with plastic wrap and keep leftovers at room temperature.

Sweet-Crust Apple Pie
Appeltaart

SWEET PASTRY DOUGH

3 cups all-purpose flour (spoon flour into dry-measure cup and level off)

½ cup sugar

1½ teaspoons baking powder

12 tablespoons (1½ sticks) unsalted butter, cold, cut into 12 pieces

2 teaspoons finely grated lemon zest

2 large eggs

2 large egg yolks

1 tablespoon milk or water

APPLE FILLING

⅓ cup (about 2½ ounces) dark raisins

⅓ cup (about 2½ ounces) dried currants

3 tablespoons dark rum

4 tablespoons (½ stick) unsalted butter

3½ pounds Golden Delicious apples, peeled, halved, cored, and sliced ¼ inch thick

1 tablespoon lemon juice

⅓ cup sugar

1 teaspoon ground cinnamon

One 9-inch springform pan 2½ inches deep, buttered

Apple pies of this type abound in the Netherlands, especially in Amsterdam, where a café called Winkel on the Nordermarkt square is reputed to produce the best pie in town. A deep, straight-sided pan is lined with a rich, sweet dough and filled with a lightly cooked apple mixture enriched with sugar, butter, rum, raisins, and currants. The top of the pie is covered with a lattice crust. The pie is usually served warm with a hefty helping of whipped cream on the side. Winkel has a captive audience in the Nordermarkt, where there are flea markets and flower markets throughout the week. ***1 deep 9-inch pie, about 12 servings***

1. For the dough, combine the dry ingredients in the bowl of a food processor fitted with the metal blade. Pulse several times to mix. Add the butter and pulse repeatedly until it is mixed in finely. Add the lemon zest, eggs, yolks, and milk and pulse until

the dough forms a ball. Invert the dough onto a floured work surface, carefully remove the blade, and form the dough into a rough cylinder. Refrigerate the dough in plastic wrap while preparing the filling. You may keep the dough refrigerated for up to 2 days before continuing.

2. For the filling, in a small bowl combine the raisins, currants, and rum and stir well to mix. Set aside while you cook the apples.

3. Melt the butter in a wide sauté pan and add the apples. Cook over medium-high heat, tossing them in the pan or gently stirring with a wooden spoon, until the apples are reduced by approximately one-third from their original volume, about 10 minutes. Scrape the apples into a bowl and cool them.

4. After the apples have cooled, stir in the lemon juice, sugar, cinnamon, and macerated raisins and currants, along with any rum not already absorbed.

5. When you are ready to bake the pie, set a rack in the lower third of the oven and preheat to 350 degrees.

6. Remove the dough from the refrigerator and gently knead it on a floured surface until it is smooth and malleable. Use a bench scraper or a knife to cut off three-quarters of the dough. Form the larger piece of dough into a disk and place it on a floured surface. Flour the dough and roll it to a 14-inch disk. Fold the dough in quarters and transfer it to the prepared pan, lining up the point with the center of the pan. Unfold the dough into the pan and press it well against the bottom and sides. Use a bench scraper or the back of a knife to trim away any excess dough at the top rim.

7. Scrape the filling into the prepared crust and smooth the top. The filling will be below the top of the crust; this is remedied later on.

8. Roll the remaining piece of dough to a 9-inch square. Use a serrated or plain pizza wheel to cut the dough into 10 strips, each ¾ inch wide. (Discard scraps.) Place a strip on the center of the filling, lining it up with the diameter of the pan. Pinch away the ends of the strip so that the dough is on the filling, but not adhering to

the edge of the bottom crust. Repeat with 4 more strips, arranging them about ¾ inch apart on either side of the first one. Repeat with the remaining 5 strips of dough, arranging them at a 45-degree angle to the first ones to create a lattice. Use a table knife to loosen the dough on the side of the pan and fold it over onto the top crust to form a border.

9. Bake the pie until the crust is baked through and the filling is gently bubbling, about 1 hour.

10. Cool the pie on a rack.

SERVING: Remove the side of the springform pan and slide the pie off the pan base onto a platter. You may need to use a long, thin spatula or knife to loosen the pie from the pan base. Serve the pie warm or at room temperature with some whipped cream.

STORAGE: Keep the pie at room temperature on the day it is baked. Store leftovers in plastic wrap at room temperature.

ITALY

Sicilian Baked Cassata

Cassata al Forno

PASTRY DOUGH (PASTA FROLLA)

2 cups all-purpose flour (spoon flour into dry-measure cup and level off)

1/3 cup sugar

1 teaspoon baking powder

1/2 teaspoon salt

8 tablespoons (1 stick) unsalted butter, cold, and cut into 10 pieces

2 teaspoons finely grated orange or lemon zest

4 large egg yolks

2 tablespoons milk or water

RICOTTA FILLING

1 1/4 pounds (20 ounces) whole-milk ricotta

1/2 cup sugar

4 large egg whites

1 1/2 teaspoons vanilla extract

1 1/2 teaspoons white rum

1/2 teaspoon ground cinnamon

1/4 cup (about 1 1/2 ounces) candied orange peel, cut into 1/4-inch dice

1/4 cup (about 1 ounce) coarsely chopped skinned pistachios

2 ounces semisweet chocolate, cut into 1/4-inch pieces and sifted in a strainer to remove the dusty particles

Confectioners' sugar for finishing

One 9-inch glass pie pan, buttered

Cassata (page 160) is a typical Sicilian cake for which a pan is lined with sponge cake and filled with a ricotta cream. The outside is covered with marzipan and decorated. The recipe here substitutes a pastry dough, pasta frolla, for the cake. The filling is mostly the same, except that some egg whites are added to help it set during baking.

Be careful not to overbake the cassata. When it is done, the dough will be golden and the filling will have puffed slightly. Overbaking will provoke water to drain from the cheese. ***One 9-inch pie, about 12 servings***

1. For the dough, combine the dry ingredients in the bowl of a food processor fitted with the metal blade. Pulse several times to mix. Add the butter and pulse about 10 times. Add the orange zest, yolks, and milk or water and pulse repeatedly until the dough forms a ball. Invert the dough onto a floured work surface and carefully remove the blade. Squeeze the dough into a rough cylinder, wrap

it in plastic, and refrigerate it while preparing the filling. You may keep the dough in the refrigerator for up to 2 days before continuing.

2. When you are ready to bake the pie, set a rack in the lower third of the oven and preheat to 350 degrees.

3. For the filling, put the ricotta in a large mixing bowl and beat it smooth with a large rubber spatula. Beat in the sugar followed by the egg whites, a little at a time, beating smooth after each addition. Stir in the remaining ingredients, one at a time.

4. Remove the dough from the refrigerator and knead it lightly on a floured surface until it is smooth and malleable. Use a bench scraper or knife to cut off a little more than half the dough for the bottom crust. Form the larger piece of dough into a disk and place it on a floured work surface. Flour the dough and roll it to a disk about 12 inches in diameter. Fold the dough in half and transfer it to the prepared pan, lining up the fold with the diameter of the pan. Unfold the dough into the pan and press it well into the bottom and sides. Trim away the excess dough at the rim with a bench scraper or the back of a knife.

5. Scrape the filling into the dough-lined pan and smooth the top.

6. Roll the remaining dough to a 9-inch disk and fold it in half. Place the dough on the filling and unfold it to cover it. Moisten the edge of the top crust with water and fold the dough on the rim of the pan over the top crust, gently pressing it into place. With the tip of a knife, cut three or four 1-inch vent holes in the top crust.

7. Bake the pie until the crust is golden and the filling has puffed slightly, about 45 minutes.

8. Cool the pie on a rack. After the pie is cool, invert a platter on the pie and invert the pie onto the platter. Lift off the pan. The bottom crust now becomes the top of the pie. Wrap the pie loosely in plastic wrap and refrigerate until you intend to serve it.

Serving: Dust the cassata lightly with confectioners' sugar immediately before serving.

Storage: As noted above, keep the pie refrigerated until you intend to serve it. Wrap and refrigerate leftovers.

SWITZERLAND

Caramelized Walnut Pie from the Engadin

Engadiner Nusstorte

CARAMEL WALNUT FILLING

1 1/4 cups sugar

1 teaspoon water

2/3 cup heavy whipping cream

1 tablespoon honey

2 cups (about 8 ounces) walnut pieces, coarsely chopped

PASTRY DOUGH

3 cups all-purpose four (spoon flour into dry-measure cups and level off)

1/2 cup sugar

1 teaspoon baking powder

16 tablespoons (2 sticks) unsalted butter, cold, cut into 16 pieces

2 large eggs

1 large egg yolk

One 9-inch round pan, 2 inches deep, buttered, and the bottom lined with a disk of buttered parchment

The Engadin is a part of canton Graubuenden, well known for St. Moritz, a ski resort filled with grand, palatial luxury hotels and elegant restaurants. During the nineteenth century, before the creation of the great resorts, rural villages in the Engadin saw the emergence of a generation of pastry cooks who emigrated to every part of the world to open Swiss pastry shops. Many of the greatest names in pastry in Italy, such as Caflisch, Caviezel, Planta, and Sandri, owe their origins to the Engadin. The same is true in many other countries.

This pie was probably an invention of one of those great pastry-making families of the Engadin, though as far as I know, no one ever claimed it as a personal triumph. Crumbly-sweet pastry layers enclose a caramelized walnut filling enriched with cream. It's a perfect dessert for cool weather, especially in the fall when the fresh crop of walnuts arrives. ***One 9-inch pie, about 12 servings***

1. For the filling, combine the sugar and water in a large saucepan and stir with a wooden spoon until the mixture has the consistency of wet sand. In a small bowl combine the cream and honey. Place the bowl near the pan on the stove. Place the sugar and water over medium heat and stir occasionally until the sugar turns a deep amber caramel. Remove the pan from the heat and immediately pour in the cream and honey mixture, a little at a time to avoid causing the caramel to boil over. Return the pan to the heat and cook, stirring occasionally, for 1 additional minute.
2. Stir the walnuts into the filling and scrape it into a buttered bowl to cool slightly.
3. For the dough, combine the dry ingredients in the bowl of a food processor fitted with the metal blade. Pulse several times to mix. Add the butter and pulse about 10 times. Add the eggs and yolk and pulse repeatedly until the dough forms a ball.
4. Invert the dough onto a floured surface and carefully remove the blade. Form the dough into a rough cylinder and use a bench scraper or knife to cut off two-thirds of it.
5. Place the larger piece of dough on a floured surface and flour the dough. Roll it to a 13-inch disk. Fold the dough in half and transfer it to the prepared pan, lining up the fold with the diameter of the pan. Unfold the dough into the pan and press it well into the bottom and sides. Use a bench scraper or the back of a knife to trim away the excess dough at the top.
6. Scrape the filling into the dough-lined pan and spread the top smooth.
7. Roll the remaining piece of dough to a 9-inch disk and slide a cookie sheet or 12-inch tart pan bottom under it. Slide the dough off the cookie sheet onto the filling. Fold over the sides of the bottom crust that extend above the top crust. Press the folded dough down against the top crust with the ends of the tines of a fork. Use the fork to poke a dozen vent holes in the top crust at 2-inch intervals.

8. Bake the pie until the dough is baked through and deep golden and the filling is firm, about 45 minutes.

9. Cool completely on a rack and wrap in plastic wrap. Wait until the next day to serve the pie, or the filling will be runny when you cut into it.

SERVING: Invert the nusstorte onto a rack or flat plate and remove the pan and paper. Replace the pan with a platter and invert everything with the nusstorte in between. Remove the rack or plate. Serve the nusstorte in wedges. It needs no accompaniment.

STORAGE: Keep the nusstorte wrapped in plastic both before and after serving.

FRANCE

Basque Custard Pie
Gâteau Basque

PASTRY DOUGH

4 cups all-purpose flour (spoon flour into dry-measure cup and level off)

2 teaspoons baking powder

½ pound (2 sticks) unsalted butter, softened

1 cup sugar

4 large eggs

2 teaspoons orange flower water

1 teaspoon vanilla extract

PASTRY CREAM

2 cups milk

½ cup sugar

6 large egg yolks

⅓ cup all-purpose flour

PIE FILLING

All the pastry cream, above

3 large eggs

½ cup blanched whole almonds, finely ground in the food processor

1 teaspoon almond extract

⅔ cup black cherry (not sour cherry) preserves

Egg wash: 1 egg beaten with a pinch of salt

One 10-inch round pan, 2 inches deep, thickly buttered

Though the name of this pie in French is *gâteau*, which usually refers to a cake, it is a pie with a top and bottom crust. The classic filling for a gâteau Basque is a flour-thickened pastry cream with almonds scented with a little almond extract. There are many versions of this pie that also include cherries. Itxassou, a village in the Basque region of France, is famous for its cherries, and they or a jam made from them often form part of this filling. The real thing is not available here, so I spread a layer of black cherry preserves on the bottom crust under the pastry cream filling. ***One 10-inch straight-sided pie, about 12 servings***

1. For the dough, stir the flour and baking powder together and set aside. Put the butter and sugar in the bowl of an electric mixer and beat with the paddle attachment on medium speed for about 2 minutes, or until very smooth. Beat in the eggs, one at a time, beating smooth after each addition.

Beat in the orange flower water and the vanilla. Remove the bowl from the mixer and use a large rubber spatula to stir in the flour mixture. Scrape the dough to a floured work surface and form it into a rough cylinder. Refrigerate the dough in plastic wrap for at least 1 hour. You may leave the dough in the refrigerator for up to 2 days before continuing.

2. For the pastry cream, bring the milk and ¼ cup of the sugar to a boil in a medium saucepan over low heat, whisking occasionally to make sure all the sugar has dissolved. In a medium mixing bowl, whisk the yolks to break them up and whisk in the remaining ¼ cup sugar. Sift and whisk in the flour. When the milk comes to a boil, whisk about a third of it into the yolk mixture. Return the remaining milk to a boil and whisk the yolk mixture into the milk, continuing to whisk constantly until the cream thickens and returns to a boil. Keep whisking for an additional 15 seconds or so while the cream boils.

3. Scrape the pastry cream into a glass or stainless steel bowl, press plastic wrap against the surface of the cream, and refrigerate it until it has cooled completely. The pastry cream may be prepared the day before you intend to bake the pie.

4. When you are ready to bake the pie, set a rack in the lower third of the oven and preheat to 350 degrees.

5. To complete the filling, whisk the eggs with the almonds and almond extract. Turn the pastry cream into a medium mixing bowl and incorporate the egg mixture into it, stirring gently with a large rubber spatula. Do not whisk the filling, or it may become too thin.

6. Remove the dough from the refrigerator and gently knead it on a floured surface until it is smooth and malleable. Using a bench scraper or a knife, cut off a little more than half the dough. Form the larger piece of dough into a disk and place it on a floured work surface. Flour the dough and roll it to a 14-inch disk. Fold the dough in quarters and transfer it to the prepared pan. Line up the point with the center of the pan and unfold the dough into the pan. Press the dough well into the bottom and sides of the pan and use a bench scraper or the back of a knife to sever any excess dough at the top of the pan.

7. Spread the cherry preserves in the bottom of the prepared crust. Scrape the filling in and smooth the top with a spatula.

8. Roll three-fourths of the remaining dough to a 10-inch disk and use a cookie sheet or a tart pan bottom larger than the dough to transfer it to the pie. Slide the disk of dough onto the filling. Egg-wash the top and fold over the sides of the bottom crust that extend above the top crust.

9. Press any dough scraps together. Roll them to a 6-inch square and cut out six or eight 2½-inch disks or crescents with a fluted cookie cutter. Position the pastry decorations symmetrically around the edge of the top crust. Brush egg wash on the decorations and use the tines of a fork to trace a crosshatch pattern on them. Brush more egg wash all over the top crust, including the decorations.

10. Bake the pie until the crust is baked through and a deep golden color, about 45 to 55 minutes.

11. Cool the pie in the pan on a rack. After the pie has cooled to room temperature, refrigerate the pan in plastic wrap, preferably overnight.

12. To unmold the pie, warm the bottom of the pan over low heat for a few seconds. Invert the pie onto a rack or flat cake cardboard and lift off the pan. Replace the pan with a platter and invert the whole stack again, removing the rack and leaving the pie on the platter.

SERVING: The pie must be refrigerated after baking so that the filling sets, but the pastry would have an awful texture if you served the pie ice-cold, so bring it to room temperature for 1 hour before you serve it. The filling will still be set, but the crust will have softened and will be much more edible. Serve the pie in thin wedges. It is quite rich and needs no accompaniment.

STORAGE: Keep the pie refrigerated, covered with plastic wrap, until 1 hour before you intend to serve it. Wrap and refrigerate leftovers.

SWITZERLAND

Chocolate Cream Tartlets
Guayaquils

PASTRY DOUGH

16 tablespoons (2 sticks) unsalted butter, softened

½ cup sugar

2 large egg yolks

2 teaspoons finely grated lemon zest

1 teaspoon vanilla extract

2½ cups cake flour (spoon flour into dry-measure cup and level off)

FILLING

¾ cup heavy whipping cream

1 tablespoon light corn syrup

6 ounces semisweet chocolate, cut into ¼-inch pieces

⅓ cup seedless raspberry preserves

FINISHING

1 cup chocolate shavings

Confectioners' sugar for dusting

Twenty-four 2½-inch-diameter round tartlet pans

The Swiss name for these tartlets might imply that they are adapted from an Ecuadorian recipe, but I think the name must derive from a brand or type of chocolate using South American cocoa beans. The tartlets are fairly simple to prepare, though they never fail to impress. They are part of an amazing array of tiny tartlets and other pastry-based confections the Swiss refer to as *Konfekt*, or confections. You'll find little pastries like these in any good-quality pastry shop in Switzerland, but my favorite place for them (and for a wide assortment of other baked goods) is Sprüngli in Zurich. ***Twenty-four 2½-inch tartlets***

1. For the dough, combine the butter and sugar in the bowl of an electric mixer. Place on the mixer fitted with the paddle attachment and beat on medium speed until very light, about 5 minutes. Beat in the egg yolks, one at a time, beating smooth after each addition. Beat in the lemon zest and vanilla. Stop the mixer and scrape down the bowl and beater with a large rubber

spatula. Add the flour and beat on lowest speed, just until the flour is absorbed. Scrape the dough to a floured surface and form it into a rectangle ½ inch thick. Refrigerate in plastic wrap until firm, about 1 hour. You may leave the dough refrigerated for up to 2 days before continuing.

2. To make the tartlet shells, remove the dough from the refrigerator and place it on a floured surface. Use a bench scraper or knife to cut the dough into 4 equal pieces. Leave 1 piece of dough out and refrigerate the rest. Flour the dough and use a rolling pin to press it with a series of close parallel strokes to soften it. Roll the dough to a 6-inch square. Use a 2¾- to 3-inch plain cutter to cut rounds of the dough. Fit them into the pans and use your thumbs to press them well into the bottom and sides. Use the back of a knife to sever any excess dough at the rims of the pans. Repeat with the remaining pieces of dough, refrigerating the scraps as they are formed. Reroll some of the scraps to make the last few tartlet crusts. Arrange the little pans in rows on a jelly-roll pan as they are lined with dough. Cover the whole pan with plastic wrap and refrigerate the tartlet crusts for at least 2 hours to help prevent excessive shrinkage during baking. (Press any remaining scraps together and refrigerate them. Roll them out within 2 days to make some simple cookies.)

3. When you are ready to bake the tartlet shells, set a rack in the middle level of the oven and preheat to 350 degrees.

4. Remove the pan of tartlet shells from the refrigerator and use a fork to pierce the dough all over at ¼-inch intervals. This eliminates the need to fill the crusts with beans or other weights while they are baking.

5. Bake the tartlet crusts until they are a pale golden color, about 15 minutes. Cool the crusts in the pans on a rack. After the crusts have completely cooled, remove them from the pans and arrange them on a clean jelly-roll pan.

6. For the chocolate filling, bring the cream and corn syrup to a boil in a small saucepan over medium heat, whisking occasionally to mix in the corn syrup. Remove from heat and add the chocolate. Wait 1 minute and whisk smooth. Pour the chocolate filling into a large measuring cup to make it easy to fill the crusts later on. Let the chocolate filling cool to lukewarm, stirring occasionally.

7. Pipe or spoon about ½ teaspoon of the raspberry preserves into each baked crust. Pour in chocolate filling until level with the top of the crust. Let the filling cool completely and set.

8. To finish the tartlets, cover the chocolate filling completely with chocolate shavings. One at a time, finish the tartlets by gently holding the blade of a small offset spatula across the middle of each tartlet. Sprinkle with confectioners' sugar and lift the blade away so that the area in the center of the tartlet has no sugar on it.

SERVING: These are a perfect tea or after-dinner pastry.

STORAGE: Keep the tartlets at room temperature until you intend to serve them. Keep leftovers in a cool place, but do not refrigerate them, or the crusts will soften and become soggy.

ITALY

Custard-Filled Tartlets
Bocconotti di Crema

1 recipe Pasta Frolla (see Cassata al Forno, page 223), chilled

PASTRY CREAM

2 cups milk

¾ cup sugar, divided

6 large egg yolks

⅓ cup all-purpose flour (spoon flour into dry-measure cup and level off)

CUSTARD FILLING

All the pastry cream, above

3 large eggs, well beaten

1 tablespoon finely grated orange zest

2 teaspoons vanilla extract

¼ teaspoon ground cinnamon

12 fluted brioche molds, 3 inches in diameter across the top, well buttered, plus a jelly-roll pan

This is probably the most frequently requested recipe on my website, www.nickmalgieri.com. Bocconotti ("little mouthfuls") di crema are deep tartlets with a sweet pastry crust and a creamy custard filling, often enhanced with some sour cherry jam at the bottom (see the variation). Widely available in Italian-American pastry shops, they are wildly popular with anyone who has ever tasted them. I've done my best to re-create the ones I remember tasting over the years in many places, both here and in Italy.

The brioche molds needed to bake these come in dozens of sizes. If the molds you have are much larger than the ones specified below, you'll just make fewer tartlets. You can also use muffin pans or small aluminum foil pie pans for baking them, but the results won't have the characteristic shape. Sometimes the filling puffs a lot and the dough on top cracks—this doesn't affect the taste in any way.

In Italian, *crema* (cream) refers to a cooked cream or a creamy sauce. Dairy cream is called *panna*. ***About twelve 3-inch tartlets, depending on the size of the molds***

1. For the pastry cream, combine the milk and half the sugar in a heavy-bottomed saucepan, preferably one made of enameled iron. Place over medium heat and bring to a boil, whisking occasionally to make sure the sugar has dissolved.

2. In a mixing bowl, whisk the egg yolks, then whisk in the remaining sugar. Sift and whisk in the flour. The mixture will be very thick. When the milk boils, whisk about a third of it into the yolk mixture. Return the remaining milk to medium heat and boil again. Whisk the yolk mixture into the milk and continue whisking constantly until the cream thickens and returns to a full boil. Cook, whisking constantly, for 15 seconds. Scrape the cream into a glass or stainless steel bowl and press plastic wrap against the surface to prevent a skin from forming. Refrigerate the cream until it has cooled completely. You may prepare the cream the day before, but no longer in advance than that.

3. To make the filling, turn the pastry cream into a large bowl and gently stir in the eggs, orange zest, vanilla, and cinnamon.

4. Set a rack in the lowest level of the oven and preheat to 350 degrees.

5. Remove the dough from the refrigerator and place it on a floured work surface. Gently knead the dough until it is smooth and malleable. Press the dough into a rectangle and use a bench scraper or a knife to divide it into 3 equal pieces. Place 1 piece of the dough on a floured surface and flour the dough. Roll it into a 10-inch square, which will be quite thin. Use a pizza wheel to cut the dough into 4 squares, each 5 inches on a side. Ease one of the squares of dough into one of the prepared pans and press it well against the bottom and sides of the pan (don't press too hard, or the fluted ridges of the pan will cut through the dough). With your fingertips, sever any excess dough at the top of the pan. Repeat with the remaining 3 pans. Arrange the dough-lined pans on the jelly-roll pan. Repeat with the second and third pieces of dough and the next 8 pans.

6. Fill the pans with the custard, leaving ¼ inch empty at the top. Reroll the scraps of dough and use a pizza wheel to cut them into ½-inch-wide strips. Place 2 strips perpendicular to each other on the top of each tartlet to form a cross. Use your fingertips to sever the ends of the strips at the edges of the pans.

7. Bake the tartlets until the dough is baked through and the filling is set and slightly puffed, about 30 minutes. Cool the tartlets on a rack.

SERVING: These are good for dessert or with tea or coffee. Italian-Americans eat them for breakfast.

STORAGE: Keep the tartlets loosely covered with plastic wrap in the refrigerator after they have cooled. Bring them to room temperature for 1 hour before serving. Refrigerate leftovers and bring to room temperature before serving again.

VARIATION: CUSTARD-FILLED TARTLETS WITH SOUR CHERRY JAM (*BOCCONOTTI DI CREMA ED AMARENE*)

Put a teaspoon of sour cherry jam in the bottom of each tartlet crust before adding the custard filling. You could use another type of jam, but it wouldn't be traditional.

FRANCE

Raspberry Tartlets
Tartelettes aux Framboises

PASTRY CREAM FILLING

1 cup milk

½ cup heavy whipping cream

⅓ cup sugar

4 large egg yolks

3 tablespoons all-purpose flour

2 teaspoons vanilla extract

RASPBERRY GLAZE

1 cup seedless raspberry jam

1 tablespoon water

CRUST

Twenty-four 2½-inch tartlet pans, lined with dough, baked, and cooled, as in Guayaquils, page 231

FINISHING

Two ½-pint baskets fresh raspberries for finishing

Twenty-four 2½-inch tartlet pans

Use this recipe as a model for any little tartlets made with raw fruit. Apples, pears, and peaches will not work, however, because they will darken, even under a glaze.

Tartlets like these are a mainstay of many pastry shops in France. They are fairly easy to assemble, since the tartlet crusts and the pastry cream filling may be made in advance. Raspberries are my favorite fruit for them, though you may also use small strawberries, or slices of kiwi or mango (cut the kiwi or mango into rounds of the same diameter as the top of the tartlet). For other than red fruits, substitute apple jelly or strained apricot preserves for the raspberry jam. ***Twenty-four 2½-inch diameter tartlets***

1. To make the pastry cream, combine the milk, cream, and about half of the sugar in a medium heavy-bottomed saucepan. Bring to a boil over medium heat, whisking occasionally to dissolve the sugar. In a medium bowl, whisk the egg yolks, then whisk the remaining sugar into the yolks. Sift and whisk in the flour. When the milk mixture boils, whisk about a third of it into the yolk mixture. Return the remaining milk mixture to a boil and whisk the yolk mixture into it, continuing to whisk constantly until the cream

thickens and returns to a full boil. Allow to boil, whisking constantly, for 15 seconds. Remove from heat and whisk in the vanilla, then scrape the pastry cream into a glass bowl or stainless steel bowl. Press plastic wrap directly against the surface of the pastry cream and refrigerate it until completely cold. You may prepare the pastry cream the day before using it.

2. For the glaze, combine the jam and water in a small saucepan and place over low heat to melt. Simmer for a few minutes, or until it is no longer watery. If you prepare the glaze in advance, pour it into a small jar, cover, and refrigerate. Reheat the glaze before using. If you prepare it a few hours before you need it, just leave it in the pan and reheat it later on.

3. To assemble the tartlets, pipe or spoon the pastry cream into the tartlet crusts, leaving ¼ inch empty at the top. Arrange the raspberries on the pastry cream, gently pressing them to the pastry cream to adhere. Brush the tops of the raspberries sparingly with the glaze.

SERVING: These are a lovely tea pastry. They also work well as part of an assortment of desserts.

STORAGE: If you prepare the tartlets more than an hour or so in advance, refrigerate them, or the pastry cream may spoil.

Tartelette aux Framboise (center right) and Linzerschnitten (page 247).

Butter Tarts

1 recipe pastry dough, as in maple syrup tart, page 192

BUTTER FILLING

4 tablespoons (½ stick) unsalted butter, softened to the consistency of mayonnaise

½ cup dark brown sugar, firmly packed

1 cup light corn syrup

2 large eggs

1 teaspoon vanilla extract

One 12-cavity muffin pan, buttered

You'll probably find these Canadian tartlets similar to an American pecan pie, though without any nuts. The recipe comes from my friend Bonnie Stern, Canada's most noted food authority. She told me that this type of tart probably originated in Scotland and became popular in Canada early in the twentieth century, when corn syrup was first marketed in Canada.

Although the flavor is different, these are similar in spirit to the maple syrup tart, page 192.

Make sure that the butter is very soft, or it will not combine evenly with the other filling ingredients. ***12 individual tarts***

1. Set a rack in the lowest level of the oven and preheat to 375 degrees.
2. Remove the dough from the refrigerator and use a bench scraper or knife to cut it in thirds. Place one of the pieces on a floured surface and flour the dough. Gently press the dough with a rolling pin in close parallel strokes to soften it slightly. Roll the dough to an 8-inch square. Use a 4-inch round cutter, plain or fluted, to cut 4 rounds from the dough. Press the rounds of dough into the cavities in one of the pans as they are cut (the rounds of dough will not come all the way up to the top of the pan). Repeat with the remaining pieces of dough. Chill the tartlet crusts while preparing the filling.

3. For the filling, place the butter in a medium bowl and whisk it smooth. Whisk in the brown sugar. Whisk in the corn syrup about a third at a time, whisking smooth after each addition. Whisk in the eggs and vanilla, one at a time.

4. Pour the filling into a measuring cup and fill the tartlet shells in the pans. Leave about ¼ inch empty at the top of each tartlet.

5. Bake the tartlets until the crusts are baked through and the filling is set, about 25 minutes.

6. Cool the tartlets in the pans on racks for about 5 minutes. Run a paring knife around each cavity and lift the tartlets from the muffin pans. Cool them completely on a rack.

SERVING: Serve these with a little whipped cream on the side, or with coffee after dinner. In Canada they are more likely to be eaten as a snack, without the whipped cream.

STORAGE: Keep the tartlets loosely covered with plastic wrap at room temperature.

VARIATION

Divide ⅓ cup each raisins and coarsely chopped walnut pieces evenly among the tartlet crusts before pouring in the butter filling.

PORTUGAL

Custard Cream Tartlets
Pasteis de Nata

1/3 batch of quickest puff pastry, page 311 (prepare a whole batch of dough and reserve the rest for another use)

CUSTARD FILLING

1 cup heavy whipping cream

1/2 cup sugar

4 large eggs yolks

1 tablespoon all-purpose flour

1 teaspoon finely grated lemon zest

Twenty-four 2½-inch tartlet pans, plus a jelly-roll pan

In North America, you would be most likely to encounter these tartlets on a dim sum cart in a Chinese teahouse, though cities with Portuguese populations have bakeries that sell them. The tartlets migrated from Portugal to its former colony, Macao, near Hong Kong—thus their presence in Chinese restaurants, especially since dim sum is an essentially Hong Kong phenomenon. The real Portuguese version is made from a kind of puff pastry, rolled into a log and cut into disks. If you don't feel like making such an effort to prepare the dough, use the flaky pastry dough for the maple syrup tart on page 192 and use a round cutter to shape the crusts. ***Twenty-four 2½-inch diameter tartlets***

1. The night before you expect to bake the tartlets, or at least 8 hours before, make the crusts. Place the puff pastry on a floured work surface and flour the dough. Press the dough with a rolling pin in close parallel strokes to soften it. Roll the dough to a 12 × 12-inch square. Starting from one of the sides, roll up the dough like a jelly roll, making sure not to stretch it as you are rolling it. Refrigerate the log of dough in plastic wrap for 1 hour.

2. After the dough is firm again, remove it from the refrigerator and cut it into 24 slices, each ½ inch thick. Press a slice of dough into one of the tartlet pans using your thumbs. Make sure the dough extends about ¼ inch above the rim of the pan. Repeat with the remaining slices of dough and pans. Arrange the pans on a jelly-roll pan and cover the whole pan loosely with plastic wrap. Refrigerate the crusts for a minimum of 8 hours, preferably overnight. If you try to bake them sooner, the crusts will shrink.

3. Shortly before you intend to bake the tartlets, make the custard filling. Bring the cream and ¼ cup of the sugar to a boil in a medium saucepan over low heat, whisking occasionally to dissolve the sugar. In a bowl, whisk the egg yolks, then whisk in the remaining ¼ cup sugar and the flour. Whisk in the lemon zest. When the cream boils, whisk the cream into the yolk mixture. Return the mixture to the saucepan and cook over low heat, stirring constantly with a flat-edged wooden spatula, until the cream thickens slightly and comes to a gentle boil. Pour the filling into a clean bowl and cool it to lukewarm, stirring occasionally.

4. Set a rack in the lowest level of the oven and preheat to 400 degrees.

5. Pour the filling into a measuring cup with a lip and fill the tartlet crusts to within ¼ inch of the top.

6. Bake the tartlets until the crust is baked through and the filling is set and colored in spots (the filling will not become a uniform brown all over), about 20 minutes.

7. Cool the tartlets in the pans on a rack. Use the point of a paring knife to loosen them from the pans. As long as the filling has not overflowed, they should pop right out of the pans.

Serving: These are a perfect tea pastry, or a little something to serve with coffee after dinner.

Storage: Keep the tartlets at room temperature on the day they are baked. Wrap and refrigerate leftovers and bring them to room temperature before serving again.

AUSTRIA

Viennese Apple Slices
Muerbteig-Apfelschnitten

VIENNESE SWEET DOUGH

2½ cups all-purpose flour (spoon flour into dry-measure cup and level off)

1½ teaspoons baking powder

16 tablespoons (2 sticks) unsalted butter, softened

1 cup confectioners' sugar

2 teaspoons vanilla extract

1 tablespoon finely grated lemon zest

¼ teaspoon salt

2 large egg yolks

APPLE FILLING

3½ pounds tart apples, such as Granny Smith, peeled, cored, halved, and sliced

½ cup sugar

4 tablespoons (½ stick) unsalted butter

2 teaspoons finely grated lemon zest

½ teaspoon ground cinnamon

1 cup dark raisins

ASSEMBLY

1 cup fresh white breadcrumbs

Egg wash: 1 egg well beaten with a pinch of salt

One 9 × 13 × 2-inch pan lined with buttered foil

This is a great, easy way to serve neat individual portions of the Viennese version of apple pie. The cooked apple filling is sandwiched between two layers of *Muerbteig*—Viennese sweet dough—and baked. ***Twenty-four 3 × 1½-inch slices***

1. For the pastry dough, in a small bowl combine flour and baking powder and set aside. Combine the butter and confectioners' sugar in the bowl of an electric mixer. Place the bowl on the mixer fitted with the paddle attachment and beat on low speed until smoothly mixed. Increase the speed to medium and beat until lightened, about 3 additional minutes. Beat in the vanilla, lemon zest, and salt. Beat in the egg yolks, one at a time, and continue beating until the mixture is smooth. Stop the mixer and scrape the bowl and paddle with a large rubber spatula. On lowest speed, beat in the flour mixture. Scrape the dough onto a floured work surface and form it into a disk. Wrap the dough in

plastic and chill it until it is firm, about 1 hour. You may leave the dough in the refrigerator for up to 2 days before continuing.

2. For the apple filling, combine the apples, sugar, butter, lemon zest, and cinnamon in a large enameled iron Dutch oven or another pan with a tight-fitting lid. Stir well to mix. Place over medium heat until the apples start to sizzle. Cover the pan and cook the apples, uncovering the pan and stirring 3 or 4 times, until the apples are swimming in water, about 15 minutes. Uncover the pan, add the raisins, and let the water evaporate, stirring occasionally—but not too often, or the apple slices will break up too much. By the time the apples have cooked down, about half the slices will have disintegrated and half should remain intact, yielding a sliced apple filling bound with apple puree. Scrape the filling into a bowl and let it cool to room temperature. Cover the bowl with plastic wrap and refrigerate the filling for up to 2 days if you do not intend to bake the apple slices immediately.

3. Set a rack in the lowest level of the oven and preheat to 350 degrees.

4. Remove the dough from the refrigerator and place it on a floured surface. Flour the dough and press it with the rolling pin in close parallel strokes to soften. Form the dough into a rectangle. Use a bench scraper or knife to cut the dough into 2 equal pieces. Place one of the pieces on a floured surface and roll it into a 9 × 13-inch rectangle. Slide a cookie sheet under the dough and transfer it to the prepared pan. Slide it off the cookie sheet into the pan.

5. With a fork, pierce the dough at 1-inch intervals, then scatter the breadcrumbs on the dough. Spread the filling on the breadcrumbs, smoothing with a medium offset spatula.

6. Roll the second piece of dough the same way as the first and use a cookie sheet to slide it onto the filling. Gently press the dough into place with the palm of one hand. Be sure not to press too hard, or the top crust will not be straight and even.

7. Brush the egg wash on the crust and use a fork to trace parallel lines about 1 inch apart. Make more lines 1 inch apart, at a 45-degree angle to the first ones. Egg-wash the crust again.

8. Bake until the crust is deep golden, about 45 minutes. Cool in the pan on a rack.

9. To unmold, place a cutting board or stiff rectangular cardboard on the pan. Holding the two together, invert the pan onto the board. Remove the pan and the foil. Replace with another pan or cardboard, then invert the whole stack. Lift off the top board.

SERVING: Cut the baked pastry lengthwise into 3 strips, each 3 inches wide. Cut across every 1½ inches to make slices. Arrange the slices on a platter.

STORAGE: Keep the slices covered with plastic wrap at room temperature before and after serving.

SWITZERLAND

Linzer Slices
Linzerschnitten

LINZER DOUGH

3 cups all-purpose flour (spoon flour into dry-measure cup and level off)

1 cup (about 4 ounces) unblanched almonds, finely ground in a food processor

2/3 cup sugar

1 teaspoon baking powder

1 teaspoon ground cinnamon

1/2 teaspoon ground cloves

2 teaspoons finely grated lemon zest

16 tablespoons (2 sticks) unsalted butter, cold, cut into 16 pieces

1 large egg

1 large egg yolk

FILLING

6 ounces canned almond paste, cut into 1/2-inch cubes

1/4 cup sugar

2 tablespoons light corn syrup

2 tablespoons Kirsch

1/2 cup seedless raspberry preserves

Egg wash: 1 egg well beaten with a pinch of salt

Linzer torte is a Viennese pastry, but this Swiss version is different from the classic torte. It is made with a dough that is firm enough to be rolled out, and it includes a layer of Kirsch-scented almond paste under the traditional raspberry jam, for a truly Swiss touch. This recipe is a re-creation of one we made at the Seehotel Meierhof in Horgen, down the lake shore from Zurich, where I worked in 1973 and 1974. Unfortunately I've had to piece together the recipe from my memory of tasting it; Armand, the despotic pastry chef, never shared his recipes. ***Twenty 3½ × 1½-inch slices***

1. To make the dough, combine all the dry ingredients, the spices, and the lemon zest in the bowl of a food processor fitted with the metal blade. Pulse several times to mix. Add the butter and pulse about 10 times. Add the egg and yolk and pulse repeatedly until the dough looks evenly moistened

but does not form a ball. Invert the dough onto a floured surface and carefully remove the blade. Gently squeeze the dough together and form it into a rough cylinder. Refrigerate the dough in plastic wrap until it is firm, about 2 hours. You may leave the dough refrigerated for up to 2 days before continuing.

2. For the filling, combine the almond paste and sugar in the bowl of an electric mixer. Place the bowl on the mixer fitted with the paddle attachment and beat on medium speed until smooth. Add the corn syrup and beat smooth. Add the Kirsch, 1 tablespoon at a time, beating smooth after each addition.

3. When you are ready to assemble the slices, set a rack in the middle level of the oven and preheat to 350 degrees.

4. Remove the dough from the refrigerator and place it on a floured surface. Gently knead the dough until is smooth and malleable. Form the dough into a rectangle. Use a bench scraper or knife to cut off about a fourth of the dough. Place the larger piece of dough on a floured surface and flour it. Roll the dough to a 9 × 15-inch rectangle. Slide the dough onto a piece of parchment paper. Use a pizza wheel to cut 4½-inch strips along one of the 15-inch sides of the dough. Cut the remaining dough in half to make two 3½ × 15-inch rectangles. Slide the ½-inch strips off the paper and position the two large rectangles 4 inches away from each other. Carefully slide the paper with the dough on it to the pan. Paint the 15-inch edges of dough with water and position one of the strips on each of the 15-inch edges. Gently press the strips in place with your fingertips to avoid leaving deep indentations in the dough. If you have time, chill the tart bases until firm before continuing.

5. With a small offset spatula, evenly spread the almond paste filling between the narrow strips on the tart bases. Spread the raspberry preserves over the almond paste.

6. Roll the remaining piece of dough to a 7 × 10-inch rectangle. Use a serrated pizza wheel to cut it into 2 rectangles, each 3½ × 10 inches. Cut across the 2 rectangles of dough to make 40 strips, each ½ inch wide. Position an X of the dough strips on the filling, every 1½ inches down the length of both filled tarts, trimming the edges even with the narrow strips on the sides of the bases. Brush the dough with egg wash.

7. Bake the tarts until they are well colored and firm to the touch, about 30 to 40 minutes. Cool the tarts on the pan on a rack.

SERVING: Trim the narrow edges even and cut each tart into 1½-inch slices. Line up the slices on a platter to serve.

STORAGE: Keep the slices loosely covered with plastic wrap at room temperature before and after serving.

FRANCE

Pear Slices
Tranches aux Poires

SWEET ALMOND PASTRY DOUGH (PÂTE SUCRÉE AUX AMANDES)

½ cup (about 2 ounces) blanched almonds

⅓ cup sugar

2½ cups all-purpose flour (spoon flour into dry-measure cup and level off)

1½ teaspoons baking powder

½ teaspoon salt

10 tablespoons (1¼ sticks) unsalted butter, cold, cut into 10 pieces

2 large eggs

2 tablespoons milk or water

POACHED PEARS

2 tablespoons lemon juice

6 firm-ripe Bartlett pears, about 2½ pounds

2 cups sugar

1 whole vanilla bean, not split

ALMOND FILLING

6 ounces canned almond paste, cut into ½-inch cubes

⅓ cup sugar

3 large eggs

6 tablespoons (¾ stick) unsalted butter, softened

1 tablespoon Kirsch

1 teaspoon vanilla extract

⅓ cup all-purpose flour (spoon flour into dry-measure cup and level off)

APRICOT GLAZE

1 cup apricot preserves

2 tablespoons water

Toasted sliced almonds for finishing

One 12 × 18-inch jelly-roll pan

Fruit slices such as these made with pears are a standard in many pastry shops in France. Sometimes they are made with puff pastry, but this one is made with a tender sweet dough—a perfect complement to the melting texture of poached pears. This is an easy way of making individual tarts because you don't need any special equipment aside from a jelly-roll pan. ***12 individual tarts***

1. To make the dough, combine the almonds and sugar in the bowl of a food processor fitted with the metal blade. Pulse repeatedly to grind the almonds very fine. Scrape the inside bottom edge of the bowl with the point of a metal spatula. Add the flour, baking powder, and salt and pulse several times to mix. Add the butter and pulse about 10 times to mix the butter in finely. Add the eggs and milk and pulse repeatedly until the dough forms a ball. Invert the dough to a floured surface and carefully remove the blade. Form the dough into a cylinder. Refrigerate the dough in plastic wrap until firm, about 1 hour. You may keep the dough refrigerated for up to 2 days before continuing.

2. Half-fill with ice water a large enameled iron casserole that has a tight-fitting lid. Add the lemon juice. Peel, halve, and core the pears, one at a time, dropping the pear halves into the acidulated ice water. After all the pears are prepared, skim out the ice and add the sugar and vanilla bean. Bring the pears to a full rolling boil over medium heat and let them boil for 30 seconds. Remove the pan from the heat, cover it, and let the pears cool in the hot syrup. The heat retained by the syrup will finish cooking the pears so that they remain firm and do not become mushy. Refrigerate the pears in the syrup.

3. For the almond filling, combine the almond paste, sugar, and 1 egg in the bowl of an electric mixer. Place the bowl on the mixer fitted with the paddle attachment and beat the mixture smooth on medium speed. Add the butter and continue beating about 2 additional minutes, or until smooth. Stop the mixer and scrape down the bowl and beater with a large rubber spatula. On medium speed, add the remaining 2 eggs, one at a time, beating smooth after each addition. Beat in the Kirsch

and vanilla. Decrease the mixer speed to lowest and add the flour, mixing just until the flour is absorbed. Remove the bowl from the mixer and give the filling a final mixing with a large rubber spatula.

4. To bake the tarts, set a rack in the lowest level of the oven and preheat to 350 degrees.

5. Remove the dough from the refrigerator and place it on a floured surface. Gently knead the dough until it is smooth and malleable. Form the dough into a rectangle. Place the dough on a floured surface and flour it. Roll the dough into a 12 × 15-inch rectangle. Slide the dough onto a piece of parchment paper. Use a pizza wheel to cut 4 strips, each ¾ inch wide, along one of the 15-inch sides of the dough. Cut the remaining dough in half to make two 4½ × 15-inch rectangles. Slide the ¾-inch strips off the paper and position the two large rectangles 4 inches away from each other. Carefully slide the paper with the dough on it to the pan. Paint the 15-inch edges of dough with water and position one of the strips on each of the 15-inch edges. Gently press the strips into place with your fingertips to avoid leaving deep indentations in the dough. If you have time, chill the tart bases until firm before continuing.

6. Spread half of the almond filling on each of the 2 tart bases in the center section between the narrow strips. Remove the pear halves from their syrup and drain them on a jelly-roll pan covered with paper towels. Slice one of the pear halves lengthwise into ¼-inch slices. Fan it out slightly, pushing with the palm of your hand toward the stem end. Slide a metal spatula under a pear half and transfer it to the tart base, positioning it at one of the ends on the almond filling. Repeat with another pear half, this time arranging it in the direction opposite to the first one. Continue alternating fanned-out pear halves on the tart bases, placing 6 on each base.

7. Bake the filled tarts until the dough is baked through and the almond filling is set, about 40 minutes. Cool the tarts on the pan on a rack.

8. For the apricot glaze, stir the preserves and water together in a small saucepan. Place over low heat and bring the mixture to a simmer, stirring occasionally. Strain the glaze into a bowl and rinse out the pan. Return the glaze to the pan and bring it to a simmer over low heat. Simmer the glaze for 2 minutes, or until it is no longer watery. For advance preparation, pour into a jar, cover, and refrigerate. Bring the glaze back to a boil before applying it to the tart.

9. Reheat the glaze if necessary and use a brush to paint it on the filling, avoiding the side strips on the tart bases. If necessary, trim the long sides of the tart bases straight. Trim the short edges and cut the tart bases into separate portions between the pears. Sprinkle the sides of the tarts at the narrow ends of the pears with a pinch of the sliced almonds.

Serving: Line up the pear tarts on a platter. These are an impressive dessert for a fancy dinner.

Storage: Before and after you serve the pear tarts, keep them at room temperature, loosely tented with aluminum foil (not with plastic wrap, which would stick to the glaze).

6. SAVORY PASTRIES

SWITZERLAND	CHEESE TART FROM BASEL *Basler Kaeswaie*
SOUTH AFRICA	CAPE MALAY CURRIED BEEF TART *Bobotietaart*
FRANCE	ALSATIAN ONION TART *Tarte à l'Oignon à l'Alsacienne*
ITALY	SPINACH, HAM, AND CHEESE PIE FROM MILAN *Pizza Rustica alla Milanese*
ITALY	ZUCCHINI PIE FROM GENOA *Torta di Zucchine alla Genovese*
EGYPT	SPICY MEAT PIE IN A FILO CRUST WITH YOGURT SAUCE *Habibi Gullash Bakari*
SPAIN	FISH IN A SPANISH PIE *Tarta de Pescado*
RUSSIA	CABBAGE PIE *Pirog s Kapustoi*
ITALY	NEAPOLITAN SALTY RING BISCUITS *Taralli Napoletani*
ITALY	HAM- AND CHEESE-FILLED BRIOCHE FROM REGALEALI IN SICILY *Sformato di Formaggi Principe di Galles*
JAPAN	SALTY AND SWEET RICE AND SESAME CRACKERS *Osenbei*
AUSTRALIA	SAUSAGE ROLLS
CHINA	BARBECUED PORK BUNS *Cha Shao Bao*
MEXICO	SPICY CHICKEN TURNOVERS *Empanadas de Pollo*
ARGENTINA	BEEF-FILLED TURNOVERS *Empanadas de Carne*

Overleaf: Tarta de Pescado

THIS IS A BRANCH OF BAKING that I particularly love. I often include savory pastries in menus for entertaining, whether as hors d'oeuvres, appetizers, or main courses. Savory pies make a great addition to a buffet, and many are very much at home on a picnic.

In addition to their versatility, many savory pastries may be prepared and baked entirely in advance and served at room temperature, taking away the stress of last-minute preparation.

For the sake of simplicity in this chapter, I have called all the large savory pastries with a top crust pies, no matter what their shape. Any with just a bottom crust I have referred to as tarts, since most of them are baked in standard tart pans with fluted sides and removable bottoms.

It's important to make sure the fillings are adequately seasoned before placing them in the crust. For this reason, I have structured most of the recipes so that raw eggs are added only at the end of the filling preparation. This way, you can safely taste the filling, overseason it very slightly, then add the eggs. Although I'm not particularly squeamish about tasting something with raw eggs in it, I know that many people like to avoid raw eggs for reasons of health. Also, I find that the taste of raw egg can dominate a filling and make it difficult to get an accurate idea of the seasoning.

The smaller savory pastries at the end of the chapter all make perfect hors d'oeuvres. Some of the slightly larger ones also function well as plated appetizers. But don't exhaust yourself preparing a large selection of baked hors d'oeuvres. One or two, accompanied by a bowl of olives and maybe some salted nuts, will make an adequate presentation at the start of any party.

SWITZERLAND

Cheese Tart from Basel
Basler Kaeswaie

PASTRY DOUGH

2 cups all-purpose flour (spoon flour into dry-measure cup and level off)

1 teaspoon salt

1 teaspoon baking powder

8 tablespoons (1 stick) unsalted butter, cold, cut into 8 to 10 pieces

5 tablespoons cold water

CHEESE FILLING

1½ cups (about 4 ounces) coarsely grated Swiss Gruyère

2 tablespoons all-purpose flour

2 cups heavy whipping cream or half and half

3 large eggs

¼ teaspoon salt

One 11- or 12-inch tart pan with removable bottom

This tart, an accompanying onion tart similar to the Alsatian onion tart on page 263, and a bowl of brown flour soup form the typical carnival breakfast in Basel. In the early hours of daylight, residents and visitors congregate in all of Basel's restaurants after the predawn Morgenstreich, the official beginning of the Basler Fasnacht, or carnival celebration. It all begins on the Monday morning after Ash Wednesday, when the carnivals in Latin countries have been over since the previous week. The following recipe is based on information from my friend Erika Lieben, a native of and frequent visitor to Basel, and the recipe in a cookbook by Amalie Schneider-Schloeth called *Basler Kochschule*, or *Basel Cooking School* (11th edition, Friedrich Reinhart, no date). ***One 11- or 12-inch tart, about 8 servings***

1. Set a rack in the lowest level of the oven and preheat to 375 degrees.

2. For the dough, combine the dry ingredients in the bowl of a food processor fitted with the steel blade and pulse several times to mix. Add the butter and pulse until the butter is in ¼-inch pieces. Add the water and pulse until the dough forms a ball. Invert the dough onto a floured work surface, carefully remove the blade, and form the dough into a thick disk.

3. Flour the dough and roll it to a 14-inch disk. Fold the dough in half and transfer it to the pan, lining up the fold with the diameter of the pan. Unfold the dough into the pan and press it well against the bottom and sides. Use a bench scraper or the back of a knife to cut away any excess dough at the rim.

4. To prepare the filling, toss the cheese with the flour and distribute it evenly over the pastry crust. Whisk the remaining ingredients together and pour over the cheese.

5. Bake the tart until the crust is baked through and the filling is set and well colored, about 30 to 40 minutes.

6. Cool the tart in the pan on a rack.

SERVING: Unmold the tart and slide it off the pan base onto a platter. Serve warm or at room temperature as a first course, or as the main course of a light meal with a mixed salad.

STORAGE: Keep the tart at room temperature on the day it is baked. Wrap and refrigerate leftovers and bring to room temperature or heat briefly at 350 degrees before serving again.

SOUTH AFRICA

Cape Malay Curried Beef Tart
Bobotietaart

One 12-inch tart crust as for the cheese tart from Basel, page 258

BOBOTIE

½ cup fresh breadcrumbs, from French or Italian bread, crust removed

⅓ cup warm milk or water

3 tablespoons vegetable oil, such as sunflower or canola

1 medium onion (about 6 ounces), peeled and minced

2 garlic cloves, peeled and finely minced or grated on the microplane

1½ teaspoons salt

1 tablespoon best-quality curry powder

1½ teaspoons ground turmeric

½ teaspoon ground cloves

¾ pound lean ground beef, such as sirloin

½ cup water

2 large eggs

1 tablespoon sugar

1 tablespoon cider vinegar

1 medium (about 6 ounces) Granny Smith apple, peeled and coarsely grated

¼ cup diced dried apricots or dark raisins

¼ cup apricot preserves or sweet mango chutney

⅓ cup slivered almonds

CUSTARD TOPPING

1 large egg

⅔ cup milk, heated to lukewarm, about 120 degrees

4 fresh lemon leaves or bay leaves

The Cape Malay community is composed of the mostly Muslim descendants of inhabitants of the island of Java who were brought to Cape Town as slaves in the seventeenth century. They are not from Malaysia but were dubbed Malay because they speak the Malay language. Bobotie, a kind of baked ground beef curry covered with a custard, is a classic Cape Malay dish. It is usually presented in a gratin or some other baking dish. I tasted several versions in Cape Town, the best of which was prepared by Manuel Davids, who, along with his partner Pieter Van Straaten, hosted a complete Cape Malay dinner in my honor. There were many different curries of meat and fish and, of course, bobotie. I was already interested in bobotie and asked the assembled guests if they thought it would be bizarre presented in a tart crust; instead, they all heartily agreed that this would be a natural way to dress it up. Fortunately my Cape Town connection, Kyra Effren, was present at the party and explained that there is a sweet-sour element to the preparation. Manuel's version, with adjustments from Kyra, uses raisins or diced dried apricots and apricot preserves or sweet mango chutney as the sweet elements and a grated tart apple and a little vinegar as the sour ones. ***One 12-inch tart, about 10 servings***

1. Set a rack in the lower third of the oven and preheat to 350 degrees.
2. To prepare the bobotie, place the breadcrumbs in a small bowl and pour the warm milk or water over them. Set aside until cooled.
3. Heat the oil in a wide sauté pan and add the onion. Cook for about 5 minutes over medium heat or until the onion starts to color. Stir in the garlic and cook just for a few seconds so that the garlic doesn't burn. Stir in the salt, curry powder, turmeric, and cloves and cook for 1 minute.
4. Add the ground beef to the pan and break it up with a wooden spoon, thoroughly mixing in the onion and spice mixture as you do. Add the water and thoroughly stir it in. Simmer the mixture over low to medium heat until about half the water has evaporated, 5 to 10 minutes. Scrape the beef mixture into a large mixing bowl and allow it to cool slightly.
5. Stir the soaked breadcrumbs into the beef mixture. Stir in the remaining ingredients, in order, one at a time.
6. Scrape the bobotie mixture into the prepared crust and smooth the top. Bake until the filling has colored nicely on top and the dough is baked through, about 30 minutes.

7. To prepare the custard topping, whisk the egg and milk together. Pull the rack out of the oven with the tart on it and pour the custard mixture evenly over the meat filling. Strew the leaves over the custard and return the tart to the oven. Bake just until the custard has set, about 10 minutes.

8. Place the tart on a rack to cool slightly. Remove and discard the leaves before serving.

SERVING: The bobotie is good hot from the oven, warm, or at room temperature. Cut the tart into wedges. This is good as a first course or main course, or as one of the dishes on a buffet for a large party.

STORAGE: Keep at room temperature on the day it is made, but don't bake the tart too far in advance of serving it, as it doesn't keep indefinitely. If you want to serve the tart hot, prepare the crust and filling and bake it about 1 hour before you intend to serve it. Wrap and refrigerate leftovers and bring them to room temperature before serving again.

FRANCE

Alsatian Onion Tart
Tarte à l'Oignon à l'Alsacienne

PASTRY DOUGH

2 cups all-purpose flour (spoon flour into dry-measure cup and level off)

1 teaspoon baking powder

½ teaspoon salt

5 ounces (about ⅔ cup) leaf lard, or regular lard from the supermarket, cut into ½-inch dice and chilled, or 10 tablespoons (1¼ sticks) unsalted butter

4 tablespoons cold water

ONION FILLING

4 ounces bacon (half of an 8-ounce package), cut into ½-inch dice

2 pounds large white onions, halved, peeled, and sliced

1 cup heavy whipping cream

Salt

Freshly ground pepper

Freshly grated nutmeg

4 large eggs

One 11- or 12-inch fluted tart pan with removable bottom

Alsace is the homeland of the onion tart—a rich combination of cooked onions, bacon, and a savory custard in a crumbly crust. Tarts like this are made all over the region and are also a traditional Carnival dish in nearby Basel, in Switzerland. I like to use lard in the crust for a rich and crumbly texture, though you may substitute butter if you like. I prefer white onions for the filling because they are a little less sugary-sweet after they are cooked. ***One 11- or 12-inch tart, about 8 servings***

1. For the dough, combine the dry ingredients in the bowl of a food processor fitted with the steel blade. Pulse several times to mix. Add the lard and pulse at 1-second intervals until the lard is in pea-size pieces, about 5 to 6 pulses. Add the water and pulse again until the dough is evenly moistened but does not form a ball. Invert the dough onto a floured work

surface, carefully remove the blade, and gently squeeze and press the dough into a disk about 5 inches in diameter. Wrap in plastic and refrigerate while preparing the filling.

2. Set a rack in the lowest level of the oven and preheat to 375 degrees.

3. To prepare the filling, put the bacon dice in a large sauté pan and place the pan over low heat. Cook until the bacon has rendered its fat and the bacon pieces color nicely. Use a slotted spoon to remove the bacon to a small plate and add the onions to the pan. Cover the pan and increase the heat to medium. Cook the onions, uncovering and stirring occasionally, until they are wilted and translucent, about 10 minutes. Uncover the pan and cook until the onions are very reduced in volume and just beginning to color, about 10 additional minutes. Scrape the onions into a medium mixing bowl.

4. Stir the cream and bacon into the onions and season with the salt, pepper, and nutmeg. At this point the filling should taste slightly oversalted. Whisk the eggs in a small bowl, then stir them into the filling.

5. Remove the dough from the refrigerator and place it on a lightly floured work surface. Lightly flour the dough and gently press it with a rolling pin to soften it slightly if it has hardened. Continue pressing on the dough, using gentle parallel strokes close to each other, until it is malleable. Roll the dough to a 13- to 14-inch disk.

6. Fold the dough in half and transfer it to the pan, lining up the fold with the diameter of the pan. Unfold the dough into the pan and press it well into the bottom and sides. Use a bench scraper or the back of a knife to cut away any excess dough at the top edge.

7. Pour the filling into the pan and use a small spoon to distribute the onions and bacon gently and evenly.

8. Bake the tart until the dough is well colored and baked through and the filling is set, about 30 minutes.

9. Cool the tart in the pan on a rack.

Serving: Remove the side of the pan and slide the tart from the pan's metal base to a platter for serving. Serve in wedges, warm or at room temperature. This makes a good first course or can be accompanied by a salad to make a light meal.

Storage: Keep the tart at a cool room temperature for a few hours before serving. Wrap and refrigerate leftovers and bring them to room temperature before serving again.

VARIATION

Sometimes I use individual 4½-inch tart pans with removable bottoms to bake this, especially when I serve it as a first course. This recipe will easily make 6 to 8 tartlets, depending on the size of your pans.

Spinach, Ham, and Cheese Pie from Milan
Pizza Rustica alla Milanese

DOUGH

3½ cups all-purpose flour (spoon flour into dry-measure cup and level off)

2 teaspoons baking powder

1 teaspoon salt

16 tablespoons (2 sticks) unsalted butter, cold, cut into 20 pieces

3 large eggs

3 large egg yolks

SPINACH FILLING

2 pounds baby spinach

3 tablespoons unsalted butter

1 cup sliced yellow onion

Salt

Freshly ground black pepper

Freshly grated nutmeg

1 pound whole-milk ricotta

4 ounces (about 1 cup) parmigiano-reggiano, finely grated

6 large eggs

12 ounces boiled ham, thinly sliced

12 ounces Emmentaler (Switzerland Swiss) cheese, rind removed and sliced thin

One 12-inch round pan, 2 inches deep, buttered

In 1988, when I was in Italy doing research for my book *Great Italian Desserts*, my friend Miriam Brickman joined me for some of the travel and visits to pastry shops. We were in the Via Montenapoleone neighborhood, Milan's fashion center. I happened on Gastronomia Montenapoleone, a fancy prepared food shop, and was immediately seduced by a slice of this exquisite savory pie. My memory of it has remained so intact that I think my version is very close to the original.

If you want to save time and effort in preparing this, use the prewashed baby spinach that comes in a sealed bag; it makes the whole process much easier.

Don't be surprised at the use of boiled ham, rather than raw ham (prosciutto), and Swiss cheese in this Italian pie; both are common ingredients in Italian cooking, especially in the area around Milan. ***One 12-inch pie, about 16 servings***

1. Set a rack in the lowest level of the oven and preheat to 350 degrees.

2. For the dough, combine the dry ingredients in the bowl of a food processor fitted with the steel blade. Pulse several times to mix. Add the butter and pulse again to mix the butter in finely. Add the eggs and yolks and pulse again, until the mixture forms a ball. Empty the bowl out onto a floured work surface and carefully remove the blade. Form the dough into a thick cylinder and keep it cool, but not necessarily in the refrigerator, while preparing the filling.

3. For the filling, pour ½ inch of water into a large pan with a tight-fitting cover and bring to a boil. Add the spinach, cover, and place over high heat. Remove the cover and stir occasionally as the spinach wilts and cooks; this will take only a few minutes. Once all the spinach is cooked and reduced, drain it in a colander and let it cool enough so that you can touch it. With your hands, wring out any excess water. Place the spinach on a cutting board and chop it fine with a stainless steel knife. Set aside.

4. Melt the butter in a large sauté pan over medium heat and add the onions. Cook until the onions wilt and begin to color, about 5 minutes. Add the spinach and stir it in thoroughly with a wooden spoon. Cook to evaporate excess moisture from the spinach, about 1 to 2 minutes, then season with salt, pepper, and just a hint of nutmeg.

5. Scrape the spinach mixture into a large mixing bowl. Use a large rubber spatula to stir the ricotta into the spinach mixture. Stir in the grated cheese. Taste for seasoning at this point, before adding the eggs. The mixture should taste slightly oversalted. Stir in the eggs, 2 at a time, and set the filling aside.

6. Cut two-thirds of the dough off the cylinder and, with the palm of your hand, flatten it into a thick disk. Lightly flour the work surface and the dough and roll the dough to a large disk, about 16 inches in diameter. Fold the dough into quarters and place it in the prepared pan so that the point is in the center of the pan. Unfold the dough to line the pan, pressing it firmly against the bottom and sides. With a bench scraper or the back of a knife, trim the dough even with the top of the pan.

7. Spread a third of the spinach filling in the dough-lined pan. Arrange about half of the slices of ham on the filling, making an even layer. Repeat with about half of the slices of cheese. Spread another third of the filling over the cheese and cover with the remaining ham and cheese. Finally, spread the remaining spinach filling over the cheese.

8. Roll the remaining dough to a 12-inch disk and place it on the filling, folding and unfolding it as above. Use a table knife to detach from the pan the dough from the bottom crust at the top edge of the pan. Fold over the sides of the bottom crust that extend above the top crust. Cut 6 vent holes in the top crust with the point of a sharp knife.

9. Bake the pie until the dough is baked through and deep golden and the filling is set and firm, about 50 to 60 minutes. Cool in the pan on a rack.

SERVING: Invert the pie onto a large platter or cutting board and lift off the pan. Reinvert the pie so that the top crust is uppermost. This makes an excellent first course, or the main course of a light meal, accompanied by a tossed salad. It's also great for a picnic.

STORAGE: Keep the pie at a cool room temperature on the day it is baked. Refrigerate leftovers in plastic wrap.

VARIATIONS

I have prepared this for large parties when I wasn't sure if everyone would want to eat meat, so I just left out the ham and used a little more cheese on each layer. There was no drastic change in quality, although the ham offers a nice contrast.

You may use a 9 × 13 × 2-inch pan instead of the 12-inch round pan, or a 12 × 18 × 1-inch half sheet pan. In the half sheet pan, make only one layer of the sliced ham and cheese between halves of the filling. This is a convenient size if you want to cut the pie into small squares for hors d'oeuvres.

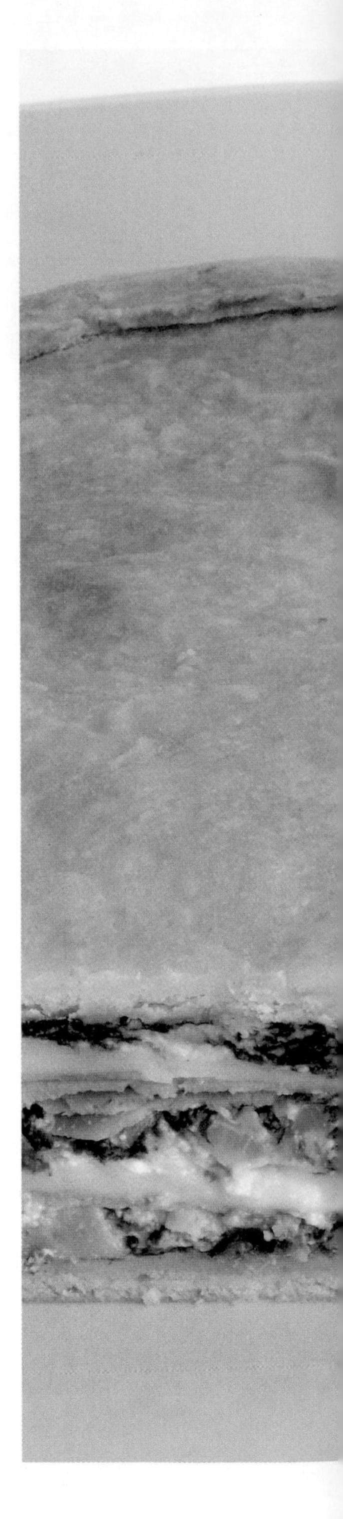

Zucchini Pie from Genoa
Torta di Zucchine alla Genovese

OLIVE OIL DOUGH

2½ cups all-purpose flour (spoon flour into dry-measure cup and level off)

1 teaspoon salt

1 teaspoon sugar

1 teaspoon baking powder

½ cup olive oil

3 large eggs

2 tablespoons water

ZUCCHINI FILLING

2½ pounds young, tender zucchini

1 teaspoon salt

½ cup arborio or long-grain rice

3 tablespoons olive oil

1 medium white or yellow onion, about 8 ounces, peeled and finely chopped

2 garlic cloves, peeled and finely chopped or grated on a microplane

1 cup (about 2 ounces) finely grated parmigiano-reggiano cheese

Salt

Freshly ground black pepper

4 large eggs

¾ cup fresh basil leaves, lightly packed

One 11- or 12-inch tart pan with removable bottom, lightly brushed with olive oil

I first tasted this delicious pie at Enrichetta Trucco in Genoa, a shop specializing in the typical savory pies of Liguria. In this type of shop, the pies are all made in large rectangular pans, then cut into slabs and sold by weight. I've adapted my re-creation to a round tart pan, which looks more appealing. ***One 11- or 12-inch pie, about 10 to 12 servings***

1. For the dough, combine the dry ingredients in the bowl of a food processor fitted with the steel blade. Pulse several times to mix. Add the oil, eggs, and water and pulse until the dough forms a ball. Invert the dough onto a floured work surface and carefully remove the blade. Form the dough into a cylinder and chill it in plastic wrap while preparing the filling.

2. For the filling, rinse the zucchini and cut away the ends. Shred the zucchini on the medium shredding disk of the food processor or grate it on the largest holes of a box grater. Put the shredded zucchini in a mixing bowl and toss it with the salt. Transfer the zucchini to a colander set over a bowl. The salt will extract the excess water, which will drain away through the holes in the colander. Let the zucchini stand for about 15 minutes, while you are cooking the rice.

3. Half fill a large saucepan with water and bring it to a boil. Salt the water lightly and stir in the rice. Return the rice to a boil and lower the heat so that the rice boils gently but does not boil over. Cook the rice until it is fully tender, about 12 minutes. Drain and cool the rice.

4. Wring out the zucchini a handful at a time to rid it of excess water. Put the oil in a wide sauté pan over medium heat. Add the onion and cook until the onion is wilted and translucent, about 5 minutes. Stir in the zucchini and cook for about 5 minutes, stirring occasionally with a wooden spoon to make sure that most of the remaining moisture has evaporated. Stir in the garlic and cook just until the scent of the garlic is apparent, about 1 minute. Scrape the cooked mixture into a mixing bowl and stir in the cooled rice.

5. Stir in the cheese and taste the filling for seasoning. The filling should taste slightly oversalted at this point. If not, add more salt. Add about 5 or 6 grindings of pepper and stir it in. Stir in the eggs, one at a time. Tear the basil leaves into ½-inch pieces and stir them in.

6. Set a rack in the lowest level of the oven and preheat to 400 degrees.

7. Unwrap the dough and use a bench scraper or a knife to cut it into 2 equal pieces. Place 1 piece cut side down on a floured work surface and press it into a disk. Flour the dough and roll it into a 14-inch disk. Roll the dough very thin, or you will not manage to line the pan and cover the pie with it. If the dough resists, cover it with a towel for 5 minutes before continuing to work with it. Fold the dough into quarters and transfer it to the pan, lining up the point with the center of the pan. Unfold the dough and press it well into the bottom and sides of the pan. Let any extra dough hang over the side of the pan. Spread the filling over the dough and smooth it with a medium offset spatula.

8. Roll the second piece of dough as you did the first and fold it in half. Brush some water on the edge of the bottom crust. Place the second disk of dough over the filling, lining up the fold with the diameter of the pan. Unfold the dough to cover the filling and press it well with your fingertips against the bottom crust, severing any excess dough at the edge as you press down. Use the point of a knife to cut several 2-inch vent holes in the top crust.

9. Bake the tart until the dough is well colored and the filling is set, about 30 minutes. Place the tart on a rack to cool.

SERVING: Unmold the tart and slide it off the metal pan base onto a platter. If necessary, you can loosen the bottom of the tart by running a long, thin knife or spatula under it between the bottom crust and the pan base. Serve the tart warm or at room temperature as a first course or as the main course of a light meal with a salad. It's also perfect for a picnic.

STORAGE: Keep the tart at room temperature for up to a few hours after it is baked before serving. Wrap and refrigerate leftovers and bring them back to room temperature before serving again.

EGYPT

Spicy Meat Pie in a Filo Crust with Yogurt Sauce
Habibi Gullash Bakari

MEAT FILLING

2 tablespoons olive oil

1 small white or yellow onion, peeled and chopped, about 1 cup

4 small garlic cloves, finely chopped or grated with a microplane

1 pound lean ground beef, such as sirloin

1 small green bell pepper, finely chopped, about 1 cup

2 tablespoons chopped hot green chili, such as a long green chili, or jalapeño

1 teaspoon salt

1 tablespoon freshly ground black pepper

¼ teaspoon ground cumin

¼ teaspoon ground coriander

½ teaspoon freshly grated nutmeg

⅛ teaspoon ground cardamom

½ teaspoon sweet Spanish paprika

FILO PASTRY CRUST

20 sheets filo dough, homemade or bought

12 tablespoons (1½ sticks) unsalted butter, melted

YOGURT SAUCE

1 quart whole-milk or low-fat (not nonfat) yogurt

2 garlic cloves, finely chopped or grated on the microplane

½ cup extra-virgin olive oil

Salt for seasoning

One 9 × 13 × 2-inch pan, generously buttered

Habibi ("darling" in Arabic) is Hong Kong's only authentic Egyptian restaurant, owned by my friends Jennifer Migliorelli and Hosni Emam, a native of Cairo. Jennifer has spent the better part of the last 20 years in Hong Kong and opened Habibi in 2000. It was an immediate success and has already branched out to a smaller café next door.

This pie is equally good hot or at room temperature. If you want to serve it hot, you may assemble the pie in advance and bake it just before serving. Make sure to drain the yogurt for the sauce the day before you intend to serve the pie. Before assembling the pie, review the instructions on working with filo dough on page 316. ***One 9 × 13 × 2-inch pie, about twenty-four 3-inch triangular servings or twelve 3-inch square servings***

1. To prepare the filling, heat the oil in a wide sauté pan over medium heat and add the onion. Cook just until the onion is beginning to color, about 5 minutes. Stir in the garlic and cook for a few seconds longer, making sure the garlic doesn't burn.

2. Use a wooden spoon to stir in and break up the ground beef. Cook for 10 minutes, continuing to break up any large lumps of the meat.

3. Stir in the bell pepper and the chili along with the seasonings. Simmer the mixture until the meat is completely cooked through, about 5 additional minutes. Scrape the mixture into a mixing bowl and cool it to room temperature. If you intend to wait longer than an hour or so to assemble the pie, cover the filling with plastic wrap and refrigerate.

4. To assemble the pie, place a filo sheet in the bottom of the prepared pan and drizzle with butter. Place another sheet on top of the first and drizzle with butter. Repeat to make a bottom crust of 10 sheets of dough.

5. Spread the meat filling evenly on the dough and top the filling with another 10 sheets of dough, drizzling butter between the layers as for the bottom crust. (Butter the top sheet.)

6. Use a sharp paring knife to cut through about half the layers of the top crust into 3-inch squares. If you intend to serve the pie as a main course, leave it in 3-inch squares. If you intend to serve smaller portions, cut across the squares in the same way to make triangles. If you do not intend to bake the pie immediately, cover and refrigerate it.

7. To make the yogurt sauce, line a strainer with wet cheesecloth or a paper towel and scrape the yogurt into it. Place the strainer over a bowl and cover loosely with plastic wrap. Refrigerate the yogurt and allow it to drain overnight. After the yogurt has drained, scrape it into the bowl of a food processor fitted with the steel blade. Add the garlic and allow the processor to run for 30 seconds. With the processor running, drizzle in the oil through the feed tube. Scrape the sauce into a bowl, whisk in salt to taste, cover it with plastic wrap, and refrigerate it until needed.

8. When you are ready to bake the pie, set a rack in the middle level of the oven and preheat to 375 degrees. Bake the pie until the dough is well baked through, about 40 minutes. Brush the top of the pie with butter or olive oil as soon as you remove it from the oven.

9. Serve the pie immediately or allow it to cool to room temperature.

SERVING: Using the markings on the top crust as your guide, cut through the filling and bottom crust with a sharp knife. Use an offset spatula or pie server to lift the triangle of pie from the pan. Place each on a plate and spoon some of the yogurt sauce next to the pastry.

STORAGE: The pie will keep at room temperature for a few hours. Wrap and refrigerate leftovers and bring them to room temperature again before serving.

SPAIN

Fish in a Spanish Pie

Tarta de Pescado

DOUGH

3 cups all-purpose flour (spoon flour into dry-measure cup and level off)

1 teaspoon salt

1 teaspoon baking powder

1/8 teaspoon ground anise (crush aniseed to a powder in a spice grinder or mortar and pestle if you cannot buy ground anise)

1/2 cup olive oil

2 large eggs

1/2 cup water

2 tablespoons brandy

FISH FILLING

2 large skinless trout fillets or fillets of another delicate freshwater or saltwater fish, about 24 ounces total

Olive oil for brushing the fish

Salt

Freshly grated nutmeg

3/4 cup whole hazelnuts, roasted, skinned, and coarsely crushed

3/4 cup dark raisins

Egg wash: 1 egg well beaten with a pinch of salt

1 cookie sheet or jelly-roll pan lined with parchment or foil

This intriguing recipe doesn't come from a Spanish source at all, though it is very Spanish in flavor and spirit. I first read about it in the *Alice B. Toklas Cookbook* (Doubleday Anchor, 1960). The name is the one Miss Toklas gave to the recipe, and I have prepared it often with great success. Gertrude Stein and Alice B. Toklas traveled extensively in Spain in the early years of the twentieth century and became enamored of the country. Miss Toklas wrote that her recipe was a modified version of yet another recipe, one given to her by a French friend. To make the pie more delicate and easier to serve, I like to use two large, or several small, skinless fish fillets, as opposed to the whole fish in the original recipe. ***About 4 main-course servings, more if served as an appetizer***

1. About 1 hour before you intend to assemble the pie, prepare the dough. Put the dry ingredients in the bowl of a food processor fitted with the steel blade. Pulse several times to mix.

Add all the remaining ingredients and pulse repeatedly until the dough forms a ball. Invert the dough onto a floured surface and carefully remove the blade. Shape the dough into a rough rectangle and wrap in plastic. Refrigerate for about 1 hour.

2. To assemble the pie, cut the dough into 2 equal pieces. Place half the dough on a floured surface and flour it lightly. Roll the dough to a rectangle about 2 to 3 inches larger all around than one of the fish fillets. Place the rectangle of dough on the prepared pan. Arrange 1 fillet on it skinned side down so that there is an equal amount of dough surrounding the fillet in all directions.

3. Brush the fish fillet with olive oil and season it with salt and nutmeg. Mix the hazelnuts and raisins together and scatter them over the fillet.

4. Brush the interior side of the second fillet with oil and season it like the first one. Place this fillet skinned side up on top of the nuts and raisins and brush and season the top of the fillet. Brush egg wash on the dough all around the fish.

5. Roll the second piece of dough slightly larger all around than the first piece and place it over the fish. With your fingertips, press the layers of dough together. Use a pizza wheel to cut the assembled pie into a fish shape, trying to stay at least 1 inch or so away from the fish in all directions so that the pie doesn't open during baking. Remove any excess dough.

6. Paint the pie all over with egg wash and use the point of a spoon to mark a gill about a quarter of the way down from the head, making a curved line from top to bottom. Press the point of the spoon into the head to make an eye and outline a mouth on the head with another curved line. Use the point of the spoon to mark scales all over the body of the fish. (Don't worry if you pierce the dough. The holes will allow steam to escape while the pie is baking.) Egg-wash the pie again and then refrigerate it until about 1 hour before you intend to serve it, and as long as half a day.

7. When you are ready to bake the pie, set a rack in the lower third of the oven and preheat to 375 degrees. Bake the pie until the crust is well colored and baked through and the fish is cooked through, about 35 to 40 minutes. The fish should reach an internal temperature of about 135 to 140 degrees on an instant-read thermometer.

8. Slide the pie onto a platter and serve it immediately.

Serving: Cut the pie into large rectangular slices. A cucumber salad is a nice accompaniment.

Storage: Wrap leftovers in plastic and refrigerate them. Bring leftovers to room temperature before serving again. Finish any leftovers within a day or so, as fish is very perishable.

RUSSIA

Cabbage Pie

Pirog s Kapustoi

BREAD DOUGH CRUST

1 cup warm water, about 110 degrees

2½ teaspoons active dry yeast

3 cups unbleached all-purpose flour (spoon flour into dry-measure cup and level off)

1 teaspoon salt

3 tablespoons unsalted butter, melted and cooled

CABBAGE FILLING

1½ pounds green cabbage, cored and finely shredded

½ teaspoon salt

2 tablespoons unsalted butter

2 teaspoons sugar

2 hard-cooked eggs, chopped (see Note)

1 cookie sheet or jelly-roll pan covered with parchment or foil

One of my oldest and dearest friends, Sandy Leonard, who lives in Watertown, Massachusetts, loves to cook and bake. He got this recipe from his friend Larissa Erokhin, who grew up in Moscow and now also lives in Massachusetts. It's a very simple pie with a filling of gently cooked cabbage and hard-cooked eggs, just the thing for a winter supper. The recipe below uses a yeast-risen dough as the crust, but you may also substitute the dough from the fish in a Spanish pie (page 276), minus the anise. ***One 10-inch pie, about 8 to 10 servings***

1. For the dough, pour the water into the bowl of an electric mixer and whisk in the yeast by hand. Add the flour, salt, and butter and stir together with a large rubber spatula. Place the dough on the mixer fitted with the dough hook and mix for 2 minutes on lowest speed. Stop the mixer and allow the dough to rest for 10 minutes.

2. Mix the dough on medium speed until it is smooth and elastic, about 3 to 4 minutes. Scrape the dough into a buttered bowl and turn it over so that the top is buttered. Cover with plastic wrap and let the dough rise at room temperature until it has doubled in bulk, about 1 hour.

3. While the dough is rising, prepare the filling. Toss the cabbage with the salt in a mixing bowl and wring out handfuls of it to rid it of excess moisture.

4. Melt the butter in a wide sauté pan and add the cabbage and sugar. Cook over medium heat for about 10 minutes, stirring occasionally with a wooden spoon, until the cabbage is wilted and somewhat reduced. Scrape the cabbage into a bowl and let it cool slightly. After the cabbage has cooled, gently fold in the chopped eggs with a rubber spatula.

5. Set a rack in the lower third of the oven and preheat to 400 degrees.

6. Scrape the dough from the bowl to a floured work surface and press it into a rough oval. Use a knife or bench scraper to cut the dough into 2 equal pieces. Avoid handling the dough too much or folding it over on itself, or it will be too elastic to roll.

7. Place 1 piece of dough on a floured work surface and lightly flour it. Roll the dough to a 10-inch disk. If the dough resists, cover it with a towel and let it rest for 5 minutes, then roll again. Fold the dough in half and transfer it to the prepared pan. Unfold the dough and press it into an even 10-inch disk.

8. Spread the filling on the dough, leaving a 1-inch border on all sides.

9. Roll the second piece of dough to a 10-inch disk, as above. Brush the edge of the bottom crust with water. Fold the top crust in half and arrange it over the filling. Unfold the dough and press the edge of the top and bottom crusts together. Fold the crusts together about ½ inch toward the center of the pie, pressing hard with your fingertips or the tines of a fork to seal.

10. Cut four or five 2-inch vent holes in the top crust and brush with water all over. Note that the dough does not rise again before baking.

11. Bake the pie until the crust is baked through and well colored, about 30 minutes.

12. Slide the pie off the pan onto a rack to cool.

NOTE: For perfect hard-cooked eggs, place the eggs in a saucepan of cold water and cook over low to medium heat until the water boils. Cook the eggs for 7 minutes from the time the water boils. Drain the eggs and immerse them in a bowl of cold water, gently cracking the shells against the side of the bowl. Leave the eggs in the water for about 5 minutes, then peel them. Refrigerate the peeled eggs in plastic wrap until they are cold.

SERVING: Slide the pie from the rack to a platter and cut it into wedges. Serve it with some sour cream on the side.

STORAGE: The pie can be kept at room temperature for a few hours between baking and serving. Wrap and refrigerate leftovers. Bring them to room temperature before serving again.

Neapolitan Salty Ring Biscuits
Taralli Napoletani

3/4 cup warm water, about 110 degrees

2 1/2 teaspoons active dry yeast

1/4 cup olive oil

3 cups unbleached all-purpose flour (spoon flour into dry-measure cup and level off)

2 teaspoons salt

1 tablespoon fennel seeds

1 teaspoon coarsely ground black pepper

2 large rectangular cooling racks, turned upside down and lightly oiled

In southern Italy, taralli come in all sizes and flavors. There are large ones, made from a dough that consists of nothing more than flour and eggs with seasonings; sweet ones, both large and small; Apulian taralli made from a dough moistened with white wine; and the typical Neapolitan ones sometimes referred to in Neapolitan dialect as scaldatelli—little boiled things. Like bagels, many, though not all, taralli are given a quick bath in boiling water before baking. It produces a nice sheen on the outside and stiffens them slightly. When we made these at home when I was a child, we baked them directly on the oven racks, a risky procedure because some always fell to the bottom of the oven or onto the floor while the racks were being pulled in and out of the oven. Nowadays, I bake them on an upside-down cooling rack. They bake just as they would on the oven rack but are much easier to handle. ***About 30 taralli***

1. For the dough, pour the water into a small bowl and whisk in the yeast. Whisk in the oil.

2. Put the remaining ingredients in the bowl of a food processor fitted with the steel blade. Pulse several times to mix. Add the liquid and pulse again until the dough forms a ball. Let the processor run continuously for about 10 seconds to knead the dough.

3. Invert the dough to an oiled bowl and carefully remove the blade. Turn the dough over so that the top is oiled, and cover the bowl with plastic wrap. Let the dough rise at room temperature until it doubles in bulk, about 1 hour.

4. After the dough has risen, scrape it out of the bowl to a lightly floured work surface and use a bench scraper or knife to cut it into 2 equal pieces. Roll each piece of dough under the palms of your hand to a 6-inch cylinder. Cut each cylinder of dough into 3 equal pieces, to make 6 pieces in all. Roll one of the cylinders to a 5-inch length and cut it into five 1-inch pieces. Repeat with the remaining pieces of dough to make 30 equal pieces in all.

5. One at a time, roll each piece of dough under the palms of your hands to make an 8-inch strand. Join the ends together to make a circle, pressing firmly to seal. Line up the formed taralli on a lightly floured work surface or floured jelly-roll pans, making sure they do not touch each other.

6. Set racks in the upper and lower thirds of the oven and preheat to 375 degrees.

7. Fill a large pot (such as one in which you would cook pasta) three-fourths full of water. Bring the water to a full rolling boil. Set one of the oiled cooling racks on the stovetop (put a pan under it to catch drips) next to the pan of boiling water. Drop the taralli, 6 or 8 at a time, into the boiling water and remove them with a skimmer as soon as they float to the surface. Arrange the taralli, about 1 inch apart in all directions, on the prepared rack. Repeat until all of the taralli have been boiled and arranged on the racks.

8. Bake the taralli until they are golden and crisp, about 30 minutes. About halfway through baking, move the rack from the upper third of the oven to the lower third, and the rack from the lower third to the upper third. Cool the taralli on the racks they baked on.

Serving: The traditional accompaniment to taralli is a glass of wine. You may serve them as hors d'oeuvres or as a snack.

Storage: After the taralli have cooled completely, store them in a tin or plastic container with a tight-fitting cover. They last indefinitely.

ITALY

Ham- and Cheese-Filled Brioche from Regaleali in Sicily

Sformato di Formaggi Principe di Galles

BRIOCHE DOUGH

½ cup milk

4 teaspoons active dry yeast

3⅓ cups unbleached all-purpose flour (spoon flour into dry-measure cup and level off)

8 tablespoons (1 stick) unsalted butter, softened

2 tablespoons sugar

1 teaspoon salt

4 large eggs

FILLING

3 cups (12 ounces) of a mixture of Gruyère, Edam, Gouda, and Fontina cheeses, cut into ½-inch dice

¾ cup (4 ounces) boiled ham, cut into ½-inch dice

1 cup green peas, fresh or frozen, brought to a boil, cooked for 3 minutes, and drained

Egg wash: 1 egg well beaten with a pinch of salt

One 10-inch springform pan, buttered

Anna Tasca Lanza is an old friend whose family's ancestral home is the Regaleali wine estate near Caltanisetta in central Sicily. For many years the family's estate has had a remarkable chef, Mario Lo Menzo, one of the last of a breed thoroughly trained in elaborate French-based cooking, who are called *monzù* (a corruption of the French *monsieur*). The monzù tradition began early in the nineteenth century, when many French chefs migrated to Naples and Sicily to work for noble houses there. By and by, the French chefs trained Italian assistants in their craft, so that later generations of monzù were native Italians. Chef Lo Menzo is one of the last living monzù, and he continued to prepare elegant meals at Regaleali, where Anna teaches cooking classes several times a year, until his recent retirement.

The recipe here is a standard in the monzù's repertoire, and he bakes it often for important occasions at the estate. The Italian name of the dish refers to the fact that he once prepared it for Charles, the prince of Wales, who, Anna says, "raved about it."

Even though this recipe is the creation of a brilliant chef, it is not particularly difficult to make. I have streamlined it even further with an easy brioche dough prepared in the food processor. Make sure the dough is chilled enough, or it will be difficult to press into the pan. ***One 10-inch pie, about 16 servings***

1. For the brioche dough, put the milk in a small saucepan and place over low heat. Bring the milk to a lukewarm temperature, about 110 degrees. Make sure not to overheat the milk, or the yeast will die and not leaven the dough. Remove the milk from the heat and pour it into a small mixing bowl, then whisk in the yeast. Stir in 1 cup of the flour and cover the bowl with plastic wrap. Set aside to rise slightly while preparing the other ingredients.

2. Put the butter, sugar, and salt in the bowl of a food processor fitted with the metal blade. Pulse to mix. Add the eggs and pulse again to mix. The mixture may appear somewhat curdled, but that doesn't matter. Scrape the yeast mixture into the bowl and pulse again to mix the yeast mixture thoroughly into the butter and egg mixture.

3. Remove the steel blade and scrape off any dough sticking to it. Ease the plastic blade into place and add the remaining 2⅓ cups flour. Pulse repeatedly until the dough is evenly mixed. Let the food processor run for 10 seconds to give the dough a final kneading.

4. Invert the dough into a buttered bowl. Scrape the inside of the bowl with a rubber spatula and add any dough clinging there to the dough in the buttered bowl. Remove the blade if it is stuck in the dough and cover the bowl with plastic wrap. Refrigerate the dough for a minimum of 1 hour, though it can stay in the refrigerator as long as overnight to chill.

5. Once the dough has chilled, scrape it from the bowl to a lightly floured work surface. Use a bench scraper or a knife to cut off two-thirds of the dough. Press the dough into a disk and flour it. Roll the dough to a 14-inch disk. Fold the dough into quarters and place it in the pan so that the point lines up with the center of the pan. Unfold the dough and press it well into the bottom and sides of the pan. Let any extra dough hang over the edge of the pan. Mix the cheeses, ham, and peas together and scrape them into the prepared crust.

6. Press the remaining dough into a disk on a floured work surface and flour the dough. Roll it to a 10-inch disk and arrange it in the pan on top of the filling. Brush the egg wash on the top crust and trim the overhanging dough to an even ½-inch length. Evenly fold the overhanging dough over the top crust all around.

7. Cover the pan with buttered plastic wrap or a towel and let it rise at room temperature until the pie fills the pan to the top, about 2 hours. The rising time will depend on the room temperature: the dough will rise more quickly if the room is warm.

8. About 15 minutes before the pie has fully risen, set a rack in the middle level of the oven and preheat to 350 degrees.

9. Bake the pie until the dough is completely baked through, about 1 hour. Cool the pie thoroughly on a rack so that the melted cheese filling sets.

Serving: Remove the side of the springform pan and slide the pie from the pan base onto a platter. Serve in small wedges as a first course.

Storage: Keep the pie at room temperature on the day it is baked. Keep leftovers, in plastic wrap, at a cool room temperature.

JAPAN

Salty and Sweet Rice and Sesame Crackers

Osenbei

½ cup uncooked Japanese sushi rice or other short-grained rice, such as Arborio

1 teaspoon salt, plus more for seasoning the dough

4 teaspoons white sesame seeds, lightly toasted

2 tablespoons black sesame seeds

¼ cup soy sauce

¼ cup mirin

2 cookie sheets or jelly-roll pans lined with lightly oiled parchment or foil

This recipe comes from my friend Reiko Akehi, a correspondent for Japanese food magazines who is based in New York. These are really simple to prepare—you just beat up some cooked rice with seasonings and roll out the resulting dough between sheets of plastic wrap (it's sticky), then dry the crackers before baking. The drying is the most important part of the recipe: If the crackers have not dried completely before they are baked, they will not remain flat or become properly crisp. The final salty-sweet brushing with soy sauce and mirin, sweet Japanese cooking wine, gives the crackers a not overpowering, very pleasant salty-sweet flavor. See Sources on page 363 for Japanese ingredients. ***About twenty 3-inch crackers, depending on the size of the cutter***

1. To cook the rice, bring a large pot of water to a boil. At the boil, stir in the rice and salt. Adjust heat so that the water is at a low boil, to keep it from boiling over. Cook for 15 minutes, or until the rice is slightly overcooked. Drain the rice, but do not rinse it. Spread the rice out on a large plate or a jelly-roll pan covered with plastic wrap and allow it to cool.

2. After the rice has cooled, put it in the bowl of an electric mixer and stir in the white and black sesame seeds. Taste the rice. It should be quite salty, much more so than for normal use. Stir in more salt as needed.

3. Put the bowl on the mixer fitted with the paddle attachment and mix on low to medium speed until the dough is quite sticky, about 2 to 3 minutes.

4. Stretch a length of plastic wrap out on a work surface and spread the rice on it. Top with another piece of plastic wrap and gently roll over the rice with a rolling pin until it is a little less than ⅛ inch thick. Carefully pull away the top piece of plastic wrap and discard it. Use a plain 2- to 3-inch cutter to cut out the crackers. As you cut each cracker, use a wide spatula to transfer it to one of the prepared pans. Press any scraps together, roll them again between fresh sheets of plastic wrap, and cut additional crackers. Repeat until you have used up all the dough. Let the crackers dry at room temperature for 24 hours.

5. When you are ready to bake the crackers, set racks in the upper and lower thirds of the oven and preheat to 300 degrees.

6. Bake the crackers for 20 minutes. Then remove the pans from the oven and use a metal spatula to turn each cracker over. Return the pans to the oven. Bake until the crackers are dry and crisp, about 20 additional minutes.

7. Immediately after you remove the crackers from the oven, stir together the soy sauce and mirin and brush the mixture on the crackers. Let the crackers dry completely.

SERVING: These are good at any time but are best with a drink before dinner.

STORAGE: Keep the crackers in a tin or plastic container with a tight-fitting cover. If the crackers become limp, bake them again at 300 degrees until they are crisp, about 10 minutes.

AUSTRALIA

Sausage Rolls

1 batch quickest puff pastry, page 311

SAUSAGE FILLING

8 ounces white bread, crusts removed, diced, about 3 cups

2/3 cup milk, scalded

12 ounces ground pork

12 ounces ground veal

2 cups (about 10 ounces) white onions, minced

1/3 cup Dijon mustard

2 tablespoons fresh rosemary, finely chopped

Salt

Freshly ground black pepper

Egg wash: 1 egg well beaten with a pinch of salt

1 jelly-roll pan lined with parchment or foil

During my first trip to Australia, I visited a great bakery café in Melbourne called Babka. When my friend Maureen McKeon and I had lunch there, I had to taste the sausage rolls. They were light and delicate and surrounded by a buttery puff pastry, and they were truly excellent. This recipe was shared by Sasha Lewis, the owner of Babka, and her son Niko, who is the head baker there. They start out with fresh ground pork and veal, with seasonings added—the right way to make these rolls. If you like, you may substitute ground beef for the pork, but the flavor will not be the same. ***Nine 6-inch sausage rolls***

1. Place the dough on a floured surface and lightly flour it. Roll the dough to an 18-inch square. Trim the edges even if necessary. Slide the dough onto a cookie sheet or the back of a jelly-roll pan, cover it with plastic wrap, and chill it while preparing the sausage mixture.

2. For the sausage mixture, soak the bread in the milk until it is completely absorbed, then gently squeeze out the excess milk. Combine the remaining sausage ingredients in a large bowl and stir well to mix. Stir in the soaked bread and season with salt and pepper.

3. To taste the mixture for seasoning, make a small, thin patty and cook it quickly on both sides in very little oil in a small sauté pan. Cool slightly and taste. Add more seasoning to the raw mixture if necessary.

4. Remove the dough from the refrigerator and slide it onto a lightly floured work surface. Use a pizza wheel to cut the dough into 3 strips, each 6 × 18 inches. Paint the right side of the 18-inch side of each strip of the dough with a ½-inch-wide strip of egg wash. Put the sausage filling into a pastry bag with no tube and a 1-inch opening at the end and pipe the sausage filling into a straight 1-inch-diameter cylinder the length of the strip of dough on the long end opposite the egg wash. Repeat with the remaining strips of dough and remaining filling.

5. Roll the strips of dough up like a jelly roll, but not too tightly, from the sausage sides, to make 3 cylinders, each 18 inches long. Roll the filled pieces of dough onto a cookie sheet, seam side down, and cover them with plastic wrap. Refrigerate for at least 30 minutes, or up to several hours. You may keep the uncut rolls in the refrigerator for most of the day, but they should be baked on the day you make the filling and form them.

6. When you are ready to bake the sausage rolls, set a rack in the middle level of the oven and preheat to 375 degrees.

7. Remove the rolls from the refrigerator and cut each into three 6-inch lengths. Arrange the pieces, seam sides down, on the prepared pan and paint the outside of each with the egg wash. With the point of a paring knife, cut three ½-inch diagonal slashes in the top of each sausage roll.

8. Bake the sausage rolls until the dough is a very dark golden color, about 30 minutes.

SERVING: Serve the sausage rolls immediately with a tossed salad or a hot green vegetable.

STORAGE: Wrap and refrigerate leftovers. Reheat in a 375-degree oven or in a toaster oven before serving again.

CHINA

Barbecued Pork Buns

Cha Shao Bao

CHINESE ROAST PORK

2½ pounds boneless Boston pork butt

4 garlic cloves, coarsely chopped

½ teaspoon Chinese five-spice powder

½ cup honey

½ cup hoisin sauce

2 tablespoons black soy sauce

4 tablespoons soy sauce

¼ cup ketchup

¼ cup Chinese rice wine or dry California sherry

2 tablespoons oil, such as corn, canola, or peanut

BUN FILLING

2 tablespoons oil

1 medium (about 8 ounces) white onion, peeled, halved, and chopped

2½ cups Chinese roast pork, above, cut into ¼-inch dice

2 tablespoons chicken stock or water

3 tablespoons soy sauce

2 teaspoons sugar

¼ teaspoon freshly ground pepper

⅓ cup finely sliced scallions, both white and green parts

2 tablespoons cornstarch dissolved in 3 tablespoons chicken stock or water

BUN DOUGH

¾ cup milk

2½ teaspoons active dry yeast

5 tablespoons unsalted butter, melted and cooled

1 large egg

4 teaspoons sugar

½ teaspoon salt

3 cups unbleached all-purpose flour (spoon flour into dry-measure cup and level off)

Egg wash: 1 egg well beaten with a pinch of salt

1 roasting pan and a cooling rack slightly larger than the pan

2 cookie sheets or jelly-roll pans lined with parchment or foil for baking the buns

I'm always happy when these appear on a dim sum cart in a teahouse, and I knew I wanted to include them here, though my skill in Chinese cooking is mostly limited to eating it. So I called on my longtime friend Norman Weinstein, a gifted teacher of Chinese cooking, and these are the result. The recipe is also loosely based on one in Florence Lin's *Complete Book of Chinese Noodles, Dumplings, and Breads* (Quill Paperback, 1986).

I've given a full recipe for these, including the preparation of the roast pork. If you live near a Chinese restaurant that has good roast pork, by all means buy some for the recipe. If you don't like pork, skinned and boned chicken thighs make an adequate, though not perfect, substitute. ***Sixteen 3-inch buns***

1. To prepare the roast pork, cut the meat into slices 1½ inches thick. Then cut across the slices every 1 to 1½ inches to make long strips. Place the meat in a rectangular glass pan or stainless steel pan that will hold it in one layer. Set the meat aside while preparing the marinade.

2. To prepare the marinade, in a small bowl combine all remaining ingredients and stir well to mix. Pour over the meat and stir the meat around in the marinade so that all the meat is well moistened with it. Cover the pan with plastic wrap and let the meat marinate for 3 to 6 hours at a cool room temperature or in the refrigerator.

3. To roast the pork, set a rack in the middle level of the oven and preheat to 375 degrees.

4. Pour about 1 inch of warm water into the roasting pan and balance the rack on top of the roasting pan. Lift the pieces of pork from the marinade and arrange them on the rack. Roast the pork for about 1 hour, basting 2 to 3 times with the remaining marinade and turning the pieces several times. Remove the pan from the oven and place the rack over a jelly-roll pan. Cool the pork to room temperature. If you are roasting the pork in advance, refrigerate it in plastic wrap before continuing. Cold pork is easier to dice.

5. To prepare the filling, heat the oil in a large sauté pan or wok and add the onion. Cook over low to medium heat for about 5 minutes, or until the onion is softened. Stir in the diced pork and chicken stock and simmer 1 minute. Add all the

remaining ingredients except the scallions and dissolved cornstarch and stir well to mix. Push the filling aside to expose some of the pan bottom and add the cornstarch mixture. Stir constantly until it thickens slightly, then stir the thickened cornstarch evenly into the filling. Cook, stirring, 1 minute longer, then stir in the scallions. Scrape the filling into a glass or stainless steel bowl and cool it to room temperature. For advance preparation, cover the bowl with plastic wrap and refrigerate it for up to a day before continuing.

6. To prepare the dough, in a small saucepan over low heat, heat the milk until it is lukewarm (about 110 degrees). Remove the pan from the heat and pour the milk into a medium bowl. Whisk in the yeast, followed by the butter. Whisk in the egg with the sugar and salt.

7. Place the flour in the bowl of a food processor fitted with the steel blade. Add the yeast and egg mixture, scraping it in with a rubber spatula. Pulse until the dough forms a very soft ball. Let the processor run continuously for 10 seconds to knead the dough.

8. Invert the dough into a buttered bowl and carefully remove the blade. Turn the dough over so that the top is buttered, and cover the bowl with plastic wrap. Let the dough rise at room temperature until it has doubled in bulk, about 1 hour.

9. To form the buns, scrape the dough onto a floured work surface and use a bench scraper or knife to cut it in half. Roll each piece of dough under the palms of your hands to an 8-inch cylinder. Cut each cylinder of dough into eight 1-inch pieces.

10. Place one of the pieces of dough on a lightly floured work surface and press and roll it to a 3-inch disk. Place a heaping tablespoon of the filling in the center and draw the sides of the disk of dough up all around the filling to meet in the center, enclosing the filling. Firmly pinch the seam closed and invert the bun, seam side down, onto one of the prepared pans. Repeat with the remaining dough and filling.

11. Cover the buns with oiled plastic wrap or a towel and let them rise at room temperature until they almost double in bulk, about 30 minutes.

12. About 15 minutes before the buns are completely risen, set racks in the upper and lower thirds of the oven and preheat to 350 degrees.
13. Immediately before baking the buns, carefully brush them with the egg wash.
14. Bake the buns until they are a deep golden color, about 20 to 25 minutes. Switch the pan from the upper rack to the lower one, and the pan from the lower rack to the upper one, about midway through the baking.
15. Cool the buns on a rack.

SERVING: These are perfect for a snack or picnic and also good for brunch or buffet.

STORAGE: Keep the buns at room temperature on the day they are baked. Wrap and freeze for longer storage. Before serving again, defrost the buns and reheat them at 350 degrees for about 10 minutes, then cool them.

MEXICO

Spicy Chicken Turnovers
Empanadas de Pollo

EMPANADA DOUGH

4 cups all-purpose flour (spoon flour into dry-measure cup and level off)

1 teaspoon salt

8 ounces (about 1 cup) leaf lard or other lard, cut into ½-inch dice and chilled, plus ⅓ cup melted lard for painting the dough

3 large eggs

3 large egg yolks

2 tablespoons water

POACHED CHICKEN

1½ pounds chicken thighs

1 medium (about 3 ounces) carrot, peeled

½ small (about 2 ounces) white onion (save the rest for the filling)

2 sprigs flat-leaf parsley or cilantro

1 teaspoon salt

CHICKEN FILLING

2 tablespoons vegetable oil, such as corn or canola

½ small (about 2 ounces) white onion, finely chopped

2 Serrano peppers or other small hot peppers, finely chopped, see Note

1 cup (about 8 ounces) fresh, ripe tomato, peeled, seeded, and chopped; or 1 cup well-drained, seeded, chopped canned tomatoes

1 teaspoon salt

¼ teaspoon freshly ground black pepper

2 tablespoons sugar for sprinkling the empanadas after baking, optional

2 cookie sheets or jelly-roll pans lined with parchment or foil

I remember buying Diana Kennedy's miraculous book *The Cuisines of Mexico* (Harper and Row, 1972) and reading it in a single sitting on a train ride back from Boston in the early 1970s. Later on, I was fortunate to meet Diana, attend her classes, and taste her delicious, authentic Mexican cooking on numerous occasions when she visited the old Peter Kump's New York Cooking School. This recipe is partly based on one of hers from *Recipes from the Regional Cooks of Mexico* (Harper and Row, 1978).

Sprinkling the savory empanadas with sugar after they have been baked might seem strange at first, but it is an essential part of the flavor of these pastries. Of course, you can make them without the sugar, but then they're not the real thing. ***About twenty-four 4-inch semicircular turnovers***

1. To prepare the dough, place the flour and salt in the bowl of a food processor fitted with the steel blade and pulse several times to mix. Add 4 tablespoons of the lard and pulse about 10 times to mix the lard in evenly. Add the remaining lard and pulse 2 times only. In a small bowl whisk the eggs, yolks, and water together thoroughly. Add egg mixture to the bowl. Pulse only until the dough forms large clumps, 3 to 4 times. (Do not continue to pulse until the dough forms a ball, or the lard will be mixed in too much.)

2. Invert the dough onto a floured work surface and carefully remove the blade. Press the dough together, gently squeezing it. Flour the dough and press it into a rough rectangle. Roll the dough (have a long, thin spatula or knife handy to run under the dough if it sticks to the work surface) to a rectangle about 12 × 18 inches. Paint the dough with about half the melted lard and fold it in thirds, folding one of the 12-inch ends in over the center third and folding the other 12-inch side over it, to form a 3-layered package that is 6 × 12 inches.

3. Flour the work surface and the dough and roll it again to 12 × 18 inches. (If the dough has become very soft, slide it onto a cookie sheet, cover it with plastic wrap, and refrigerate for 30 minutes.) Paint the dough with the remaining lard and roll it up like a jelly roll, from one of the 12-inch ends, to make a fairly tight cylinder of dough about 12 inches long and about 2 inches in diameter. Refrigerate the dough in plastic wrap while preparing the filling. You may wait until the next day to use the dough.

4. To poach the chicken, put it into a large Dutch oven and add the carrot, onion, and parsley or cilantro. Cover with cold water and bring to a boil over medium heat, skimming the foam that rises to the surface as it accumulates. When the water

reaches a boil, lower the heat so it just simmers gently in one corner of the pan. Add the salt. Cook the chicken until it is almost cooked through, about 15 minutes. Remove the pan from the heat, remove and dice the carrot, and let the chicken cool in the liquid. When the chicken is cold, skin it and remove the bones. Chill the chicken in the liquid if you are not going to make the filling immediately.

5. To prepare the filling, heat the oil in a medium sauté pan and add the onion and hot peppers. Cook over medium to low heat until the onion is limp and translucent. Add the tomato and continue to cook until the tomato has rendered its water and the water has evaporated. Drain and dice the chicken and gently stir it in along with the diced carrot and the seasonings and cook for 1 additional minute. Taste the filling and stir in more salt and pepper if necessary. Scrape the filling into a bowl and cool it to room temperature. If you are not going to assemble the empanadas immediately, cover the bowl with plastic wrap and refrigerate the filling.

6. Before you begin to assemble the empanadas, set racks in the upper and lower thirds of the oven and preheat to 400 degrees.

7. Remove the dough from the refrigerator and cut it into 24 slices, each ½ inch thick. Keep most of the slices of dough refrigerated on a cookie sheet while you are assembling the empanadas, or the dough will soften and become difficult to work with.

8. Place 1 piece of dough, cut side down, on a floured work surface. Lightly flour the dough and press it into a disk with the palm of your hand. Roll the dough to an even 4-inch disk. Use a plate or a cardboard pattern to trim the dough to a 4-inch round. Place a heaping tablespoon of the filling on the bottom half of the disk of dough. Moisten the bottom circumference of the dough with water and fold the top half over the filling so that it meets the other edge. Use your fingertips or the end of the tines of a fork to seal the 2 layers of dough together firmly. Arrange on one of the prepared pans, placing 12 empanadas on each pan. Repeat with the remaining dough and filling.

9. Bake the empanadas until they are a deep golden color, about 20 to 25 minutes. Remove them from the oven and sprinkle evenly with the sugar. Cool the empanadas on the pans for 10 minutes. Be careful in removing the empanadas from the baking pans (use a spatula); they are very fragile.

NOTE: If you want the filling to be spicy, chop the chiles seeds and all. For less heat, scrape away the seeds and veins inside the chiles.

SERVING: Serve as an hors d'oeuvre with drinks or as a first course.

STORAGE: Serve the empanadas immediately after they are baked, or chill them covered with plastic wrap before baking, but bake them on the day they are assembled. Wrap and refrigerate leftovers and reheat on a cookie sheet in a 350-degree oven before serving again.

ARGENTINA

Beef-Filled Turnovers
Empanadas de Carne

EMPANADA DOUGH

4 cups all-purpose flour (spoon flour into dry-measure cup and level off)

3 teaspoons baking powder

3 teaspoons salt

12 tablespoons (1½ sticks) unsalted butter, softened

1 egg yolk

Cold water

BEEF FILLING

3 tablespoons vegetable oil

1 large white onion (about 12 ounces), finely chopped

1 pound ground chuck

1 bunch scallions, white and half the green part, thinly sliced, about ¾ cup

1 teaspoon salt

¼ cup sugar

1 teaspoon ground cumin, optional

1 tablespoon aji molido or sweet Spanish paprika

¾ cup pitted Spanish green olives

½ cup dark raisins

5 large eggs, hard-cooked and chopped (see Note on page 281)

SUGAR SYRUP FOR SEALING THE EMPANADAS

¾ cup water

2 tablespoons sugar

1½ quarts vegetable oil, such as corn or canola, for frying the empanadas

2 jelly-roll pans lined with paper towels

Ana Rambaldi is one of the most gifted home cooks and bakers I know. She often stays up half the night preparing her specialties, such as these empanadas from her native Argentina. All but one of the ingredients are easy to find wherever you shop. The filling is flavored with an Argentine type of crushed red pepper that is not hot, called aji molido, or ground pepper. Ana says you can substitute sweet Spanish paprika, but the taste will not be exactly the same. In typical South American fashion, the meat filling here is sweetened with sugar. Most Americans would probably prefer less sugar or none at all—the choice is up to you.

This recipe makes a lot of empanadas. Ana stacks up the disks of dough between squares of parchment paper, wraps the package in a double layer of plastic wrap, and freezes it. When she wants to make some empanadas from the frozen dough, she separates as many pieces of dough as she needs from the package and places them individually on the countertop. They defrost in a few seconds. I don't recommend freezing the filling, but there is no reason you can't prepare half a batch if you want to make fewer empanadas.

Make sure to review the instructions for deep-frying on page 343, before proceeding.

Thirty-two 5-inch semicircular turnovers

1. To prepare the dough, mix all the dry ingredients in a large bowl and rub in the butter, rubbing the flour and butter between the palms of your hands and scooping down to the bottom of the bowl to bring up any unmixed flour. With a fork, beat the egg yolk in a 1-cup liquid measure and fill it up with cold tap water to make 1 cup. Stir the liquid into the dough with a large rubber spatula, continuing to stir until the dough is evenly moistened and is in large clumps. If there is any dry flour left in the bottom of the bowl, push the dough aside and moisten the dry flour with a few more drops of water.

2. Knead the dough on a lightly floured work surface until it is smooth and elastic, about 5 minutes.

3. Alternatively, to mix the dough by machine, perform step 1 in the bowl of an electric mixer. Place the dough on the mixer fitted with the dough hook and mix on lowest speed for about 2 minutes. Stop the mixer and let the dough rest for 10 minutes. Mix again on medium speed until the dough is smooth and elastic, about 2 minutes.

4. Chill the dough in plastic wrap for 1 hour.

5. Remove the dough from the refrigerator and use a knife or bench scraper to cut it in half. Return one half of the dough to the refrigerator.

6. Place the other half of the dough on a floured surface and lightly flour it. Roll the dough to a 20-inch square. Fold the dough into thirds, from the right and left side inward over the center. Fold the top third down over the center and the bottom up

over the center. Wrap and refrigerate the dough and repeat the rolling and folding with the second piece of dough. Wrap and chill the second piece of dough and refrigerate both for about 1 hour.

7. To prepare the filling, heat the oil over medium heat in a large sauté pan and add the onion. Cook, stirring occasionally, until the onion is limp and translucent, about 4 to 5 minutes. Stir in the ground beef with a wooden spoon and break up any lumps with the spoon. Cook the beef until it is no longer raw-looking, or until any accumulated water in the pan evaporates and the beef is sizzling, about 10 minutes. Scrape the beef mixture into a large mixing bowl and stir in the remaining ingredients, one at a time. Taste the filling for seasoning and add more salt if necessary. Cover the bowl and refrigerate the filling until you are ready to form the empanadas. The filling will keep well for up to 3 days.

8. To prepare the sugar syrup, bring the water and sugar to a boil in a small saucepan, stirring a couple of times to make sure the sugar has dissolved. Cool the syrup and store it in a covered jar in the refrigerator until you are ready to use it.

9. To form the empanada crusts, remove 1 piece of dough from the refrigerator and place it on a floured surface. Flour the dough and roll it to a 20-inch square. Use a plate or a cardboard pattern as a guide to cut the dough into 5-inch disks. Repeat with the second piece of dough. Wrap and freeze any crusts you don't intend to use immediately (see headnote). Reserve any scraps of dough for another use, such as the one suggested on page 361. The dough recipe makes enough disks of dough for all the filling, so the scraps don't need to be rerolled to make empanadas.

10. To fill the empanadas, place 2 tablespoons of the filling on the lower half of 1 disk of dough. Use a brush or fingertip to moisten the edge of the dough with the sugar syrup. Fold the dough over to cover the filling and meet the other end of the crust. Press firmly with fingertips to seal the 2 layers of dough together. Starting at one side of the edge, make a small fold about ¼ inch deep from the outside of the empanada toward the center, or seal by pressing hard with the tines of a fork, as in the illustrations on the next page. Continue making little folds until you reach the other end of the semicircular side of the empanada. Repeat with the remaining crusts and filling.

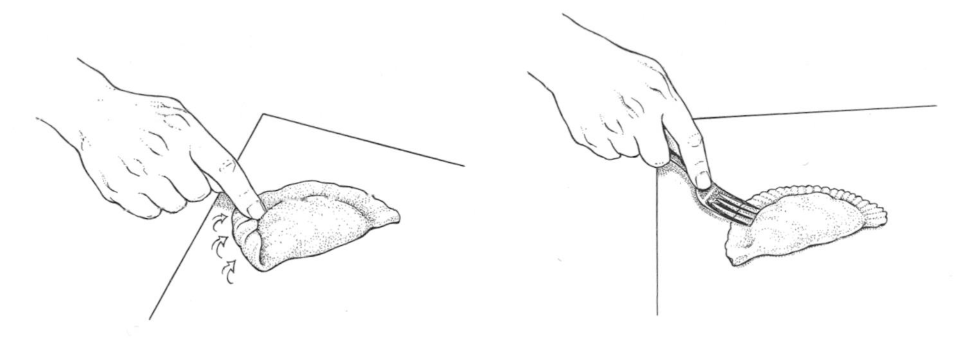

11. To fry the empanadas, heat the oil in a large Dutch oven to 375 degrees. Fry 3 or 4 empanadas at a time. As they are fried, drain them on one of the prepared pans. Repeat with the remaining empanadas, making sure that the oil does not start to foam and boil over.

12. When you are finished with the frying, cover the pan and move it off the hot burner. Leave the oil to cool completely before discarding it or saving it to fry more empanadas later on. If you intend to keep the oil, strain it into a jar, cover tightly, and refrigerate.

Serving: Serve the empanadas as soon as they are fried. These are perfect for a very informal or family occasion, when your guests can be in the kitchen with you and enjoy the empanadas piping hot.

Storage: Fill and fry only as many empanadas as you need at any given time. See instructions above for freezing the crusts. The filling will keep for several days tightly wrapped and refrigerated.

7. PUFF PASTRY, STRUDEL, AND FILO DOUGH

FRANCE	TRADITIONAL PUFF PASTRY *Pâte Feuilletée*
	QUICKEST PUFF PASTRY
AUSTRIA	STRUDEL DOUGH *Strudelteig*
GREECE	FILO DOUGH *Zimi Gia Filo*
FRANCE	APPLE GRILL TART *Grille aux Pommes*
FRANCE	THREE KINGS PUFF PASTRY CAKE *Galette des Rois*
MONACO	PUFF PASTRY CAKE WITH LIGHTENED PASTRY CREAM FILLING *Prince Albert*
SWITZERLAND	PUFF PASTRY DIAMONDS *Diamanten*
AUSTRIA	VIENNESE APPLE STRUDEL *Wiener Apfelstrudel*
AUSTRIA	VIENNESE CHEESE STRUDEL *Wiener Topfenstrudel*
GREECE	FILO PIE WITH SEMOLINA-THICKENED CREAM FILLING *Galaktoboureko*
EGYPT	CREAM- AND NUT-FILLED PASTRY *Habibi Baklava*
SYRIA	SWEET CHEESE PURSES *Sh'eab-Ee-Yat*
RHODES	SEPHARDIC BAKLAVA *Trigonas*

Overleaf: Wiener Apfelstrudel

SHATTERINGLY CRISP FLAKY PASTRIES have universal appeal. What can equal the combination of delicate puff pastry layers and a smooth cream filling in a mile-feuille or Napoleon? Strudels tend to be more tender, with their outer leaves flaky and the inner leaves moist and tender from contact with the filling. Most filo pastries, even those soaked with flavored syrup after baking, retain some crispness, providing the bit of crunch that everyone loves. In this chapter there are recipes for all three types of dough.

The two puff pastry recipes here give you options, since one ("quickest puff pastry") is extremely quick and easy to prepare while the other ("traditional puff pastry") uses the more time-consuming classic method. Each has its merits, and even if you don't have the time for the classic preparation, you can whip up a batch of "quickest puff pastry" in about 15 minutes from start to finish. This eliminates the need to use commercially prepared puff pastry, some of which has no butter in it at all.

Strudel dough is magic, pure and simple. The first time you make a traditional hand-pulled strudel and see a lifeless mass of dough pulled more than paper-thin, you'll be amazed—not only because the dough is actually transparent, but also because it was so easy to do.

Filo dough is usually bought commercially prepared, though I do give a recipe for making it yourself if you have the time and inclination to do so. Filo is stretched to transparent thinness in single small sheets, rather than into a large sheet of dough as strudel is.

All the recipes in this chapter have show-stopping results. They'll be greeted by all who taste them with disbelief that you made them yourself—something we bakers delight in.

FRANCE

Traditional Puff Pastry
Pâte Feuilletée

DOUGH

3 cups unbleached all-purpose flour (spoon flour into dry-measure cup and level off)

2/3 cup cake flour, not self-rising

8 tablespoons (1 stick) unsalted butter, softened, cut into 8 pieces

1 1/2 teaspoons salt

1 cup cold water, plus more if necessary

BUTTER BLOCK

1/3 cup unbleached all-purpose flour (spoon flour into dry-measure cup and level off)

1 pound (4 sticks) unsalted butter, cold

Known technically as a laminated dough, and with a French name that means "leaved" or "leafy," puff pastry takes layers of butter and alternates them with layers of dough. The puff happens when the butter melts and is absorbed by the dough and the steam generated by the evaporation of the water in the dough pushes the layers apart.

Traditional French puff pastry is somewhat more complicated than the following recipe, but not really difficult. First you make a dough with flour, a small amount of butter, water, and salt. After that, you soften the remaining large quantity of butter with a little flour to prevent it from melting on contact with your hands. Both dough and butter are shaped into a square, the dough being larger than the butter. The dough is then wrapped around the butter, and you flatten the package and roll it into a large rectangle. Then you fold and roll the package repeatedly to increase the number of layers of dough and butter alternating in the dough.

Remember one word when you make or use puff pastry: cold. Preparing or trying to use this dough in a warm room will be a nightmare, because the dough is 40 percent butter. In most cases you will chill the dough after it has been rolled as well so that it cuts evenly. If the dough is soft, its top and bottom layers will fuse together, and you won't be able to see the delicate leafing or separation of the layers of dough on the side of your baked pastry.

This recipe does have a lot of steps, all of which you need to complete exactly in order to achieve the almost miraculous result of the layers rising and separating from each other as the dough is baking. The first time you make puff pastry, leave enough time to study the steps and thoroughly understand what you are doing while preparing the dough. It takes a bit of effort, but the results are more than worth it. You'll be rewarded with dough that is beautiful in appearance, pleasing in texture, and with a fine buttery flavor after baking. ***About 2½ pounds of dough***

1. To make the dough, sift the flours together into a large mixing bowl. Rub the butter finely into the flour so that no lumps of butter remain but the mixture stays cool and powdery. Stir the salt into the water and mix well to dissolve it completely.

2. Make a well in the center of the flour and add the salted water. Use a large rubber spatula to mix the water into the dough, without pressing on it. Fold it in, much the same way as you might fold egg whites into a batter. The dough will form several large ropy-looking curds and will not be smooth. Use the spatula to push the moistened pieces of dough to one side and see if there are any unmoistened bits of flour in the bottom of the bowl. If there are, add drops of water to moisten them. Don't try to press the dough together into a smooth mass, or it will become too elastic to roll later on. Cover the bowl of dough with plastic wrap or a towel and set aside while preparing the butter.

3. To make the butter block, scatter about half the flour on the work surface and place the butter on it. Scatter the rest of the flour on the butter. Gently pound the butter with a rolling pin to soften it and make it malleable. Use your hands to squeeze the butter and flour together and form it into a square about 1 inch thick. Pressing against the sides of the mass of butter with a bench scraper helps to make flat, even sides. Scrape any bits off the work surface and place them on the block of butter. Set the butter aside.

4. Flour the work surface and scrape the dough from the bowl onto it. Use the palms of your hands to press the dough into a square. Lightly flour the dough and roll the 4 corners of the square to about a third of their original thickness into 4 flaps, about 3 inches long, leaving an unrolled square of dough in the middle. Press on the unrolled square of dough if necessary to make it the same size as the block of butter. Place the block of butter on the dough, positioning it so that the corners are between the flaps.

5. Fold the flaps of dough over the square of butter to enclose it without stretching them. If you see any butter between the flaps of dough, pinch the dough together to cover the butter.

6. Flour the work surface and the dough and butter and gently press the dough, beginning with the end closest to you, with a rolling pin in close parallel strokes to lengthen it into a rectangle about ⅜ inch thick. Check to see that there is enough flour underneath and on the dough and roll over it once away from you without rolling over the end. Roll back toward you once. The dough should now be about ¼ inch thick. Adjust the corners of the dough to make them into true 90-degree angles, then fold both short ends of dough into the middle, leaving a ½-inch space. Fold it in half at the middle to make 4 layers of dough.

7. Flour the work surface and the dough, and position the dough on the work surface so that the folded, closed end of the dough is on the left. Press and roll as in step 6, rolling once or twice also in the width, to make a sheet that is about 9 × 18 inches. Fold the dough again as in step 6.

8. Wrap the dough in plastic and refrigerate it for at least 2 hours or as long as overnight before continuing.

9. When you are ready to complete the rolling and folding of the dough, remove it from the refrigerator and unwrap it. Let it soften for about 10 minutes before you start to press and roll again. Repeat step 6 twice more, making sure to roll out in the width so that the package of dough doesn't become too narrow.

10. Refrigerate the dough in plastic wrap for at least 4 hours or as long as overnight before using it.

Storage: You may keep the dough refrigerated for up to 2 days before using it. For longer storage, double-wrap and freeze the dough after it has rested for at least 4 hours in the refrigerator. Defrost the dough in the refrigerator overnight before using it.

Quickest Puff Pastry

¾ cup cold water

1½ teaspoons salt

3 cups unbleached all-purpose flour (spoon flour into dry-measure cup and level off)

1 pound (4 sticks) unsalted butter, cold, cut into ½-inch cubes

This is the best way to prepare the dough easily and quickly. It's really a machine-made version of quick puff pastry: large cubes, as opposed to a single block, of butter are incorporated into the dough to create the layers that will later puff apart. After you've prepared this dough once or twice, you'll be able to go from start to finish in about 15 minutes—maybe a world record for puff pastry production.

Quickest puff pastry works like this: Large pieces of butter are embedded in a dough made from flour, water, salt, and a little extra butter. Incorporating this small amount of butter into the dough before introducing the large pieces of butter helps to make a slightly less elastic dough that is easier to roll out. After the large pieces of butter are added, the dough is rolled out into a sheet. The sheet is folded in three, then rolled up from the end and pressed into a square—one-step puff pastry. The layers are fairly uneven compared with those in the previous recipe, but the dough rises and becomes delicate and flaky nonetheless. Traditional puff pastry rises higher, but none of the recipes in this chapter call for a toweringly high rise from the dough, so you're safe with either. Make sure everything is cold. Don't attempt this recipe if the kitchen is warm, or the dough will turn to unmanageable goo. (Most recipes call for chilling the dough after it has been rolled so it cuts evenly and doesn't distort during baking.)

The only other precaution regards pulsing the pieces of butter into the flour in the food processor. Be careful to follow the directions. Pulse only 2 or 3 times before and after adding the water, or the butter will be incorporated too finely and not form the desired layers in the dough. ***About 2½ pounds of dough***

1. Combine the water and salt in a measuring cup or small bowl and stir well to dissolve the salt completely. Set aside.

2. Place the flour in the bowl of a food processor fitted with the metal blade. Add a fourth of the butter and pulse repeatedly to mix in finely. Add the remaining butter and pulse just until it is distributed in the flour mixture, 2 or 3 times.

3. Add the salted water and pulse 2 or 3 times again. The dough will not form a ball.

4. Invert the dough onto a floured work surface and carefully remove the blade. Lightly flour the dough and form it into a rough rectangle.

5. Gently roll the dough, making sure there is always enough flour between the work surface and the dough to prevent it from sticking, until it is a rectangle about 15 × 24 inches.

6. Fold the top long edge over the middle section, and then fold the bottom edge over that to make 3 equal layers, as in the illustration. Roll the dough up like a jelly roll from one of the short edges. Use the palm of your hand to flatten the rolled dough into a rectangular shape, about 6 × 10 inches and about 1 inch thick.

7. Refrigerate the dough in plastic wrap until it is firm, at least 2 hours. It is then ready to use in any of the recipes that call for it.

STORAGE: You may keep the dough in the refrigerator for up to 2 days before using it. If you are preparing the dough longer in advance, double-wrap and freeze it. Defrost the dough in the refrigerator overnight before using.

AUSTRIA

Strudel Dough
Strudelteig

DOUGH

3 cups unbleached all-purpose flour (spoon flour into dry-measure cup and level off)

½ teaspoon salt

2 large eggs

1 tablespoon vegetable oil, such as canola or corn

Warm water

STRETCHING THE DOUGH

Flour for the cloth and the dough

Oil for painting the dough

12 tablespoons (1½ sticks) unsalted butter, melted

⅓ cup dry breadcrumbs

1 cloth or clean sheet to cover a table whose top is at least 2 × 4 feet and no more than 2½ × 6 feet

Most Viennese strudels use this dough. Technically known as gezogenem, or pulled strudel, this dough will stretch to many square feet of transparent thinness. I like to prepare the dough by hand; the warmth of human hands makes the dough respond better than when it is prepared by machine. The kneading is easy—it's just a repeated slapping of the dough against the work surface to develop a strong structure of gluten, which enables the paper-thin pulling later on. After it has been kneaded, strudel dough must rest at least 1 hour so that the elasticity of the gluten relaxes. Two hours is even better.

After the instructions for preparing the dough, you will find instructions for pulling it—the starting point for any of the strudel recipes in this chapter. Remember always to prepare the filling first so that you may fill and roll the strudel soon after the dough is pulled. If it waits more than a few minutes, it may dry out and become brittle, breaking apart when the strudel is rolled.

Unlike puff pastry, strudel dough likes a warm atmosphere to be pulled to its transparent thinness. If the room is cool, don't worry—you needn't raise the heat or try any makeshift methods for raising the temperature. Patience is the most important thing in preparing strudel. You need to wait until the dough has rested before trying to stretch it. If the dough should resist while you are stretching it, stop and wait for a few minutes so that the dough can relax and be stretched again. Don't try to rush the process, or you'll wind up with strudel dough riddled with holes and tears.

The dough here makes enough for 2 strudels. The large yield of both dough and finished strudels is appropriate to the amount of work it takes to prepare them. Remember to remove your rings, wristwatch, and bracelets before stretching the dough—they may break through the dough and tear it. ***About 1½ pounds of dough, enough to make two 16-inch-long strudels***

1. In a medium bowl, stir the flour and salt together with a large rubber spatula. In a 2-cup measuring cup, mix with a fork the eggs, the oil, and enough warm water to make 1¼ cups liquid, 10 fluid ounces, total.

2. Use the rubber spatula to stir the liquid into the flour, continuing to stir until the flour is evenly moistened and forms a shaggy dough.

3. Scrape the dough out onto a lightly floured work surface and press it together with your hands. The dough will become sticky, but don't add any extra flour to it. Begin kneading the dough by lifting it with your left hand and smacking it against the work surface. Detach the dough from the work surface with a bench scraper and fold it over on itself. Grasp the dough from the open side at the bottom left of the fold and repeat. You'll need to slap the dough this way 100 times, stopping after every 10 strokes to knead the dough. The whole process takes only a few minutes—just don't lose count.

4. At the end of the slapping and kneading process, the dough will have become smooth and elastic. Oil a small bowl and put the dough into it, turning it over so that the top is also oiled. Press plastic wrap directly against the surface of the dough. Let the dough rest at room temperature about 2 hours before trying to stretch it.

5. Before you start to stretch the dough, make sure your filling is ready. Cover the table with the cloth and scatter flour on it. Rub the flour into the cloth with the palm of your hand. Put some extra flour in the center of the cloth and scrape the dough onto it. Do not fold the dough over on itself as you remove it from the bowl. Flour the

dough and roll over it in all directions to make it a disk about 12 inches in diameter. Paint the rolled dough all over the top surface with oil to prevent the dough from drying out.

6. Make both hands into a fist and slide them, knuckles up, directly under the center of the dough. Gently stretch the dough over the backs of your hands, pulling them apart from each other in all directions from the center of the dough. If the dough resists, let it rest for a few minutes.

7. Once the dough is about 50 percent larger than it was when you started, begin stretching it to the shape of the table: slide your fists under the dough and gently pull in one direction. As the dough becomes thinner, its color will lighten, so you'll need to concentrate on the darker areas for more pulling. As soon as the dough is large enough, anchor it over the corners of the table on one side. Continue gently pulling and stretching the dough until it covers the entire table, anchoring it over opposite edges of the table as soon as you can.

8. Pull on any dough hanging over the edge of the table to make it longer and thinner. You might not need this extra dough, but it will be useful if you need to patch any tears or holes in the larger piece of dough. Use scissors to cut away excess dough overhanging the table.

9. Let the dough dry for about 5 minutes. Then drizzle the butter all over the surface, using a brush. Scatter the breadcrumbs evenly all over the dough. The dough is now ready to be filled and rolled.

GREECE

Filo Dough
Zimi Gia Filo

4¼ cups unbleached all-purpose flour (spoon flour into dry-measure cup and level off)

2 teaspoons salt

3 tablespoons mild olive oil, not extra-virgin

1½ cups warm water

1 jelly-roll pan

Though excellent industrially made filo dough is available, many Greek and Middle Eastern households make their own; and while store-bought dough will do a perfectly good job in any of these recipes (and they include instructions for using the packaged kind), I did want to include a recipe so that you will know how the dough is prepared.

Made in much the same way as strudel dough, filo dough is stretched into individual small sheets, rather than one large sheet. Although I almost always prepare strudel dough by hand, I like to use the food processor for filo dough. Machine mixing makes the dough somewhat more elastic than hand mixing does, and I find that this enables the dough to be pulled more efficiently. Also, the strong motor kneads the dough more efficiently than you can knead it by hand.

As with strudel, make sure your filling is ready before you start stretching the dough, or it may become dry and brittle before you can shape your pastries. Carefully follow the directions for stacking the dough between sheets of foil so that it doesn't dry out. When you are about to use the dough, keep the top layer of foil on the stack of dough and cover the entire stack with a damp towel. You don't want the damp cloth to touch the dough directly, however, so always leave a layer of foil on top of the stack. If you are using industrially made filo, do the same thing. Unwrap the sheets of dough, cover them with foil, then cover the foil with a damp towel to prevent the sheets of dough from drying out while you are working with them. ***About sixteen 12-inch square sheets of dough***

1. Combine the flour and salt in the bowl of a food processor fitted with the plastic blade. Pulse several times to mix. Add the oil and pulse several times again to mix it evenly.

2. Add the water to the bowl and pulse repeatedly until the dough forms a ball. Let the dough rest in the bowl for 5 minutes. Turn the food processor back on and mix the dough for 15 seconds. Stop the machine and let the dough rest for 5 minutes.

3. Mix the dough again for 15 seconds. Invert the dough onto a floured surface and remove the blade. Lightly flour the dough and form it into a thick sausage shape, rolling it under the palms of your hands. Use a bench scraper or a knife to cut the dough into 16 equal pieces.

4. Round each piece of dough under the palm of your hand, as in the illustration on page 13. Use your hands to lightly oil the outside of each piece. Wrap each piece individually in plastic. Line up the pieces of dough on the jelly-roll pan and let them rest for 2 hours.

5. After the dough has rested, unwrap 1 piece of dough and place it on a floured work surface. Lightly flour the dough and roll it as thin as possible, rolling over the ends too. Pick up the piece of dough and stretch it into a square, a little larger than 12 inches on each side, gently pulling the dough from the center outward. Set the dough back down and trim away the thick edges with a sharp pizza wheel.

6. Cover the jelly-roll pan with foil and scatter some flour on it. Place the pieces of stretched dough on the floured foil and lightly flour the dough. Immediately top with another piece of foil. Repeat with the remaining pieces of dough, flouring the foil and the dough as you are stacking up the sheets. You can't use parchment paper between the pieces, because the paper absorbs moisture from the dough and causes it to dry out.

7. After you have finished stretching all the pieces of dough, flour the last piece and cover it with a sheet of foil. Wrap the whole pan in plastic and keep the dough at room temperature until you intend to use it.

8. When you use the dough to prepare one of the pastries in this chapter, use a soft, dry pastry brush to sweep away excess flour from the dough before buttering it.

Storage: You may keep the dough in the refrigerator overnight before using it. Unlike industrially made filo dough, this does not freeze well.

FRANCE

Apple Grill Tart
Grille aux Pommes

1/3 batch traditional puff pastry, page 308; or quickest puff pastry, page 311

APPLE FILLING

2 tablespoons lemon juice

8 large (about 4 pounds) Granny Smith apples

1/4 cup sugar

2 tablespoons light corn syrup

CARAMEL SAUCE

1 cup sugar

1 teaspoon water

3/4 cup heavy whipping cream, scalded

2 large cookie sheets, one lined with parchment paper and one floured

This is loosely based on a recipe from Alain Passard's restaurant L'Arpège in Paris. My friend Jeffrey Steingarten, the food critic for *Vogue*, visited this restaurant and watched the staff prepare the tart for a story he was doing, then shared the recipe with me. It is an intriguing and not particularly difficult recipe. A lattice or grill of thin strips of puff pastry is topped with shredded apples. After the initial baking, the tart is flipped over so that the lattice is uppermost, and it is finished off and served like this. ***One 12-inch tart, about 12 servings***

1. Place the dough on a floured surface and flour it. Press the dough to soften it, and roll it to a 12-inch square. Slide the dough to the floured cookie sheet and refrigerate it while preparing the apples.

2. Fill a large bowl with cold water and add the lemon juice. Use a food processor fitted with the fine or medium grating blade to grate the apples. Add them to the acidulated water. Allow the apples to stand in the water while you are preparing the crust.

3. Remove the dough from the refrigerator and, leaving it on the cookie sheet, trim it to an even 12-inch disk, using a platter or cardboard disk as a guide. Use a ruler to cut the disk of dough into strips 1/4 inch wide. Remove alternate strips and set them aside, in order, to the right of the cookie sheet. Replace the removed strips, again in order,

perpendicular to the ones on the pan and 1/4 inch apart to form a lattice. Try not to stretch the strips of dough as you are lifting them. Chill the lattice until it is firm.

4. Set a rack in the upper third of the oven and preheat to 400 degrees.

5. Remove the lattice from the refrigerator and cover it with a sheet of buttered parchment paper, buttered side down. Cover the paper with the other cookie sheet, invert the stack, and remove the top cookie sheet.

6. A small handful at a time, squeeze out the soaked apples and arrange the shredded apples evenly all over the prepared lattice. Sprinkle evenly with the sugar.

7. Bake the tart until the dough is quite firm, about 20 minutes.

8. Cool the tart slightly, then cover the apple filling with a sheet of buttered parchment, buttered side down. Cover with a cookie sheet, invert again, and remove the top pan and paper. The lattice is now uppermost on the tart. Paint the dough with the corn syrup and return the tart to the oven. Bake until the dough is baked through and well glazed, about 10 to 15 additional minutes.

9. Cool the tart on the pan on a rack.

10. While the tart is cooling, prepare the caramel sauce. Combine the sugar and water in a medium heavy-bottom saucepan and stir well to mix. Place over medium heat and cook until the sugar begins to melt and caramelize. Stir occasionally with a metal kitchen spoon so that the sugar caramelizes evenly. As soon as the sugar is a light amber caramel, remove it from the heat and add the heated cream, a little at a time, being careful that the sauce doesn't boil over from adding the cream too quickly. As soon as all the cream has been added, bring the sauce to a boil. Then cool it to room temperature.

Serving: Slide the tart from the pan to a platter to serve it. Cut the tart into wedges and serve with some of the caramel sauce on the side.

Storage: Keep the tart at room temperature on the day it is made. To serve leftovers, reheat both tart and sauce and cool to room temperature before serving again.

FRANCE

Three Kings Puff Pastry Cake
Galette des Rois

2/3 batch quickest puff pastry, page 308; or traditional French puff pastry, page 311

ALMOND FILLING

6 ounces canned almond paste, cut into 1/2-inch cubes

1/3 cup sugar

3 large eggs

6 tablespoons (3/4 stick) unsalted butter, softened

1 tablespoon Kirsch

1 teaspoon vanilla extract

1/3 cup unbleached all-purpose flour (spoon flour into dry-measure cup and level off)

1 whole unblanched almond, optional

Egg wash: 1 egg well beaten with a pinch of salt

1 cookie sheet or jelly-roll pan lined with parchment or foil

There is a difference between gâteau des rois, or "kings cake," and galette des rois. The gâteau is usually made from a sweet yeast-risen dough, but the galette is made from puff pastry, sometimes a puff pastry enriched with milk at the initial mixing. The recipe here uses an almond filling and is a traditional Parisian galette. The Feast of the Three Kings, celebrated on January 6, commemorates the arrival of the Magi bearing gifts for the newborn Christ. In many countries, it is the day on which gifts for the Christmas season are exchanged.

The French custom is fun: a bean or *fève* (usually a tiny heat-resistant plastic statuette of a cartoon or historical character) is hidden in the cake. When you buy a gâteau or galette des rois at a pastry shop, you also get a gold paper crown. The person who finds the *fève* in his or her portion is the "king" for the evening. If the party is in a restaurant, the king buys a round of drinks. In a home, the king's responsibility is to provide a gâteau or galette for the next gathering. In some parts of France the tradition starts right after Christmas and continues until the end of January. I like to use a whole almond as the *fève*—it's easy to spot and won't break any teeth if accidentally chewed.

This recipe will give you the kind of scraps of dough you can use to make the diamonds on page 326. ***One 12-inch round cake***

1. Place the dough on a floured surface and lightly flour it. Gently press the dough with a rolling pin to soften it. Roll the dough to a 12 × 18-inch rectangle. Cut the dough into 2 rectangles, each 9 × 12 inches. Roll each to a 12-inch square. Slide the squares of dough onto cookie sheets and refrigerate them while preparing the filling.

2. For the almond filling, in the bowl of an electric mixer combine the almond paste, sugar, and 1 egg. Place the bowl on the mixer fitted with the paddle attachment and beat on medium speed until smooth. Add the butter and continue beating until the butter is smoothly incorporated, about 2 minutes. Stop the mixer and scrape down the bowl and beater with a large rubber spatula. On medium speed again, add the remaining 2 eggs, one at a time, beating smooth after each addition. Beat in the Kirsch and vanilla. Decrease the mixer speed to lowest and add the flour, mixing only until the flour is absorbed. Remove the bowl from the mixer and give the filling a final mixing with a large rubber spatula.

3. Set a rack in the lower third of the oven and preheat to 350 degrees.

4. Remove 1 square of dough from the refrigerator and place it on the prepared pan. Put a plate or another 12-inch round pattern, such as a cake cardboard, on the dough and cut the dough into a 12-inch disk, using a sharp pizza wheel. Remove and reserve the scraps of dough for another use. Spread the almond filling over the dough, leaving a 1½-inch border without almond paste around the perimeter. Add the whole almond if you are using it.

5. Cut the other square of dough into a 12-inch disk. Paint the edge of the dough around the filling with the egg wash and place the other disk of dough over the filling, lining it up with the side of the bottom disk of dough all around. Press the 2 layers of dough together well to seal, using your fingertips. Use the back of a paring knife to indent the dough at ½-inch intervals. Paint the top of the pastry with the egg wash and let it rest for 10 minutes.

6. Paint the pastry with egg wash again, then use the point of a paring knife to trace a series of parallel lines about 1 inch apart on the top of the pastry, cutting only about a third of the way through the dough. Repeat with another 12 lines or so at 45-degree angles to the first ones.

7. Bake the galette until it is well risen and the dough is well colored on the outside, about 45 minutes. Use a toothpick to check for dryness in the center of the galette.

SERVING: This is a casual dessert, meant to be cut into wedges and served with a glass of sweet wine.

STORAGE: Keep the galette at room temperature on the day it is baked. Wrap leftovers in plastic and keep at room temperature.

MONACO

Puff Pastry Cake with Lightened Pastry Cream Filling
Prince Albert

2/3 batch of quickest puff pastry, page 308; or traditional French puff pastry, page 311

PASTRY CREAM

1 cup milk

1/2 cup heavy whipping cream

1/3 cup sugar

4 large egg yolks

3 tablespoons unbleached all-purpose flour

2 teaspoons vanilla extract

FILLING

2 tablespoons Grand Marnier or another orange liqueur

1/2 cup heavy whipping cream

1/2 cup seedless raspberry preserves, heated to melt and cooled to room temperature

Confectioners' sugar for finishing

Four 12 × 18-inch jelly-roll pans lined with parchment

In the mid-1970s, when I worked summer seasons in the Sporting Club in Monte Carlo, Prince Albert was a dessert we often prepared. I'm sure the dessert, named after the son of Prince Rainier and Princess Grace, had been created in honor of his birth. A very simple version of a mille-feuille, it is made from three layers of puff pastry stacked with a pastry cream that has orange liqueur and whipped cream folded into it. The cream is drizzled with some melted raspberry preserves, and the top is lightly dusted with confectioners' sugar—simple, elegant, and not too difficult to prepare. For best results, assemble the dessert soon before you intend to serve it. You may have the puff pastry layers baked and trimmed and the cream filling already enriched with the whipped cream. You'll need only a few minutes to assemble it, and you'll have the satisfaction of knowing that the puff pastry layers are as crisp and buttery as possible.

One 10-inch round cake, about 8 to 10 servings

1. Place the puff pastry on a floured surface and lightly flour it. Press the dough with a rolling pin to soften it. Roll the dough to a 12 × 18-inch rectangle. Cut the dough into 2 rectangles, each 9 × 12 inches, then roll each to 12 × 18 inches. Slide each onto a cookie sheet or the back of a jelly-roll pan and chill until firm, about 30 minutes.
2. Set racks in the upper and lower thirds of the oven and preheat to 350 degrees.
3. Remove the sheets of dough from the refrigerator and pierce them all over with a fork at 1-inch intervals to prevent them from puffing up too much while they are baking. Slide each onto a parchment-lined pan. Cover the dough with another sheet of parchment and another pan. (Baking the sheets of dough between the pans helps to keep them straight and flat.) Bake the sheets of dough for about 20 minutes, then turn them over, still between the two pans, and bake for an additional 10 minutes. While the sheets of dough are baking, check them every 10 minutes or so to see how they are coloring. Make sure to bake the dough only until it is a deep golden color and no more, or the butter will burn and impart a bitter flavor to the dough. As soon as they are baked through, place the sheets of dough between the pans on a rack and cool the dough between the pans to prevent it from warping.
4. While the layers are baking, prepare the pastry cream. Combine the milk, cream, and half the sugar in a medium heavy-bottomed saucepan. Bring to a boil over medium heat, whisking occasionally to dissolve the sugar. Whisk the egg yolks in a bowl and whisk in the remaining sugar. Sift and whisk in the flour. When the milk mixture boils, whisk a third of it into the yolk mixture. Return the remaining milk mixture to a boil and whisk in the yolk mixture, continuing to whisk constantly until the cream thickens and returns to a full boil. Allow to boil, whisking constantly, for 15 seconds. Remove the pan from the heat and whisk in the vanilla. Scrape the pastry cream into a glass or stainless steel bowl. Press plastic wrap directly against the surface of the pastry cream and refrigerate it until it is completely cold.
5. To trim the cooled layers to the correct size, use a 10-inch round cake cardboard or a plate. Place the cardboard at the edge of 1 rectangle of baked dough and cut out a 10-inch disk. Repeat with the second piece of dough. Cut 2 half-disks, which will form the middle layer of the dessert, from the remaining baked pastry. Evenly crumble any scraps of baked puff pastry to use for finishing the side of the dessert, and set aside.

6. To prepare the filling, gently stir the Grand Marnier into the cooled pastry cream. Whip the cream until it holds a firm peak and fold it in. Cover and chill the filling.

7. To assemble, place 1 puff pastry layer on a 10-inch round cake cardboard and spread it with about half the pastry cream. Drizzle the melted preserves onto the pastry cream. Top the filling with the 2 half-disks and repeat with the pastry cream and preserves. Top with the last disk of pastry and gently press to make all the layers stick together. Use an offset spatula to smooth the sides of the dessert with any of the cream that oozes out, then press the reserved puff pastry crumbs against the side of the cake, all around. Lightly dust the top with confectioners' sugar immediately before serving.

SERVING: Place the cake on a platter and use a sharp serrated knife, wiped after each cut, to divide it into wedges.

STORAGE: Keep the cake at a cool room temperature up to several hours after assembling it. If you try to keep it longer, it may become soggy. Wrap and refrigerate leftovers.

SWITZERLAND

Puff Pastry Diamonds
Diamanten

1/3 batch quickest puff pastry, page 308; or traditional French puff pastry, page 311

1 cup sugar, plus more for sprinkling

2 cookies sheets or jelly-roll pans lined with parchment or foil

This recipe is just one of dozens of variations on caramelized puff pastry. The dough is rolled out in a large quantity of sugar so that while it is baking, the sugar caramelizes and combines with the buttery dough to make an utterly delicious pastry. This recipe is a good way of using up puff pastry scraps. Just bunch the scraps together and wrap and refrigerate them overnight before attempting to use them.

About 30 small pastries

1. Scatter half the sugar on the work surface and place the dough on it. Cover the dough with the remaining sugar and press the dough with a rolling pin to soften it. Roll the dough to a 12-inch square.
2. Slide the dough onto a cookie sheet and refrigerate it until it is firm, about 20 to 30 minutes.
3. After the dough has chilled, set racks in the upper and lower thirds of the oven and preheat to 350 degrees.
4. Slide the chilled dough onto a sugared work surface and use a sharp pizza wheel to cut it into 2-inch-wide strips. Cut across the strips diagonally to make diamond shapes.
5. Scatter more sugar on the diamonds and transfer them to the baking pans, spacing them about 1 inch apart from each other.

6. Use the same pizza wheel to make a little ½-inch slash in the center of each diamond.

7. Bake the pastries for about 10 minutes, then switch the top pan to the bottom rack and the bottom pan to the top rack, also turning them back to front at the same time. Continue baking until the diamonds take on a deep amber caramel color. Don't let them turn dark brown, or they will be bitter.

8. Cool the diamonds on the pans on racks.

SERVING: These are especially good with a fruit or any creamy dessert.

STORAGE: Keep the diamonds between sheets of wax paper in a tin or plastic container with a tight-fitting cover. They are really best within 24 hours of baking, when the butter flavor is still fresh.

AUSTRIA

Viennese Apple Strudel
Wiener Apfelstrudel

APPLE FILLING

6 tablespoons unsalted butter

5 pounds Golden Delicious apples, peeled, halved, cored, and each half cut into 4 or 5 wedges

3/4 cup sugar

1 teaspoon ground cinnamon

2 teaspoons finely grated lemon zest

2/3 cup (about 2 ounces) dark raisins or currants

2/3 cup (about 2 1/2 ounces) walnut pieces, toasted and coarsely chopped

DOUGH

1 batch strudel dough, page 313

One 12 × 18-inch pan lined with parchment or foil

This is a real classic—perfectly cooked apples in a crisp-tender strudel crust. This recipe will make 2 large strudels, which are well worth the time and trouble it takes to stretch the dough. If you don't want to bake both strudels at the same time, double-wrap one of them in plastic and place it on a cookie sheet. Freeze solid and remove from the pan. When you want to bake it, just place the frozen strudel on a parchment-lined pan and bake as below. If you're getting ready for a large party, there's no reason not to make both strudels ahead of time, freeze them, and bake them on the day you intend to serve them.

It's not traditionally Viennese to cook the apples for the strudel filling, but I think the results are infinitely better this way. ***Two 15-inch-long strudels, about 12 servings each***

1. For the apple filling, melt the butter over medium heat in a large Dutch oven that has a tight-fitting lid. Add the apples, sugar, cinnamon, and lemon zest and stir well to mix. Wait until the apples start to sizzle, then cover the pan and let the apples cook undisturbed for 10 to 15 minutes. At the end of that time, the apples should be swimming in water. Uncover the pan, decrease the heat to medium low, and

continue cooking the apples until the water has almost entirely evaporated, about 10 to 15 minutes. Stir in the raisins and walnuts, spread the filling out on a large nonreactive platter or tray, and allow it to cool completely. If you prepare the filling the day before, cover and refrigerate it until you are ready to roll and fill the strudel.

2. Set a rack in the middle level of the oven and preheat to 375 degrees.

3. Stretch and butter the dough as on page 315, strewing it with breadcrumbs. Arrange the filling in two 16-inch cylinders the length of the dough, leaving at least a 4-inch space between the 2 batches of filling, and arranging them about 3 inches in from the edge of the table. Pick up the cloth and let the dough cover the filling, then, grasping the cloth, roll the strudels up in the dough. Use scissors to trim excess dough at the ends and to cut the 2 strudels apart from each other. Twist the dough on the ends and turn it under the strudel to seal. Pick up each strudel, sliding your forearm under it for support, and transfer it to the prepared pan. Paint the outside of the strudels with any remaining melted butter.

4. Bake the strudels until the dough is baked through and crisp, about 45 minutes.

5. Cool the strudels on the pan on a rack.

Serving: Use a long metal spatula to transfer the strudels to a platter. Or cut the strudels into portions on the baking pan and re-form them on the platter after they have been cut. Serve with unsweetened whipped cream, as is done in Vienna.

Storage: Keep the strudel at room temperature for a few hours after baking it. Wrap leftovers and reheat them before serving.

AUSTRIA

Viennese Cheese Strudel

Wiener Topfenstrudel

CHEESE FILLING

4 slices (about 4 ounces) good-quality white bread, crusts removed and diced

½ cup milk, scalded

2 pounds salted farmer cheese (see Note)

⅔ cup (about 2½ ounces) golden raisins

3 large egg yolks

½ cup sugar

⅔ cup sour cream

4 tablespoons (½ stick) unsalted butter, melted

2 teaspoons finely grated lemon zest

2 teaspoons vanilla extract

DOUGH

1 batch strudel dough, page 313

Topfen, the type of pot cheese used in Vienna to make this strudel, is not available here. In other recipes I have successfully substituted part-skim-milk ricotta, but in this strudel filling, I like to use farmer cheese, a fairly dry curd cheese available both salted and unsalted. I use the salted version for strudel. A few layers of dough on the outside of the strudel will remain crisp for an hour or so after the strudel is baked, but a cheese strudel is a moist, tender dessert—don't expect excessive crispness. ***Two 16-inch-long strudels, about 12 servings each***

1. For the cheese filling, add the diced bread to the hot milk and let it cool. Force the mixture through a strainer into a mixing bowl. Force the cheese through the strainer over the bread.

2. In a saucepan cover the raisins with water. Bring to a boil, then drain and cool them.

3. In a large mixing bowl, whisk the yolks, then whisk in the sugar. Whisk until light, about 2 minutes. Use a large rubber spatula to stir in the cheese and bread mixture. Stir in the sour cream, butter, lemon zest, and vanilla, one at a time. Stir in the cooled raisins.

4. Spread the filling in 2 rectangles about 12 × 15 inches, about 5 inches apart from each other, and about 3 inches in from the edge of the table on the stretched, buttered, crumb-covered strudel dough. Pick up the cloth and let the dough cover the filling, then, grasping the cloth, roll the strudels up in the dough. Use scissors to trim excess dough at the ends and to cut the 2 strudels apart from each other. Twist the dough on the ends and turn it under the strudels to seal. Pick up each strudel, sliding your forearm under it for support, and transfer to the prepared pan. Paint the outside of the strudels with any remaining melted butter.

5. Bake the strudels until the dough is baked through and crisp on the outside, about 45 minutes. Cool the strudels on the pan on a rack.

NOTE: If you can't find farmer chese, substitute part–skim milk ricotta.

SERVING: Use a long metal spatula to transfer the strudels to a platter. Or cut the strudels into portions on the baking pan and re-form them on the platter after they have been cut. Serve with unsweetened whipped cream, as in Vienna.

STORAGE: Keep the strudel at room temperature for a few hours after baking it. Wrap leftovers and re-heat them before serving.

GREECE

Filo Pie with Semolina-Thickened Cream Filling
Galaktoboureko

SUGAR SYRUP

1½ cups water

1½ cups sugar

¼ cup honey

1 cinnamon stick

1 3-inch strip lemon zest, removed with a vegetable peeler

SEMOLINA CUSTARD

1 quart milk

1 vanilla bean, split

1¼ cups (about 5 ounces) semolina or Cream of Wheat

1 cup sugar

5 large eggs

ASSEMBLY

32 sheets filo dough

½ pound (2 sticks) unsalted butter, melted and skimmed (see Note)

One 9 × 13 × 2-inch metal or Pyrex pan, buttered

Some filo pastries have become common American fare—certainly many versions of baklava (see page 338) fall into that category. That's one reason I find galaktoboureko so good—it's a bit unusual as well as being really delicious. Thickening a cream filling with semolina instead of flour or cornstarch is typically Greek and Middle Eastern. The bonus is that this method results in an unusually flavorful and stable cream.

This pastry requires quite a lot of filo leaves, so it can be made only with commercial dough. ***One 9 × 13 × 2-inch pie, about twenty-four 2-inch square or diamond-shaped pieces***

1. For the sugar syrup, combine all ingredients in a large saucepan. Bring to a boil over medium heat, stirring occasionally, until all the sugar dissolves. Insert a candy thermometer and cook the syrup until it registers 220 degrees. Remove the cinnamon stick and lemon zest and cool the syrup to room temperature.

2. For the cream filling, combine 3 cups of the milk and the vanilla bean in a heavy-bottom saucepan. Bring to a boil over low to medium heat. Meanwhile, in a medium

bowl, whisk the remaining milk with the semolina, sugar, and eggs. When the milk boils, use a slotted spoon to remove the vanilla bean. Whisk a third of the milk mixture into the egg mixture. Return the remaining milk to a boil and whisk the egg mixture into it, continuing to whisk constantly until the cream thickens and returns to a boil. Let the cream boil, whisking constantly, for about 20 seconds.

3. Scrape the cream into a stainless steel or glass bowl and press plastic wrap against the surface. Refrigerate the cream until you are ready to use it. Do not allow the cream to chill for more than an hour or it will become too thick to spread.

4. When you are ready to bake the pastry, set a rack in the middle level of the oven and preheat to 375 degrees.

5. Use scissors to cut the filo sheets so that they are the same size as the pan. Place a sheet in the bottom of the prepared pan and drizzle it with butter. Repeat to make a total of 16 sheets on the bottom of the pan. Butter the top sheet and spread it with the cream filling.

6. Repeat layering another 16 sheets on top of the filling, sprinkling every sheet in between with butter. Evenly butter the top sheet of dough. Use a sharp paring knife to mark 2-inch squares or diamonds in the top few layers of dough.

7. Bake the pastry until it is deep golden and crisp, about 40 minutes.

8. Remove the pan from the oven, place it on a rack, and immediately pour the syrup over the pie. Let the pastry cool.

NOTE: It's easy to clarify large quantities of butter, but when you need only a little, the process isn't as easy. Melt the butter over fairly high heat and let it simmer a little—not enough to color it, but just enough to evaporate most of the watery part. Most of the solids will stick to the bottom of the pan, so you'll be able to pour off the yellow fat easily. If there is still a little foam on the surface, skim it off with a soup spoon.

SERVING: Cut through the scoring on the top of the pastry to separate it into portions. Use a thin offset spatula to remove them from the pan in which they baked.

STORAGE: Keep at room temperature on the day it is baked. Wrap and refrigerate leftovers and bring them to room temperature before serving again.

EGYPT

Cream- and Nut-Filled Pastry

Habibi Baklava

1 batch syrup as in galaktoboureko, page 332

CREAM FILLING

1 cup milk

One 1-inch piece cinnamon stick

3 tablespoons sugar

1/4 cup heavy whipping cream

2 tablespoons cornstarch

NUT FILLING

1/4 cup (about 1 ounce) blanched almonds, toasted

1/4 cup (about 1 ounce) hazelnuts, toasted and skinned

2 tablespoons (about 1/2 ounce) whole pistachios, lightly toasted

4 tablespoons (about 1/2 ounce) sweetened, shredded coconut, lightly toasted

3 tablespoons dark raisins or dried currants

1/4 cup sugar

ASSEMBLY

16 sheets filo dough

12 tablespoons (1 1/2 sticks) unsalted butter, melted and skimmed (see Note)

1 cookie sheet or jelly-roll pan lined with parchment or foil

This unusual version of baklava comes from my friends Jennifer Migliorelli and Hosni Emam, who own Habibi, an Egyptian restaurant in Hong Kong. Here the pastry is filled with a sweetened nut mixture and a cream filling. Instead of being stacked in a pan and cut into diamonds, these baklava are rolled and coiled, making their shape as unusual as their filling. Of course, like all Middle Eastern filo pastries, they are drenched with syrup after baking. Please remember to have the syrup ready and cold when the pastries come out of the oven. The pastries will remain crisp if they are hot and the syrup is cold. ***About 8 individual baklava***

1. For the cream filling, bring the milk, cinnamon stick, and sugar to a simmer in a heavy-bottom saucepan over low heat. Meanwhile whisk the cream and cornstarch together. When the milk boils, use a slotted spoon to remove the cinnamon stick. Whisk a third of the boiling milk into the cornstarch

mixture. Return the remaining milk to a boil and whisk in the cornstarch mixture, continuing to whisk until the cream thickens and returns to a boil. Boil, whisking constantly, for 15 seconds. Scrape the cooked cream into a glass or stainless steel bowl and press plastic wrap against the surface. Refrigerate the cream until it is cold. You can prepare the cream the day before assembling the pastries.

2. For the nut filling, combine the almonds, hazelnuts, pistachios, and coconut in the bowl of a food processor fitted with the metal blade. Pulse to a medium-coarse grind, making sure not to grind the nuts to powder. Pour the nuts into a bowl and stir in the raisins and sugar.

3. Set a rack in the middle level of the oven and preheat to 350 degrees.

4. To assemble the baklava, place a sheet of filo on the work surface and drizzle with butter. Place a second sheet on top and repeat. Spread about 2 tablespoons of the cream filling in a line 1 inch wide at one of the short ends of the dough, facing you. Add 3 tablespoons of the nut mixture, sprinkling it over the cream filling. Roll up, not too tightly, and use a little of the cream filling on the end of the dough to seal the pastry closed. Make sure the seam is underneath, then roll the cylinder of dough into a loose spiral. Transfer to the prepared pan. Repeat with the remaining dough, butter, cream filling, and nut filling.

5. After all the pastries have been arranged on the pan, bake them until they are deep golden and baked all the way through, about 30 to 40 minutes.

6. Use a spatula to transfer the pastries to a rack set inside a roasting pan. Pour the cold syrup over the hot pastries and allow them to cool in the syrup.

7. Remove the pastries from the syrup and drain them on a rack set over the pan of syrup.

Note: See page 333 for comments on clarifying butter.

Serving: I like this type of sweet, rich pastry with tea or coffee in the afternoon, but it can also be served as dessert after a meal.

Storage: Keep the drained pastries at room temperature on the day they are baked. Cover with plastic and refrigerate leftovers. Bring them to room temperature before serving again.

SYRIA

Sweet Cheese Purses
Sh'eab-Ee-Yat

SUGAR SYRUP

1 batch syrup as in galaktoboureko, page 332, made without honey or cinnamon, cold

1 tablespoon lemon juice

1 teaspoon orange flower water

FILLING

1 pound whole-milk ricotta

Ground cinnamon for sprinkling

ASSEMBLY

24 sheets filo dough

½ pound (2 sticks) unsalted butter, melted and skimmed (see Note)

2 jelly-roll pans lined with parchment or foil

The name of these pastries may come from the fact that they were traditionally prepared during the eighth month, Sh'aban in Arabic. The name also refers to a purse or backpack. The recipe comes from my friend and associate Andrea Tutunjian. Her father, John Tutunjian, provided the interpretations of the Arabic name. ***About 72 individual pastries***

1. Set racks in the upper and lower thirds of the oven and preheat to 350 degrees.
2. Stir the lemon juice and orange flower water into the syrup and set aside until the pastries are baked.
3. To form the pastries, cut a sheet of filo dough in thirds lengthwise. Drizzle it with butter and place 1 tablespoon of the ricotta in one corner of the dough closest to you. Sprinkle the ricotta with a little cinnamon. Follow the illustration, opposite, and fold the dough like a flag to enclose the ricotta and cinnamon. Arrange on one of the prepared pans.
4. After all the pastries have been formed, butter the top of each.

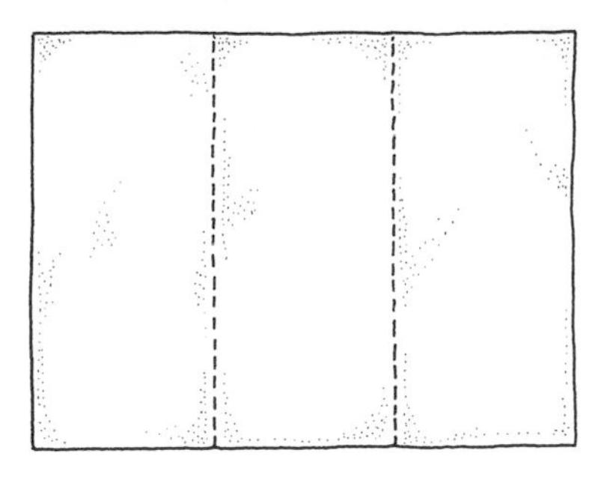

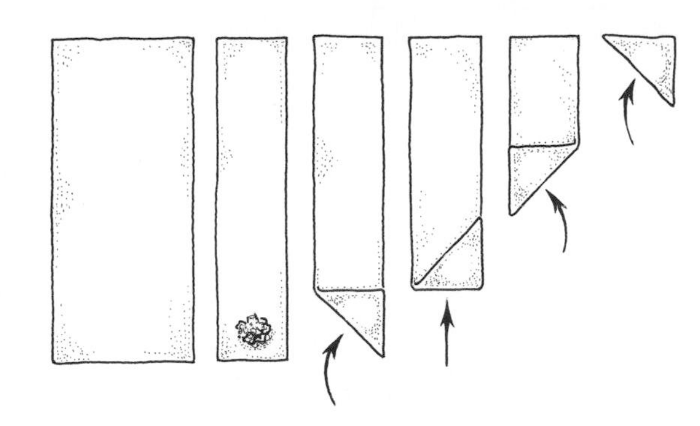

5. Bake for about 10 minutes, then switch the pans from the top rack to the bottom rack and the bottom rack to the top rack, turning the pans back to front at the same time. Continue baking until the pastries are deep golden, about 10 to 15 additional minutes.

6. Remove the pans from the oven and place them on racks. Drizzle the cold syrup over the hot pastries.

NOTE: See page 333 for comments on clarifying butter.

SERVING: Try to time these so that they are still a little warm when you serve them. You can form and chill them ahead of time and bake them about 1 hour before you want to serve them.

STORAGE: Keep the pastries at room temperature on the day they are baked. Cover leftovers and keep in a cool place.

RHODES

Sephardic Baklava
Trigonas

ALMOND FILLING

2 cups (about 8 ounces) blanched almonds, lightly toasted and finely chopped

½ teaspoon ground cinnamon

¼ teaspoon ground cloves

ASSEMBLY

16 sheets filo dough

½ pound (2 sticks) unsalted butter, melted and skimmed (see Note)

SYRUP

1½ cups water

1 cup honey

1 cup sugar

Ground toasted almonds for finishing

2 jelly-roll pans lined with parchment or foil

This recipe comes from Elsie Menasce, whom I met on my first trip to South Africa in June 2004. Elsie is the author of *The Sephardi Culinary Tradition* (Sephardic Cookbook Corporation, 1984), a book about the cuisine of the Sephardim—the Iberian, southern European, and Middle Eastern branch of Judaism, whose culinary traditions differ markedly from those of the Ashkenazi, or eastern European and Russian Jews.

The triangular baklava here is from Rhodes, the island off Greece that was alternately Turkish, Italian, and now Greek. Before and during World War II many Sephardi families fled Rhodes to Rhodesia, now Zambia and Zimbabwe, in Africa, which is where Elsie was born.

About 40 to 48 small pastries

1. For the almond filling, combine all ingredients in a bowl.
2. Set racks in the upper and lower thirds of the oven and preheat to 350 degrees.

3. To assemble the pastries, place a sheet of filo dough on the work surface and drizzle it with butter. Place another sheet on top and repeat. Use a sharp pizza wheel to cut them lengthwise into 2½-inch-wide strips. Place 1 tablespoon of the almond mixture at the short end of each strip and fold each up like a flag, as in the illustration on page 337. As the pastries are formed, arrange them on the prepared pans. Brush the tops with butter.

4. Bake the pastries until they are light golden, about 20 minutes.

5. While the pastries are baking, combine all the ingredients for the syrup in a large saucepan and bring to a boil. Lower to a simmer and continue cooking gently until the pastries are baked, then turn off the heat under the syrup.

6. Cool the pastries completely. Reheat the syrup to a boil and add 4 or 5 of the baked pastries. Cook for about 2 minutes, then remove the pastries from the syrup and place on a rack set inside a pan. Immediately sprinkle the tops of the pastries with a pinch of the ground almonds.

7. Repeat until all the pastries have been cooked in the syrup.

NOTE: See page 333 for comments on clarifying butter.

SERVING: These are good after dinner with coffee or as an accompaniment to a creamy dessert.

STORAGE: Keep the pastries in a tin or plastic container with a tight-fitting cover, between layers of aluminum foil.

8. FRIED PASTRIES

SPAIN	CRISP FRITTERS FROM CORDOBA *Buñuelos de Cordoba*
CZECH REPUBLIC AND SLOVAKIA	CELESTIAL LEAVES *Listi*
AUSTRIA	VIENNESE FRITTERS MADE FROM CREAM-PUFF DOUGH *Spritzkrapfen*
ITALY	SICILIAN TURNOVERS FILLED WITH CHICKPEAS AND CHOCOLATE *Casateddi di Ciciri*
SOUTH AFRICA	BRAIDED CRULLERS IN SYRUP *Koeksisters*
ITALY	SICILIAN RICOTTA-FILLED PASTRIES *Cannoli alla Siciliana*

Overleaf: Cannoli alla Siciliana

SOME OF THE WORLD'S BEST and most interesting pastries are baked not in an oven but in hot fat. The tradition of deep-frying is an ancient one, and recipes for fried pastries are common throughout the world. The reason is simple: until the proliferation of gas and electric appliances in the twentieth century, many home kitchens had no ovens. Homemade cakes and pastries were brought to the local baker, who baked them in his oven after he had finished his own baking. Consequently the only pastries actually baked in the home were cooked on the stove in hot oil.

The first time I visited my mother's hometown in southern Italy, some cousins took me to see a communal oven—one where you paid a small amount to the keepers of the oven to bake your cakes or biscotti for you. This was in 1974, but the tradition was still ingrained. I went one morning to visit an aunt, and she said that she would have offered me some biscotti with my coffee, but they were still down the street at the oven being baked. Old habits die hard.

In southern Europe, there is a widespread tradition of frying in lard. Lard, like beef suet, can withstand high temperatures for a long time without breaking down and foaming. Also, many southern European fried pastries are associated with Carnival, the period of feasting before Lent, when Catholics abstained from eating meat. Carnival would have been the last time for a while that they could indulge in pastries fried in animal fat, and they took advantage of it.

Deep-frying presents safety issues that you need to consider before attempting it. A large pan of fat heated to between 300 and 400 degrees can be a dangerous thing. Bear the following instructions in mind, and deep-frying will be a pleasure.

USE THE RIGHT PAN

I like to use a large (about 8-quart) enameled iron Dutch oven that has a cover. That way the pan is never more than a third to half full of oil, and there is no risk that the oil will foam and boil over. Also, there is more room to fry multiple items at one time, so that the frying process goes more quickly. The cover comes in handy at the end of frying: turn off the heat, cover the pan, and leave it in place. When it cools completely, dispose of the oil. It's not a good idea to carry around a pan filled with hot oil. Covering the pan also prevents further pungent fumes from the hot oil from escaping into the air—a plus if you live in an apartment and you don't want to smell as though you work in a doughnut shop after you've made some fried pastries.

USE THE RIGHT OIL

Most vegetable oil has a fairly high smoking point, making it safe to use for deep-frying. Some people like to use solid vegetable shortening, but I think pastries fried in vegetable shortening are too greasy. When I was a child my family always used peanut oil for frying, as the Chinese do. Peanut oil will withstand high temperatures for a long time without beginning to foam.

USE A THERMOMETER

Don't guess whether your oil is at the right temperature. Use a thermometer. The right kind of thermometer looks like a ruler and has a clip on the back to attach it to the rim of the pan so that you can safely keep it away from the items you are frying. This ruler-type thermometer also has a temperature gauge attached to it, about half an inch from the bottom, so that the bottom of the thermometer can be positioned to touch the bottom of the pan. The type of thermometer that has a round dial with a stem attached at the bottom is much less accurate. It's almost impossible to keep the stem from touching the bottom of the pan and registering a temperature higher than that of the actual fat.

Using a thermometer also makes it easy to see when the temperature is dropping or increasing too much, so that you can adjust the heat to compensate.

GET ORGANIZED

Before you place the pan on the stove to heat the fat, make sure you have several jelly-roll pans lined with multiple layers of paper towels already positioned near the stove. Also have tongs or a skimmer in place. Once you put your pastries in the oil, they will bake quickly, and you won't have time to look for a skimmer or a pan to put them on.

Neatly line up the items to be fried on a pan near the stove, too. Make sure there isn't an excessive amount of flour on the outside of the pastries. Flour can accumulate in the pan and cause the fat to foam up dangerously as the flour burns. Use your skimmer or a slotted spoon to lower the items to be fried into the fat. If you just drop them in, you may splatter your hands with hot fat.

CONCENTRATE

It's great to have a helper on hand when deep-frying, but keep the crowds away. This isn't the time to have a toddler crawling around on the floor near the stove. Let the phone ring—distractions can cause you to leave the pastries in the fat too long, and they will burn.

SPAIN

Crisp Fritters from Cordoba
Buñuelos de Cordoba

3 large eggs

¼ cup light or pure (not extra-virgin) olive oil, preferably Spanish

¼ teaspoon salt

1 teaspoon baking powder

2 cups all-purpose flour (spoon flour into dry-measure cup and level off)

1½ quarts vegetable or mild olive oil for frying

1½ cups sugar for finishing

2 jelly-roll pans lined with parchment paper for holding the buñuelos before frying, and 2 more lined with paper towels for draining them

These delicate fritters from southwestern Spain are popular throughout the Hispanic world in many different forms. In Mexico, they may be made flat like tortillas, or shaped like doughnuts, often with cheese in the dough. In Cuba, yucca is added to the dough for a moist-textured buñuelo. It wouldn't be uncommon in Spain to fry these in a light-flavored olive oil, but vegetable oil will do just as well. Like many European fried pastries, these have no sugar in the dough, but rely for sweetness on the sugar in which they are rolled after frying. ***About forty-eight 2-inch round fritters***

1. Whisk the eggs in a mixing bowl, then whisk in the oil and salt. Use a large rubber spatula to stir in the flour and baking powder to make a soft dough.

2. Scrape the dough from the bowl to a floured work surface and fold the dough over on itself, using a bench scraper to flip it, to make the dough smoother and somewhat elastic. Form the dough into a ball, flour the outside, and wrap it in plastic. Refrigerate the dough for a minimum of 1 hour, or as long as overnight.

3. When you are ready to fry the buñuelos, remove the dough from the refrigerator and place it on a lightly floured work surface. Use a bench scraper or knife to cut the dough into 4 equal pieces. Roll each piece to a cylinder 12 inches long. Cut each

cylinder into 1-inch pieces. Roll each 1-inch piece of dough under the palms of your hand to a 3-inch length. Pass a rolling pin over the dough to flatten and lengthen it slightly. Moisten one end of the dough and join it to the other, pressing to make the 2 pieces of dough stick together, forming a circle. Repeat with the remaining pieces of dough, arranging them on one of the prepared pans, not touching each other.

4. To fry the buñuelos, heat the oil to 350 degrees in a large Dutch oven. Fry 5 or 6 buñuelos at a time, turning them over once they have turned a deep golden color on the bottom. Remove and place on one of the paper-towel-lined pans to drain. Repeat with the remaining buñuelos.

5. After all the buñuelos have been fried, put the sugar in a shallow bowl and roll the warm buñuelos in it.

Serving: Pile the buñuelos on a platter. They are a good snack or a very casual dessert.

Storage: Keep the buñuelos for up to 6 hours after frying before serving them. Fried pastries such as this don't make good leftovers.

Celestial Leaves
Listi

1 large egg

4 large egg yolks

½ teaspoon salt

2 teaspoons sugar

1 teaspoon vanilla extract

1 cup all-purpose flour (spoon flour into dry-measure cup and level off)

1½ quarts vegetable oil for frying

Confectioners' sugar for finishing

1 jelly-roll pan lined with parchment paper and another 1 or 2 lined with paper towels for draining the fritters

Fritters like these are popular throughout eastern Europe. I know of Polish, Hungarian, and Austrian versions. This recipe comes from Milli De Conti Link, who gave the recipe to my friend Shirley Nachman in Detroit. Since the dough is fairly lean, these keep well for a couple of days—just dust them with the confectioners' sugar right before serving.

About thirty 1½ × 5-inch fritters

1. In a medium mixing bowl, whisk the egg and yolks together. Whisk in the salt, sugar, and vanilla. Use a large rubber spatula to stir in the flour to form a fairly stiff dough. Scrape the dough out onto a floured work surface and knead it until it is smooth, about 3 minutes. Wrap the dough in plastic and let it rest at room temperature for about 1 hour.

2. After the dough has rested, place it on a floured work surface and press it into a rough rectangle. Flour the dough and roll it to a 15-inch square. If the dough resists, cover it with a towel and let it rest for 5 to 10 minutes, then resume rolling.

3. Use a serrated cutting wheel to trim the edges of the dough evenly. Cut the dough across the middle to make 3 rectangles, each 15 × 5 inches. Cut the dough into 1½ × 5-inch strips, making 10 from each rectangle of dough. Make 2 slits in the center of each piece of dough in the length, using the cutting wheel. Transfer the cut pieces of dough to the parchment-covered pan.

4. In a large Dutch oven, heat the oil to 350 degrees. Place 5 or 6 pieces of dough on your skimmer and lower them into the hot oil. Gently stir the oil with the skimmer so that the fritters cook evenly all over. They will curl up somewhat and not remain flat. Fry the fritters until they are a light golden color. Drain the fritters on the paper-towel-lined pan.
5. Cool the fritters completely before dusting them with the confectioners' sugar.

SERVING: These are a great snack or something to serve with coffee or tea.

STORAGE: Keep unsugared fritters in a tin or plastic container with a tight-fitting cover. Dust with confectioners' sugar immediately before serving. Don't try to keep them more than a few days, or they will taste stale.

AUSTRIA

Viennese Fritters Made from Cream-Puff Dough
Spritzkrapfen

CREAM-PUFF DOUGH

1¼ cups milk

5 tablespoons unsalted butter, cut into 5 pieces

¼ teaspoon salt

1¼ cups all-purpose flour (spoon flour into dry-measure cup and level off)

5 large eggs

1 tablespoon dark rum

2 teaspoons sugar

FINISHING

2 cups confectioners' sugar

½ teaspoon cinnamon

1 jelly-roll pan lined with parchment paper, plus 1 lined with paper towels for draining the fritters

Krapfen is a general term encompassing all individual round pastries, whether fried or baked. A *Spritz* is a squirt; the term refers to the act of using a pastry bag to pipe something out. So these are round piped pastries. They're quite delicate and an old Viennese specialty, available in some of the city's finest coffeehouses. Spritzkrapfen are meant to be eaten as soon as they are fried, so plan on preparing them for a casual occasion when leaving the table to fry them won't be bothersome. For this reason they're probably best suited to being prepared as a snack, rather than as a full-scale dessert. ***About twenty-four 3-inch round fritters***

1. To make the dough, in a heavy-bottom saucepan combine the milk, butter, and salt. Bring to a boil over medium heat, stirring occasionally until the butter melts. Remove from heat, stir in the flour with a wooden spatula, and continue stirring until the dough is smooth. Return the pan to the heat and beat the dough vigorously until it leaves the sides of the pan and the bottom of the pan is lightly filmed with the dough. Scrape the dough into a bowl and stir for a minute or so to cool it slightly. Beat in the eggs one at a time, beating smooth after each addition. Beat in the rum and the sugar.

2. Place half the dough into a pastry bag fitted with an open star tube (Ateco #824). On the prepared pan lined with parchment, pipe out circles of dough 2½ inches in diameter, in straight rows. Use the point of a paring knife to cut the paper into 5 or 6 pieces, cutting around the piped dough.

3. In a large Dutch oven, heat the oil to 350 degrees. When the oil is hot, carefully invert 1 piece of paper into the oil. Use a large kitchen spoon to baste the top side of the paper with hot oil so that the fritters float away from the paper. Use tongs to remove the paper from the pan. Cook the fritters on both sides to a delicate golden color. Remove and drain on the paper-towel-lined pan. Repeat with the remaining piped dough.

4. Mix the confectioners' sugar and cinnamon together and sift a thick layer over the fritters.

Serving: Serve the spritzkrapfen as soon as possible after they are fried, while they are still warm.

Storage: As with a soufflé, you have only one opportunity to eat these. If left to cool, they will become heavy and greasy in just a few hours.

Sicilian Turnovers Filled with Chickpeas and Chocolate
Casateddi di Ciciri

There are dozens of variations of this type of pastry throughout southern Italy and Sicily. Some use a filling made from cooked chestnuts, but these very Sicilian ones substitute cooked chickpeas for the chestnuts. The filling may be flavored with either honey or vino cotto, a kind of thick syrup usually made from must, the freshly pressed grape juice destined to be fermented into wine. In the fall, throughout southern Italy and Sicily, must is abundant and every family that clings to old cooking traditions makes a supply of vino cotto for flavoring and drizzling on baked and fried pastries during the coming year. Originally used as an economical sugar substitute, vino cotto has become a symbol of antique baking traditions. Here, where must is not readily available, I cook down some red jug wine with sugar until it becomes thick and syrupy. It's easy to do, and the results last forever in the refrigerator. If you don't feel like bothering with the vino cotto, just substitute honey, as specified below. ***About 30 turnovers***

DOUGH

3 cups all-purpose flour (spoon flour into dry-measure cup and level off)

1/4 cup sugar

1 teaspoon baking powder

1/4 teaspoon salt

5 tablespoons lard or butter

2 large eggs

1/3 cup white wine or dry white vermouth

FILLING

2/3 cup (about 3 ounces) dried chickpeas, soaked in cold water overnight; or 1 1/2 cups (one 15 1/2-ounce can) canned chickpeas, rinsed and drained

1/3 cup sugar

3 tablespoons honey or vino cotto (see Note)

2 teaspoons vanilla extract

1/2 teaspoon ground cinnamon

1/4 teaspoon ground cloves

2 ounces semisweet chocolate, finely chopped

1/4 cup (about 1 ounce) blanched almonds, toasted and chopped

1/4 cup (about 1 ounce) pine nuts, lightly toasted and chopped

1 egg white, well beaten with a fork, for sealing the pastries

1 1/2 quarts vegetable oil for frying

Honey or vino cotto for drizzling on the pastries before serving

1 cookie sheet or jelly-roll pan lined with parchment for holding the pastries before frying, and another jelly-roll pan lined with paper towels for draining the fried pastries

1. For the dough, combine the dry ingredients in the bowl of a food processor fitted with the metal blade. Pulse several times to mix. Add the lard or butter and pulse until it is finely mixed in, about 10 times. Add the eggs and wine and pulse repeatedly until the dough forms a ball. Invert the dough onto a floured surface and carefully remove the blade. Press the dough into a rectangle, flour it, and wrap it in plastic. Refrigerate the dough for 2 hours to relax it. You can leave the dough in the refrigerator overnight.

2. If you are using dried chickpeas, drain the water they soaked in and place them in a medium saucepan. Add about 1 1/2 quarts of fresh water and place the pan over low heat. Let the chickpeas slowly come to a simmer, then regulate the heat so that they just simmer gently. Cook until they are quite soft, about 30 minutes. Drain the chickpeas, cool them, and puree them in a food processor.

3. To make the filling, scrape the chickpea puree into a bowl and stir in the remaining filling ingredients, one at a time.

4. To form the pastries, remove the dough from the refrigerator and use a bench scraper or knife to cut it into 3 equal pieces. Place 1 piece of dough on a floured surface and flour the dough. Roll it to a 9-inch square. Use a plain or fluted 2 1/2- to 3-inch cutter to cut the dough into disks. Repeat with the remaining pieces of dough.

5. To form a turnover, place 1 disk of dough on the work surface and place 1 tablespoon of the filling on the lower half of the disk. Paint the circumference of the lower half with the egg white. Fold the top half down to cover the filling. Seal the seam by pressing down well with your fingertips. Arrange the formed turnover on the prepared

parchment-lined pan. Repeat with the remaining pieces of dough and filling. You may reroll the scraps of dough, but it will be difficult. If you really want to use them, it's best to pass them through a pasta machine (see the cannoli recipe on page 358 for instructions), because the dough will be too elastic to roll by hand a second time.

6. After all the turnovers have been formed, let them dry at room temperature for 1 hour before frying.

7. To fry the turnovers, in a large Dutch oven heat the oil to 350 degrees. Place 4 or 5 of the turnovers on your skimmer and lower them into the hot fat. Cook them on both sides until they are a deep golden color. Drain them on the prepared paper-towel-lined pan.

Note: Vino cotto is easy to make and can be kept for months in the refrigerator. Bring 2 bottles of inexpensive red wine to a boil with 2 cups of sugar in an enameled iron or stainless steel–lined pan, stirring occasionally to make sure the sugar is dissolved. Let the syrup boil down until it thickens slightly and reaches about 220 degrees on a candy thermometer. Cool the syrup in the pan, then pour it into a plastic container with a tight-fitting cover. Before using, bring it to room temperature or heat it slightly to make it more liquid.

Serving: Arrange the casateddi on a platter and drizzle them with honey or vino cotto. They are usually served as a Christmas dessert.

Storage: Like all fried pastries, these are best on the day they are made. For advance preparation, cover with plastic and refrigerate them for up to a day before frying, but serve them on the day they are fried.

SOUTH AFRICA

Braided Crullers in Syrup
Koeksisters

DOUGH

4 cups all-purpose flour (spoon flour into dry-measure cup and level off)

4 teaspoons baking powder

1 teaspoon salt

4 tablespoons (½ stick) butter, cut into 8 pieces

1½ cups milk

1 large egg

SYRUP

4 cups water

8 cups sugar

¼ cup honey or Lyle's Golden Syrup (see Sources)

2 teaspoons cream of tartar

1 tablespoon lemon juice

2 quarts vegetable oil for frying

2 jelly-roll pans lined with parchment paper for holding the pastries before frying, and 2 more jelly-roll pans with cooling racks set on them for draining the syrup-dipped pastries

I became acquainted with this delicious pastry when I visited South Africa for the first time. Afrikaners are the descendents of South Africa's Dutch settlers and preserve many of their original culinary traditions. Koeksisters are widely available in the Cape Town area, and I tasted them at several pastry shops. These are a bit of a production to prepare, and are best done by a two-person team. One can do the frying while the other attends to immersing the hot koeksisters in the cold syrup. They must be soaked with the syrup immediately after they are fried so that they will absorb it well and won't be dry. Your reward for all this work is the taste and texture of these exotic pastries. Thanks to Engela Matthee for the recipe.

Remember to make both the dough and the syrup the day before. Each needs to chill overnight before you form, fry, and dip the koeksisters. ***About 48 koeksisters, each about 4 inches long***

1. For the dough, in a large bowl stir together the flour, baking powder, and salt. Cut the butter into small pieces and rub it evenly into the flour, rubbing the mixture back and forth between the palms of your hands. Whisk the milk and egg together and use a large rubber spatula to stir the liquid into the flour. Continue stirring until the dough is evenly moistened. Scrape the dough out onto a floured work surface and knead it until it is smooth, 2 to 3 minutes. Refrigerate the dough in plastic wrap overnight.

2. To make the syrup, combine all ingredients except the lemon juice in a large Dutch oven. Bring to a boil, stirring occasionally to dissolve the sugar. Boil the syrup for 8 minutes to allow it to concentrate and thicken. Remove from heat and stir in the lemon juice. Pour the syrup into a large bowl and cool it to room temperature. Cover the bowl with plastic wrap and refrigerate the syrup overnight.

3. To form the koeksisters, remove the dough from the refrigerator and use a bench scraper or knife to divide it into 3 pieces. Roll 1 piece of dough to a 4 × 12-inch rectangle. Use a pizza wheel to cut the dough crosswise into ¼-inch strips, making 48 strips, each ¼ inch by 4 inches. To form 1 pastry, group 3 strands and pinch them together at the top. Loosely braid the 3 strands together, as in the illustration below. Pinch the strands together at the other end and arrange the braided pastry on 1 parchment-covered pan. Repeat with the remaining strands and then the remaining pieces of dough to make 48 individual braids.

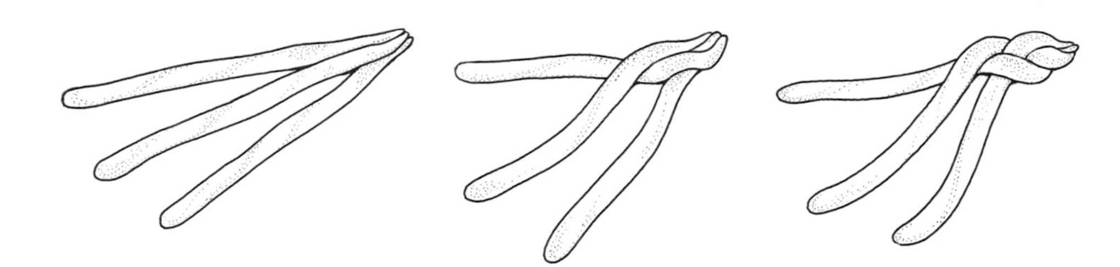

4. In a large Dutch oven, heat the oil to 350 degrees. Pour half the syrup into a large bowl and set over another larger bowl of ice water. Place the bowls on the stove near the pan in which you will fry the pastries. Leave the rest of the syrup in the refrigerator. Place 4 or 5 of the braids on your skimmer and lower them into the hot oil, cooking them on both sides until they are a deep golden color. Skim them out of the oil and let the excess oil drip back into the pan. Immediately add the hot pastries to the bowl of iced syrup. Allow them to remain in the syrup for about 3 minutes, to soak up as much as possible. Use tongs to lift them from the syrup to drain on one of the racks. As you fry more braids, add some of the refrigerated syrup to the iced syrup to keep its temperature low.

SERVING: Arrange the drained koeksisters on a platter. These are a casual food and are meant to be eaten with the hands. Have plenty of paper napkins available for sticky fingers.

STORAGE: Keep the koeksisters loosely covered with plastic wrap on the day they are made. They are best when fresh and moist and tend to dry out if kept over to a second day.

Sicilian Ricotta-Filled Pastries
Cannoli alla Siciliana

CANNOLI DOUGH

3 cups all-purpose flour (spoon flour into dry-measure cup and level off)

3 tablespoons sugar

1 teaspoon salt

1 teaspoon ground cinnamon

3 tablespoons lard or butter

1 large egg

1 large egg yolk

½ cup dry white wine or dry vermouth

1 egg white, beaten with a fork, for sealing the shells

RICOTTA FILLING

3 pounds whole-milk ricotta (see headnote)

1½ cups confectioners' sugar

2 teaspoons vanilla extract

½ teaspoon ground cinnamon or 1 to 2 drops oil of cinnamon (see Sources)

½ cup (about 2 ounces) candied orange peel, cut into ¼-inch dice

3 ounces semisweet chocolate, cut into ¼-inch pieces and sifted in a strainer to remove any dusty particles

FINISHING

1 cup (about 4 ounces) unsalted very green pistachios, skinned, dried out (but not toasted) in the oven, and chopped medium-fine

Confectioners' sugar for dusting

8 or more cannoli tubes, plus two jelly-roll pans lined with paper towels for draining the fried shells

Cannoli probably developed from an Arab pastry, as is the case with many other Sicilian dishes. Usually fried in lard in Sicily, they were originally a Carnival pastry, though nowadays they are available throughout the year.

Pastry shops here in the United States use a special kind of ricotta for the filling, called ricotta impastata, a very smooth, dry-textured ricotta made by pureeing well-drained ricotta with very dry whey cheese. In Sicily, the ricotta commonly available is dry-textured enough to make a fairly firm filling on its own. Freshly made ricotta from an Italian grocery store is an adequate substitute, and sometimes such a store will even order you some ricotta impastata, if you can use the whole 10-pound package. If you have access only to the kind of ricotta available in the supermarket, drain it well in a strainer lined with cheesecloth or a wet paper towel set over a bowl in the refrigerator overnight. It's also best to let the filling chill as long as possible to firm it up before filling the cannoli. Real cannoli filling is flavored with a drop of cinnamon oil, which contributes a characteristic flavor. (See Sources on page 363.)

You'll need 8 or 12 cannoli tubes for frying the pastry shells. These are cylindrical metal tubes about 1 inch in diameter and about 5 or 6 inches long. They're not difficult to find in cookware shops or department stores. See Sources on page 367 if you would like to order them by mail. If you are using the tubes for the first time, fry them briefly in the oil heated to cook the cannoli shells, to season them and prevent the dough from sticking. Let them cool and wipe them clean with paper towels before using. ***About 24 cannoli***

1. To make the dough, in a medium mixing bowl, combine the flour, sugar, salt, and cinnamon. Rub in the lard or butter by hand until it is finely incorporated. Whisk the egg, yolk, and wine together and use a large rubber spatula to stir the liquid into the flour mixture. Continue stirring until all the flour is evenly moistened, and then scrape the dough out onto a floured work surface. Knead the dough briefly by folding it over on itself repeatedly until it becomes too firm and elastic to knead further. Use a bench scraper or a knife to divide the dough into 3 pieces. Flour 1 piece and pass it through the widest setting on a pasta machine. Fold the dough in thirds and pass it through again from the open side. Repeat until the dough is smooth and elastic and no longer shreds as you are putting it through the machine. Fold the dough in thirds again, wrap it in plastic wrap, and repeat with the remaining pieces of dough. After all the pieces of dough have been passed through the pasta machine, fold each in thirds again, wrap them in plastic wrap, and refrigerate them for at least 1 hour or as long as overnight before continuing.

2. To form the cannoli shells, remove the dough from the refrigerator and flour 1 piece. Pass it through the pasta machine open end first, as before. Decrease the size of the opening by two notches and pass through again, flouring the dough as necessary to

keep it from sticking. Pass through every other setting, ending with the next-to-last setting on the machine. Place the strip of dough on a lightly floured work surface and cover it with plastic wrap. Repeat with the remaining 2 pieces of dough.

3. Use a plain round cutter or a stiff cardboard pattern and the point of a paring knife to cut the dough into 4-inch disks. If using a cutter, slide a couple of folded sheets of parchment paper under the dough to act as a cushion. Cut straight down without twisting the cutter, which would seal the cut edge of the dough and make it puff up like a balloon while frying. Overlap the disks of dough on the work surface until you have cut them all. See the variation at the end of the recipe for using the scraps of dough.

4. Roll over 1 disk of dough with a rolling pin to make it slightly oval. Position 1 cannoli tube lengthwise on the oval and draw 1 side of it up to the top. Carefully moisten about ½ inch of the top edge of the dough with egg white, using a brush. Make sure not to get any of the egg white on the metal tube, or it will make the fried shell stick. Draw the other edge of the dough disk up to meet the first one and overlap them slightly. Holding the tube above the work surface to prevent pressure from cutting through the bottom of the dough, press the overlapped dough firmly together with your fingertips. Repeat with as many disks of dough as you have cannoli tubes.

5. To fry the cannoli, in a large Dutch oven heat the oil to 375 degrees. Fry 3 or 4 cannoli at a time to a deep golden color. Drain them on a paper-towel-lined pan. As soon as you've removed all the cannoli, immediately remove the tubes. (This must be done while the shells are still hot, or they will contract on cooling and stick to the tubes.) Use an oven mitt to grasp the end of the tube and use a towel or several thicknesses of paper towel in the other hand to gently twist the shell off the tube. Return the shell to the pan to drain and cool. Repeat with remaining pieces of dough and tubes. If you have only a few tubes and need to reuse them, make sure to let them cool before wrapping more dough around them.

6. While the shells are cooling, make the filling. Place the ricotta in the bowl of an electric mixer. Place the bowl on the mixer fitted with the paddle attachment and beat on lowest speed for 30 seconds. Beat in the confectioners' sugar and continue

beating just until it is absorbed. Beat in the vanilla and the cinnamon or cinnamon oil. Remove the bowl from the mixer and use a large rubber spatula to stir in the candied peel and the chocolate.

7. To fill the cannoli, put some of the filling in a pastry bag that has a 1-inch opening at the end, but no tube. Squeeze filling into the shell from one end, releasing the pressure when the filling reaches the end of the shell you are squeezing from. Pull the pastry bag away in a downward motion to leave the filling straight against the end of the shell. Repeat with the other end of the shell. Repeat with as many of the shells as you want to fill at one time.

8. Sprinkle the chopped pistachios on the filling at the ends of the shells. Dust the cannoli with confectioners' sugar right before serving.

SERVING: Cannoli are excellent at any time of the day or night. They are especially good for a large party, because you can get all the work done the day before and just leave the filling until the day you intend to serve them.

STORAGE: Keep the shells loosely covered with plastic wrap at a cool room temperature for up to 1 or 2 days before filling. If kept any longer than that, the cannoli shells will develop a stale taste. Fill the shells only a few hours before serving, or they may soften and become soggy.

VARIATION: RAGS (*STRACCE*)

These are fritters you make with the leftover dough after cutting out the disks to make the cannoli shells. Press the dough together and pass it through the pasta machine again at the widest setting, as in kneading the freshly made dough. When the dough is smooth, take it through every other setting, ending with the next to last (again, as above). Use a serrated cutting wheel to cut the dough into 4-inch lengths. Cut each 4-inch piece of dough lengthwise into strips 1 inch wide. Fry and drain as above and dust heavily with confectioners' sugar before serving. You can do the same thing with scraps of the Argentine empanada dough on page 300.

SOURCES

American Almond
103 Walworth Street
Brooklyn, NY 11205
Telephone: (800) 825-6663
Website: www.americanalmond.com
One-pound cans of almond paste and praline paste.

The Baker's Catalogue
P.O. Box 876
Norwich, VT 05055-0876
Telephone: (800) 827-6836
Website: www.bakerscatalogue.com
General baking ingredients and equipment. Also, pearl sugar, candied fruit, oil of cinnamon.

Bonnie Slotnick Cookbooks
163 West 10th Street
New York, NY 10014
Telephone: (212) 989-8962
Website: www.bonnieslotnickbooks.com
Out-of-print and antiquarian cookbooks.

Bridge Kitchenware
214 East 52nd Street
New York, NY 10022
Telephone: (212) 688-4220
Website: www.bridgekitchenware.com
Cookware, chocolate, bakeware, including tart pans, brioche molds, madeleine pans, and cannoli tubes.

Calphalon Corporation
P.O. Box 583
Toledo, OH 43697
Telephone: (800) 809-7267
Website: www.calphalon.com
Bakeware and other baking tools.

Guittard Chocolate Company
10 Guittard Road
Burlingame, CA 94010
Telephone: (650) 697-4424
Website: www.guittard.com
A range of interesting chocolate products.

Kaiser Bakeware
3512 Faith Church Road
Indian Trail, NC 28079
Telephone: (800) 966-3009
Website: www.kaiserbakeware.com
Bakeware, including excellent springform pans and madeleine pans.

Kalustyan's
123 Lexington Avenue
New York, NY 10016
Telephone: (212) 685-3451
Website: www.kalustyan.com
Herbs, spices, nuts, and seeds, including black sesame seeds and onion seeds. Condiments such as several varieties of soy sauce and mirin, and other Chinese and Japanese ingredients.

Myers of Keswick
634 Hudson Street
New York, NY 10014
Telephone: (212) 691-4194
Website: www.myersofkeswick.com
Wide selection of British products, including Lyle's Golden Syrup.

New York Cake and Baking Distributors
56 West 22nd Street
New York, NY 10010
Telephone: (212) 675-2253; (800) 942-2539
Website: nycake.com

A full line of pans, decorating equipment, chocolate. Also, dragées, molds, Silpat nonstick baking mats, offset spatulas, and madeleine pans.

NORDICWARE
Highway 7 at Highway 100
Minneapolis, MN 55416
Telephone: (952) 920-2888; (800) 328-4310
Website: www.nordicware.com
Bakeware, including a variety of Bundt pans.

PENZEY'S SPICES
P.O. Box 933
Muskego, WI 53150
Telephone: (262) 785-7678; (800) 741-7787
Website: www.penzeys.com
Herbs, spices, extracts, including oil of cinnamon.

SCHARFFEN BERGER
914 Heinz Avenue
Berkeley, CA 94710
Telephone: (510) 981-4050; (800) 930-4528
Website: www.scharffenberger.com
Numerous chocolates and chocolate baking products.

SEPP LEAF PRODUCTS
381 Park Avenue South
New York, NY 10016
Telephone: (212) 683-2840
Website: www.seppleaf.com
Gold leaf for the millennium torte (page 133).

SUR LA TABLE
Pike Place Farmers Market
84 Pine Street
Seattle, WA 98101
Telephone: (206) 448-2245; (800) 243-0852
Website: www.surlatable.com
Pans, molds, and assorted baking equipment and cookware, including tart pans, tartlet pans, and cannoli tubes.

SWEET CELEBRATIONS
(formerly Maid of Scandinavia)
P.O. Box 39426
Edina, MN 55439
Telephone: (952) 943-1508; (800) 328-6722
Website: www.sweetc.com
Wide variety of decorating supplies. Also, cannoli tubes.

VALRHONA
Website: www.valrhona.com
Chocolate blocks and bars for baking, as well as cocoa.

WILLIAMS-SONOMA
100 North Point Street
San Francisco, CA 94133
Telephone: (877) 812-6235
Website: www.williams-sonoma.com
Pans, molds, and assorted baking equipment and cookware.

BIBLIOGRAPHY

Alexander, Stephanie. *The Cook's Companion: The Complete Book of Ingredients and Recipes for the Australian Kitchen.* Melbourne: Viking, 1996.

Allen, Darina. *Irish Traditional Cooking.* London: Kyle Cathie, 1995.

Annunciato, Ofélia Ramos. *O Sabor do Brasil.* São Paulo: Melhoramentos, 1996.

Bau, Frédéric. *Au Coeur des Saveurs.* Barcelona: Montagud Editores, 1998.

Benton, Peggy. *Cooking with Pomiane.* New York: Roy, 1961.

Clement, Gaston. *Gastronomie et Folklore de Chez Nous.* Brussels: Éditions Le Sphinx, 1957.

Couet, A., and E. Kayser. *Pains Spéciaux et Décorés.* Paris: Éditions St. Honoré, 1989.

Darenne, E., and E. Duval. *Traité de Pâtisserie Moderne* (rev. ed.). Paris: Flammarion, 1974.

David, Elizabeth. *English Bread and Yeast Cookery.* New York: Viking, 1977.

Day, Avanelle, and Lillie Stuckey. *The Spice Cookbook.* New York: David White, 1964.

École Professionelle Richemont. *La Boulangerie Suisse.* Lucerne: Richemont, 1983.

Ferber, Christine. *Mes Tartes Sucrées et Salées.* Paris: Payot, 1998.

Greenspan, Dorie. *Paris Sweets.* New York: Broadway Books, 2002.

Grigson, Jane. *Jane Grigson's Fruit Book.* New York: Atheneum, 1982.

Kennedy, Diana. *Recipes from the Regional Cooks of Mexico.* New York: Harper and Row, 1978.

Lacam, Pierre. *Memorial Historique et Géographique de la Pâtisserie.* Paris: Chez l'Auteur, 1895.

Lagorre, Sylvie Girard. *Gaston Le Nôtre's Gourmandises.* Paris: Flammarion, 2000.

Le Nôtre, Gaston. *Desserts Traditionnels de France.* Paris: Flammarion, 1991.

Lin, Florence. *Complete Book of Chinese Noodles, Dumplings, and Breads.* New York: Quill Paperback, 1986.

McNeill, F. Marian. *The Scots Kitchen.* Glasgow and London: Blackie and Son, 1929–1955.

Menasce, Elsie. *The Sephardi Culinary Tradition.* Cape Town: Sephardic Cookbook Corporation, 1984.

Modesto, Maria de Lourdes. *Cozinha Tradicional Portuguesa.* São Paulo: Editorial Verbo, 1982.

Pellaprat, Henri-Paul. *Modern French Culinary Art.* Cleveland: World, 1966.

Schneider-Schloeth, Amalie. *Basler Kochschule,* 11th ed. Basel: Friedrich Reinhart, undated.

Schumacher, Karl. *Wiener Suss-speisen.* Linz: Trauner Verlag, 1990.

Thuriès, Yves. *Les Recettes d'un Compagnon de Tour de France.* Cordes-sur-Ciel: Société Editar, 1982.

Toklas, Alice. *The Alice B. Toklas Cookbook.* New York: Doubleday Anchor, 1960.

ACKNOWLEDGMENTS

I wish to extend my heartfelt thanks to so many people who have been part of producing this book. First of all, my agent Phyllis Wender and her associate Sonia Pabley have been infinitely helpful and supportive. Natalie Danford edited the manuscript and helped me with every stage of writing the book.

At HarperCollins, Susan Friedland's editorial vision guided this book every step of the way, and Hugh Van Dusen and his associate editor, Marie Estrada, have embraced this project with open arms. Special thanks to copy editor Susan Gamer, design manager Jessica Shatan Heslin, production editor John Jusino, and production director Roni Axelrod, and to publicists Carrie Bachman and Jonathan Schwartz for their efforts in promoting the book.

Joel Avirom once again provided an outstanding design, with his associates Jason Snyder and Meghan Day Healey. Thanks to Tom Eckerle and Ceci Gallini for beautiful photography and props, and to Laura Hartman Maestro for her wonderful line drawings.

Andrea Tutunjian acted as "general contractor" and kept me organized during the whole process. Special thanks are due to Cara Tannenbaum, who tested most of the recipes and made sure all of our changes and additions made it into their final versions. Studio food styling and preparation of food for photography were done by Barbara Bria Pugliese, Faith Drobbin, Rebecca Millican, Cara Tannenbaum, and Andrea Tutunjian.

Rick Smilow, president of the Institute of Culinary Education, again generously provided space for recipe testing and food production. ICE director of purchasing, Josh Pappas, was so helpful and patient with last-minute requests for specialty food and equipment.

My thanks to the many friends and associates who contributed recipes: Eva Abplanalp, Reiko Akehi, Darina Allen, Stephanie Alexander, Jean Anderson, Gregor Bachmann, Tim Brennan, Floyd Cardoz, Marta Curro, Thea Cvijanovich, Manuel Davids and Pieter Van Straaten, Kyra Effren, Hosni Emam, Larissa Erokhin, Dorie Greenspan, Josef Haslinger, Yocheved Hirsch, Mohammed Hussein, Diana Kennedy, Albert Kumin, Anna Tasca Lanza, Sandy Leonard, Sasha Lewis, Niko Lewis, Erika Lieben, Milli De Conti Link, Mario Lo Menzo, Engela Matthee, Maureen McKeon, Elsie Menasce, Jennifer Migliorelli, Max Muller, Shirley Nachman, Nancy Nicholas, Gary Peese, Martin Picard, Sheri Portwood, Ana Rambaldi, Roberto Santibañez, Bonnie Slotnick, Jeffrey Steingarten, Bonnie Stern, Michelle Tampakis, Andrea Tutunjian, John Tutunjian, Norman Weinstein, and Dirk-Jan Zonneveld.

Special thanks to all my friends at Switzerland Tourism, especially Erika Lieben, and to my Viennese connection, Daniel Kennedy. I wouldn't know Melbourne or Cape Town if it were not for the kindness of my friends Maureen McKeon and Kyra Effren.

A last special thank you to Nancy Nicholas, whose idea it was to do an international baking book, and to Maida Heatter, without whom I wouldn't know Nancy.

RECIPE INDEX BY COUNTRY

INDEX

(Page references in *italic* refer to illustrations.)

C

G

N

O

P

Q

R

S